Korean Studies Guide

槿域攷

Korean studies guide

COMPILED FOR THE INSTITUTE OF EAST ASIATIC STUDIES,
UNIVERSITY OF CALIFORNIA, BY B. H. HAZARD, JR.,
JAMES HOYT, H. T. KIM, AND W. W. SMITH, JR.
EDITED BY RICHARD MARCUS

1954
BERKELEY AND LOS ANGELES
UNIVERSITY OF CALIFORNIA PRESS

UNIVERSITY OF CALIFORNIA PRESS
BERKELEY AND LOS ANGELES

CAMBRIDGE UNIVERSITY PRESS
LONDON, ENGLAND

COPYRIGHT, 1954, BY
THE REGENTS OF THE UNIVERSITY OF CALIFORNIA

LIBRARY OF CONGRESS
CATALOG CARD NUMBER: 54-7843

Foreword

The Korean Studies Guide is a direct outgrowth of work done by Professor George M. McCune before his untimely death in 1948. He, his wife, Evelyn McCune, and his brother, Shannon McCune, were pioneers in Korean studies in this country. Without George McCune we should be much further in the dark concerning that country and its rich background than we are today. Thus, although the actual writing of the Guide has been the work of others, the inspiration for it, and much of the basic training of those who have participated in its compilation, came from the McCune family. The Institute is happy to acknowledge this debt.

The Guide was written by four specialists working under the direction of the Institute of East Asiatic Studies at Berkeley. The basic planning of the Guide and compilation of the material on bibliography and reference works, as well as the gathering of the other material, was the work of Mr. Warren W. Smith, Jr. under a grant from the Rockefeller Foundation as part of a special Korean studies program in 1951. During 1952-53 the compilation was carried on by a group employed by the University of California for this special purpose. Mr. Benjamin H. Hazard, Jr. has prepared the material on archaeology in chapter iv, and the chapters on Korean history, government, and economics, with the exception of the one on the Yi dynasty. He has also taken the responsibility for the final checking of sources and Oriental language references throughout the Guide. Mr. James Hoyt has compiled the parts dealing with the Yi dynasty, Korean art, music, education, geography, and sociology. Dr. Ha Tai Kim (Kim Ha-t'ae) has written the sections on religion and philosophy, language, and literature. Each of these four men has surveyed the material as a whole and has contributed to the sections prepared by the others. Finally, the manuscript has been prepared for publication by the editor, Mr.

Richard Marcus, whose diligent and thorough revision has made possible greater unity in the assembly of the work of several different individuals, in this work the editor was assisted by Mr. John Gildersleeve, of the University of California Press. The result is a product of team research in which all have participated through an interchange of ideas and information.

The institute is particularly grateful to Dr. L. George Paik (Paek Nak-chun), President of Chosun (Chosŏn) Christian University, whose unique knowledge of Korean history and bibliography was made available to the group in Berkeley, and to Mr. Lee Hi-seung (Yi Hi-sŭng), Professor of Literature at Seoul National University, for his suggestions and corrections in the chapters on literature and language. Professor Shannon McCune, Chairman of the Department of Geography, Colgate University, took as his particular responsibility the chapter on geography and made many valuable suggestions for the other sections which have been incorporated into the Guide. For the Institute of East Asiatic Studies a committee composed of Professor Delmer M. Brown, Professor Peter A. Boodberg, Mr. Richard J. Miller, and Professor Woodbridge Bingham, chairman, have supervised the work of compilation.

In offering the Guide to students of the Far East it is felt that an urgency exists which has made important the production of some sort of guide in a field where nothing of its kind has been previously available. This handbook is not a definitive work and suggestions for its improvement will be welcomed. In fact, only by making this tool available to those who may wish to use it and then receiving their comments can there be a solid basis for revision. Revision we know there must be: the Institute takes full responsibility for issuing the Guide in its present form, and it is hoped that those who find it useful will send in their suggestions.

Woodbridge Bingham, Director
Institute of East Asiatic Studies

Contents

	Introduction	ix
I.	Libraries, General Bibliographies, and Periodicals	1
II.	Reference Materials	16
III.	Geography	29
IV.	Art and Archaeology	38
V.	General History	56
VI.	Ancient Korea	74
VII.	Three Kingdoms and Unified Silla	79
VIII.	Koryŏ Period	85
IX.	Yi Dynasty	90
X.	Government, Economics, and Recent History	106
XI.	Sociology	125
XII.	Religion and Philosophy	129
XIII.	Music	142
XIV.	Language	145
XV	Literature	153
XVI.	Education	164
XVII.	Special Reference Materials and Addenda	169

Appendices

    Chronological List of Rulers and Dynasties 177
    Publishing Houses and Societies 186
    Glossary 192

Maps 199

Index of Titles 209

Index of Authors 217

Introduction

Modern Korean studies began before the turn of the century, when a few books on Korea were written by foreign missionaries, diplomatic personnel, and visitors, but Japan's annexation of Korea in 1910 brought this pioneer period to an end. Thereafter, the peninsula was viewed by many Westerners as but an appendage of the Japanese Empire, and there was little incentive to study Korea. Meanwhile the Japanese entered upon a broad program of research on Korean subjects. Although their purpose was practical—to equip themselves with all available knowledge of Korea, and thereby to gain concrete advantage in their dealings with the Korean people—the Japanese were greatly impressed by the cultural treasures that they discovered: the heritage of a people who have played an important role in the development of Far Eastern civilization. The Japanese have never lost their interest, they have continued to publish widely, even after 1945, in the field of Korean studies.

The Russo-American occupation in 1945 and the outbreak of the Korean War in 1950 awakened a long-neglected Occidental interest in Korean affairs. This interest, like that of the Japanese, was inspired by practicality. And the West has found, as did the Japanese, that "practical" information is not enough, that it is often difficult to separate the practical from the academic, or rather, that an academic knowledge of Korean civilization is patently practical.

In view of this new interest in things Korean, the Institute of East Asiatic Studies of the University of California initiated, as part of its Summer Program on Korea in 1951, with financial assistance from the Rockefeller Foundation, the compilation of the <u>Korean Studies Guide</u>. The University of California was particularly well-equipped to undertake this task, not only because of its long tradition in the field of Korean studies, but also because

x   Introduction

the Asami collection of Korean literature, the largest aggregate of old Korean books outside the Orient, is in the University's East Asiatic Library.

The purpose of this Guide is to provide a handbook of basic information necessary for pursuing the study of the various aspects of Korean culture. In general, the chapters are divided topically and begin with brief statements outlining the subjects treated. The selection of topics and the thoroughness of the treatment accorded have been determined on the basis of (1) the value and volume of academic publications in the field, (2) the availability of source materials to the compilers, (3) the fields of specialization of the scholars who have contributed, and (4) the obvious limitation of time.

There has been some admittedly arbitrary arranging of the Guide. Emphasis, for example, has been centered upon historical materials, and the natural sciences have been almost entirely excluded. It was found most convenient to group art and archaeology in the same chapter, since many of the best examples of Korean art have been obtained from archaeological sites. Government, economics, and recent history have been similarly grouped because most source books do not readily fall into the category of a single discipline, but contain material relevant to all three.

The greater part of each chapter consists of annotated bibliographies which seek to include the most valuable works, both Western and Oriental, on the various aspects of Korean culture. The annotations indicate the contents of the books listed, they are not intended as reviews, and critical statements have been kept to a minimum. The fact that a book is listed is an indication that it is regarded as of at least some merit. The comparatively small number of Western works—especially of current Western works— should be noted, for this poverty suggests at once the failure of the West to study Korea adequately and the opportunity for work to be done.

It should also be noted that many of the important works on Korea are in Japanese or Chinese rather than Korean. This trilingual situation arises from the nature of Korea's relations with these two neighboring powers and is one of the unfortunate complications of Korean studies. However, the Korean national language has become an increasingly important medium of expression, and the nature of the Korean language—its history and relationship to other Asiatic languages—is itself a field that offers great opportunity for investigation.

Anyone acquainted with the history of Korea, ancient or modern, will be aware of the close relationship which Korea has had with China and Japan. The annals of these two countries have provided from the earliest times important primary source materials for the study of Korean history. Moreover, much of the literature of Korea itself (especially history, philosophy, and belles-lettres) has been written partly or entirely in classical Chinese. The vast amount of secondary material published in Japanese has already been mentioned.

The compilers of the Guide have essayed to mitigate language difficulties whenever possible. Standard romanization has been used throughout: McCune-Reischauer system for Korean, Wade-Giles for Chinese, Hepburn for Japanese, and Lessing-Poppe[1] for Mongolian. Descriptions of the various bibliographical entries are designed to give basic information even to those without a knowledge of the language in question. Works have been classified by the languages in which they are written—Western, Korean, Japanese, Chinese, and Mongolian—so that users with a knowledge of only certain languages can quickly find materials they can read. For the benefit of those who read han-gŭl, but do not know Chinese characters, Korean proper names (including the titles of Korean works) have been given in both scripts whenever it was possible to do so.

The breadth of the materials in the different languages indicates that studies on Korea can never be carried out without referring to the general context of Far Eastern culture. On the one hand, Korean historical sources can be of value to an understanding of the historical development of the entire Far East. On the other, Korean history and culture have an individuality and a value of their own; as a nation which has maintained its identity for

---

[1] As employed in the Mongolian-English Dictionary being prepared by the Institute of East Asiatic Studies, University of California.

over two thousand years and which today ranks among the twenty most populous nations in the world, Korea, past and present, is well worth examination.

Libraries, General Bibliographies, and Periodicals

The purpose of this chapter is to list the libraries, both in America and abroad, where strong collections bearing upon Korea are housed; to list the basic bibliographies necessary for Korean studies; and to list the more important or comprehensive magazines and journals dealing with Korea.

LIBRARIES

Library of Congress, Washington, D. C. Has perhaps the largest collection of books on Korea in Western and Oriental languages in the United States. The library has published three bibliographies of its holdings of modern works on Korea:

(1) Korea: An Annotated Bibliography of Publications in Western Languages. Washington, 1950. Emphasizes works published after 1930; covers most completely books on history, government, and economics. The index lists authors, significant titles, and subjects of special interest.

(2) Korea: An Annotated Bibliography of Publications in the Russian Language. Washington, 1950. Covers a wide range of subjects and indicates the nature of Russian research on Korea both before and after the revolution of 1917. The index lists authors, titles, and subjects.

(3) Korea: An Annotated Bibliography of Publications in Far Eastern Languages. Washington, 1950. Includes Japanese and Chinese titles, and many Korean titles published since 1945. It is arranged topically, and is strongest in bibliographies and in works on government and economics. There is an index of authors and titles.

The Library of Congress has also compiled a bibliography of Korean publications from 1946 to 1952, classified by subject. It has not yet been published but is available in photostat on special request. Most entries are in the Korean language.

The National Archives, Washington, D.C. Contains the diplomatic correspondence between Korea and America, legation messages, instructions to envoys, etc. from 1883 to 1905, the period during which America had official relations with the Korean monarchy.

The New York Public Library, New York City. The papers of Horace Allen, the American representative to Korea from 1884 to 1905, and the correspondence of George C. Foulk, who was attached to the Korean Mission of the United States and later to the American Consulate in Seoul from 1883 to 1887, are here. Includes a file of the Seoul Daily Independent. See entry 259 for a full description of the Allen collection.

The University of California, Berkeley. Its East Asiatic Library has one of the world's largest collections of Korean works since it recently purchased the Asami (Asami Rintarō 淺見倫太郎) collection, which has some 4,000 fascicles of Korean works including a set of the Yijo Sillok (289) in 888 fascicles. The East Asiatic Library also possesses a valuable collection for the study of Korean economic development from 1945 to 1950—books, pamphlets, and folders containing directives, ordinances, and memoranda related to economic problems—given to the University by Edgar A. J. Johnson, former Civil Administrator of Korea and head of the Korea branch of the ECA.

Columbia University, New York City. Has many of the important reference works for Korean studies, and has issued a bibliography of 535 titles of Chinese, Japanese, and Korean works available in its East Asiatic Library:

(4)   Kŭmsu Kangsan 錦繡江山 금수 강산 (Works on Korea). New York, 1950.

Cornell University, Ithaca, New York. Has a good collection of Western books on Korea, and some books in Japanese and Chinese, most of them on Korean art and archaeology.

Harvard University, Cambridge, Massachusetts. Has recently begun a collection of Korean works, and has outstanding Chinese and Japanese collections in which many books on Korea may be found, including most of the basic reference works for the study of Korea before 1910.

The University of Hawaii, Honolulu. Has an adequate collection, including most of the basic reference works in English, Japanese, and Chinese. It has some 300 Korean works, and has also files of the Korea Review (38) and the Korean Repository (39).

Stanford University, Stanford, California. Its Hoover Library of War, Revolution, and Peace has some 200 Korean titles, most of them written after 1945; files of Japanese newspapers published during the war and of Korean newspapers published since 1945; many Government General publications; and, perhaps most important, a collection of the photographs made of documents taken from the Japanese consulate in Korea, 1895-1910. Stanford has recently acquired the rare Kojong Sillok (289) and Sunjong Sillok (289), and also the Kanaseki 金 関 collection (see 122), which consists mainly of works on ethnology, anthropology, and archaeology of the Far East, including many items about Korea.

The University of Washington, Seattle. Has most of the basic works in both Western and Oriental languages.

Tōyō Bunko (Oriental Library), Tōkyō. Has the best collection on Korea in Japan.

Colleges and libraries in Korea have been closed or destroyed by the Korean War, and their facilities will be unavailable until they are restored and reorganized.

GENERAL BIBLIOGRAPHIES
Western

(5) Bulletin of Far Eastern Bibliography [five times a year]. Washington: American Council of Learned Societies, 1936-1941. Covers books on Korea published during these years. See also Far Eastern Quarterly (8).

(6)   Cordier, Henri. **Biblioteca Sinica, dictionnaire bibliographique des ouvrages relatifs à l'émpire chinois.** Paris, 1904-1907. 4 vols. Also **Supplément et Index.** Paris, 1924.   List under "les pays tributaires de la Chine" titles on Korea, most of them Western works published before 1900. Cordier also gives the table of contents of the **Korea Review** (38) and the **Korean Repository** (39).

(7)   Courant, Maurice. **Bibliographie Coréene.** Publications de l'École des langues orientales vivantes, XVIII-XX. Paris, 1894-1897. 3 vols. Also **Supplément.** Publications . . . , XXI. Paris, 1901.   The best Western compilation of Korean books from earliest times until 1899, a total of some 3,200 titles. The volumes are arranged topically, and there are valuable detailed indices giving titles, authors, and important dates and places mentioned in the bibliography. Courant gives whenever possible a complete bibliographical history for each title, a summary of its contents, and critical remarks on it. Names and titles are identified by Chinese characters, and Courant indicates those European collections, private or institutional, in which copies of the books may be found.

Care should be used in reading this book, for Courant had opinions about Korea's intellectual history which have been shown to be fallacious. His bibliography remains nevertheless a monumental and invaluable reference for Korean studies, the work of a diligent scholar who had first-hand contact with the materials he treats.

The introduction, a valuable essay on Korean literature, libraries, and book stores in the late nineteenth century, has been translated into English by Mrs. W. M. Royds and published in **TAKBRAS,** XXV (1936), 1-99.

(8)   **Far Eastern Quarterly.** Lancaster, Pennsylvania: Far Eastern Association, 1941- .   Continues the bibliographical work of the **Bulletin of Far Eastern Bibliography** (5). Until May, 1947, material on Korea appeared under various groupings, e.g., "Manchuria and Korea" and "Central and Northeastern Asia"; but beginning with Vol. VI, no. 3 (May, 1947) there was a separate section for Korea. Starting with the bibliography for 1949, the entire bibliography for the year is published in the August issue of the succeeding year.

The Quarterly also reviews recent books on Korea in both Western and Oriental languages. Vol. V, no. 3 (May, 1946) is entirely on Korea.

(9)   K. B S. Bibliographical Register of Important Works Written in Japanese on Japan and the Far East, Published During the Year 1932-1937. Tōkyō: Kokusai Bunka Shinkō-kai, 1937-1943. 6 vols. Has a special section for books and articles on Korea, usually listed with brief annotations. The Registers are highly selective, so that anyone using them should refer also to other sources.

(10)   Kerner, Robert. Northeast Asia, a Selected Bibliography. Berkeley: University of California Press, 1939. 2 vols. Lists in Vol. II primary and secondary source materials on Korea in Western (including Russian) and Oriental languages, some 450 entries arranged topically.

(11)   McCune, Shannon. Bibliography of Western Language Material on Korea. Rev. and enl. New York: International Secretariat, Institute of Pacific Relations, 1950. General coverage of the most recent and accessible titles, and a commentary on the content and value of the books listed.

(12)   Nachod, Oscar. Bibliography of the Japanese Empire, 1906-26. London and Leipzig, 1928. 2 vols. Also supplements: Bibliographie von Japan, 1927-29. Leipzig, 1931; and Bibliographie von Japan, 1930-32. Leipzig, 1935. See Praesent (13).

(13)   Praesent, Hans, and Wolf Haenish. Bibliographie von Japan, 1933-35. Leipzig, 1937. This work and the two later volumes by Nachod (12) contain together some 655 references to material on Korea published from 1930 to 1935.

(14)   Trollope, Mark N. "Corean Books and Their Authors," TAKBRAS, XXI (1932), 1-104. A historical treatment of Korean literature classified as classics, history, philosophy, and collected works. The article is one of the best introductions in a Western language to Korean intellectual and literary activities. During his stay in Korea Bishop Trollope collected some 10,000 Korean books, and his article is based upon lecture notes he had intended to ex-

pand into a book before his sudden death in Seoul in 1933.

(15)   Underwood, Horace. "A Partial Bibliography of Occidental Literature on Korea," <u>TAKBRAS</u>, XX (1931), 1-186.   Divides its material into fourteen sections, the titles in each section arranged by date of publication. It lists some 2,882 items and has an author index. It gives quite thorough coverage and is one of the basic bibliographies of Western books and articles on Korea before 1931. The listing was expanded and brought down to 1935 in a supplement which follows Underwood's method of classification: Gompertz, E. and G. "Supplement to 'A Partial Bibliography. . . on Korea' by H. H. Underwood, Ph. D., 1931," <u>TAKBRAS</u>, XXIV (1935), 23-48.

Korean

(16)   <u>Ch'ulp'an Taegam</u> 出版大鑑 출판대감 (Register of Publications). Seoul: Chosŏn Ch'ulp'an Munhwa Hyŏphoe, 1949. An index and a guide to the publishing trade of Korea from 1945 to 1949. It lists monographs (arranged according to subject), periodicals and newspapers, book dealers, authors and their fields of literature, pseudonyms used by famous Koreans, statistics for the publishing trade, texts of laws related to publishing, and gives a short history of the Korean Association of Cultural Publishing.

Japanese: Bibliographies and Guides to Old Works

(17)   <u>Chōsen Sōtokufu Kotosho Mokuroku</u> 朝鮮總督府古圖書目錄 (Government General Catalogue of Old Books). Keijō: Chōsen Sōtokufu, 1921.   Essentially a catalogue of old Korean and Chinese books possessed by the Government General in 1921, classified as classics, history, philosophy, and collected works. There are separate sections for Chinese and Korean books.

While it is probably one of the most comprehensive lists of old Korean books available, including many titles not found in Courant's bibliography (7), the work omits some important titles and lacks a satisfactory index. Despite these defects, the book is one of the essential reference books for the study of Korea before 1910.

Libraries, Bibliographies, Periodicals

(18)   Chōsen Tosho Kaidai 朝鮮圖書解題 (Annotated Bibliography
of Korean Books). Keijō: Chōsen Sōtokufu, 1919. Reprinted in 1932.
A selected collection of old Korean books. It gives brief annotations
of all books listed, information on their authors, and other data.
The basic information is made readily available through excellent
indices, one listing titles according to traditional Chinese divisions,
another, by the kana order of the first character of their titles.
There is also a special index of authors arranged by number of
strokes which makes it possible rapidly to look up all writings of
a particular man included in the catalogue and to find his biography.
   The Chōsen Tosho Kaidai is the best and most inclusive work
of its kind available, an essential tool for a study of Korean history
and literature, not only for bibliographical purposes, but for identification of books and authors cited in historical texts.

(19)   Hirose Bin. 廣瀬敏 Nippon Sōsho Sakuin 日本叢書索引
(Index to Japanese Collectanea). Tōkyō: Musashino Shoin, 1939.
A complete index to all the important modern collections printed
in Japan before 1931. Since many Korean books and shorter works
of Korean authors were included in collections printed in Japan
from the late Meiji period onward, it is often possible to find here
works listed nowhere else.

(20)   Oda Shōgo. 小田省吾 "Chōsen Shiseki Kaidai Kōgi" 朝鮮史籍
解題講義 (Lectures on Korean Historical Sources), Seikyū
Gakusō, XXIII (1936), 145-161. Lists and evaluates six Japanese
works which describe Korean historical works and which can be
used as guides in studying them; summarizes the history of the
Kyuchanggak 奎章閣 규장각, the royal library founded in the
last years of the Yi dynasty, which became part of the Keijō Imperial University library in 1930; and briefly describes the traditional Chinese methods of writing history, methods which the
Koreans followed.

(21)   Tōyō Bunko Chōsen-hon Bunrui Mokuroku, fu Annan-hon Moku-
roku 東洋文庫朝鮮本分類目錄附安南本目錄 (Oriental
Library Classified Catalogue of Korean Books, with a Catalogue of
Annamese Books Appended). Tōkyō: Tōyō Bunko, 1939.   A cata-

logue of all the old books on Korea in the Oriental Library in Tōkyō in 1939, classified by the traditional Chinese system, with an index of titles by number of strokes. The information on modern editions of old Korean books is one of the catalogue's most useful features. There is also a special section on sōsho 叢書 (collectanea), and titles of the individual works in each collected edition are listed.

Japanese: Bibliographies of Secondary Works and Recent Publications

(22)   Chōsen Sōtokufu Tosho Mokuroku 朝鮮總督府圖書目錄 (Government General Catalogue of Books). Keijō: Chōsen Sōtokufu, 1927. Lists the holdings of the Government General as of March, 1927, omitting old Korean books. It is much less extensive than the Shinshobu Bunrui Mokuroku (26), but it includes a few Korean and Chinese titles although the majority are Japanese. Official government publications are especially well represented. There are no annotations. Titles are arranged alphabetically under topics, and there is an alphabetical index of all the books.

(23)   Keijō Teikoku Daigaku Fuzoku Toshokan, Wakan Shomei Mokuroku 京城帝國大學附屬圖書館和漢書名目錄 (Keijō Imperial University Library Catalogue of Japanese and Chinese Books). Keijō: Keijō Teikoku Daigaku Fuzoku Toshokan, 1933-1936. 3 vols. Lists all Japanese and Chinese books at Keijō Imperial University in 1936, omitting old Korean books of the former Royal Library, medical books, and miscellaneous Korean books published before 1900 Books on Korea are scattered throughout the sections of this listing.

(24)   Sakurai Yoshiyuki 櫻井義之 Meiji Nenkan Chōsen Kenkyū Bunken-shi 明治年間朝鮮研究文獻誌 (Annotated Bibliography of Korean Studies in the Meiji Era). Keijō: Shomotsu Dōkō-kai, 1941. Contains 579 titles of selected studies on Korea, almost all in Japanese, written during 1868-1912, arranged in eight general classifications. Each entry gives general bibliographical data, a brief biography of the author, a statement (usually taken from the book itself) about the book's scope and aim, and the table of contents. There is an author index and a title index, both in kana order. In

general, this bibliography is the best one for the period it covers for individual studies, reports, and secondary works.

(25) Shigaku Bunken Mokuroku 史學文獻目錄(Catalogue of Historiographical Literature). Tōkyō: Yamagawa Shuppan-sha, 1952. A catalogue edited by the Shigak-kai 史學會 (Historical Studies Society) at Tōkyō University which lists most books, articles, and other studies on history and related subjects published in Japan from 1946 to 1950. Forty-three articles and about ten books on Korea are listed.

(26) Shinshobu Bunrui Mokuroku 新書部分類目錄(Classified Catalogue of New Books). Keijō: Chōsen Sōtokufu Toshokan, 1938. 3 vols. Lists holdings in Western bindings of the Library of the Government General as of July, 1937. Books on Korea are listed in Vol. III. The books are arranged according to topics listed in a key at the front. Some periodicals and reprints of old Korean books are listed, but the main value of the volume is for indicating recent studies in such fields as Korean history, politics, law, economics, etc. Unannotated.

Japanese: Publishers Catalogues.

(27) Bunken Hōkoku 文獻報國(National Bibliography) [monthly]. Keijō: Chōsen Sōtokufu Toshokan, 1935-1945. Records Korean publications; gives information on Korean libraries; lists important Japanese periodical literature on Korea and Manchuria; and lists copies of all publications in Korean and Japanese of which samples were submitted to the Police Affairs Bureau.

(28) Nippon Shuppan Nenkan 日本出版年鑑(Japan Publishers Yearbook). Tōkyō: Nippon Shuppan Kyōdō Kabushiki Kaisha, 1943 and 1947. 2 vols. Lists Japanese publications on Korea from 1942 to 1945. Entries are arranged by author under a detailed topical scheme and are unannotated. There is a classified list of important periodicals, with statements of their general emphasis and content.

(29) Shuppan Nenkan 出版年鑑(Publishers Yearbook). Tōkyō: Tōkyō-dō, 1930-1941. Covers publications of member firms of the Tōkyō-dō during the calendar year preceding each issue, a coverage

which except for some government publications and subscription works includes the majority of books published in the Japanese Empire. Annotated.

(30) **Shuppan Nenkan** (Publishers Yearbook). Tōkyō: Shuppan Nyūshū-sha, 1948- . Lists books and periodicals published in Japan for each preceding year, and contains essays on trends in the study of history, philosophy, economics, and other fields.

(31) **Tosho Sōmokuroku** 圖書總目金彔(General Catalogue of Books). Tōkyō: Tōkyō Shosekishō Kumiai Jimusho, 1893-1940. Separate volumes were issued in 1893, 1896, 1906, 1911, 1918, 1923, 1929, 1933, and 1940. Lists titles published or handled by the Tōkyō Bookdealers Association in print as of date of publication of each volume, a coverage of most books published in the Japanese Empire. Most volumes have three parts—title catalogue, publisher catalogue, and classified catalogue, the last covering in some detail publications in the social sciences. There is a subject index in each volume, and indices in the 1911, 1918, 1923, 1929, and 1933 volumes are especially valuable for books on Korea.

PERIODICALS
Western

(32) **Chinese Social and Political Science Review** [quarterly]. Peiping: Chinese Social and Political Science Association, 1916-1941. Contains studies of Korean problems related to Chinese history and politics, particularly in the nineteenth century, many of these studies derived from sources which have not been studied in the West.

(33) **Far Eastern Survey** [fortnightly]. New York: American Council of the Institute of Pacific Relations, 1932- . This research journal has many articles on Korea, most of them about current political, social, and economic problems. A subject index to the issues of each year is published.

(34) **Harvard Journal of Asiatic Studies** [quarterly]. Cambridge: Harvard-Yenching Institute, 1936- . Reviews books and other publications about Korea.

(35)   Japan Weekly Mail. Yokohama, 1870-1917. Edited after 1880 by Frank Brinkley, R. A., the Yokohama correspondent for the Times (London) and a student of Japanese and Chinese history. It contains articles about Korea although Brinkley's primary interest was Japan. The issues after 1900 should be read with an awareness that at that time Brinkley accepted a subsidy from the Imperial government and consequently became a firm supporter of all government measures. An index for every six months was published.

(36)   Korea Magazine [irregular]. Seoul, 1917-1919. Valuable articles for study of Korea's history, and translations of Korean books.

(37)   Korea Mission Field [monthly]. Seoul: General Council of Evangelical Missions in Korea, 1904-1941. Some good articles on Korean life and history. Published serially Gale's History (167) from July, 1924, to September, 1927.

(38)   Korea Review [monthly]. Seoul: The Methodist Publishing House, 1901-1906. Edited by Homer Hulbert. Carried scholarly articles on Korean life and history, including Hulbert's History of Korea (169).

(39)   Korean Repository [monthly]. Seoul: The Trilingual Press, 1892; 1895-1898. Published throughout 1892; suspended until January, 1895, from which date it continued until July, 1898. Edited by Homer Hulbert. It has articles of general interest on Korea and excellent coverage of some contemporary political events like the Independence Club's activities and the murder of Queen Min 閔 민 .

(40)   Korean Review [irregular]. Seattle: Korean-American Cultural Association, 1948-1949. Articles on Korean history, geography, and language.

(41)   Korean Survey [monthly]. Washington: Washington Bureau of the Korean Pacific Press, 1952- . Edited by Robert Oliver, one-time adviser to the Republic of Korea. Contains articles on current problems in Korea, and gives Korean news digests and announcements of current publications on Korea. The magazine reflects the politics and position of the Republic of Korea.

(42) **Monumentica Nipponica** [annual]. Tōkyō: Sophia University, 1938- . Suspended from 1943 to 1951. Studies of Japanese history and current affairs. Occasional articles on Korea.

(43) **Pacific Affairs** [quarterly]. New York: The American Council of the Institute of Pacific Relations, 1928- . Contains in issues since 1945 an increasing number of articles on Korea and reviews of books about Korea.

(44) **Research Monographs on Korea** [irregular]. Hamilton, New York: Korean Research Associates, 1941- . Individual studies, particularly on Korean geography and climate.

(45) **Transactions of the Asiatic Society of Japan** [annual]. Tōkyō: The Society, 1874- . Suspended from 1920 to 1924, and from 1940 to 1948. Occasional articles which bear upon Korea.

(46) **Transactions of the Korean Branch of the Royal Asiatic Society** [irregular]. Seoul: The Society, 1900-1941; 1948- . One of the best continually published sources of scholarly information on Korea. (The journal was suspended from 1941 to 1948 because of war.) Many of its articles were written by missionaries and other residents in Korea. Vol. XXXI (1949) has a brief history of the Society, and an index to Vols. I-XXX. Referred to throughout as **TAKBRAS.**

(47) **Voice of Korea** [bi-monthly]. Washington: Korean Affairs Institute, 1942- . Published monthly in 1942 and 1943. Chiefly current events, and some articles of a more general nature on Korean life and history.

Korean

(48) **Chayu Sege** 自由世界 자유세계 [irregular]. Pusan: Hongmun-sa, 1952- . Articles on history and current events. Published as part of Korea's cultural reconstruction after the destruction of publishing houses in Seoul.

(49) **Chindan Hakpo** 震檀學報 진단학보 [irregular]. Seoul: Chindan Hakhoe, 1934-1950. Published semi-annually, 1934-1941; occasionally, 1945-1950. Suspended in 1941 by order of the Govern-

ment General. Articles by many of Korea's best scholars on Korean history written in kukhanmun with footnotes which follow Western format.

The Chindan Hakpo was, in effect, a Korean language journal published by Korean scholars in an effort to make Koreans aware of their national history. It is not hard to see why the Government General looked with jaundiced eye upon the publication, and used the excuse of the paper shortage caused by the war to suspend the journal. It is unquestionably the best Korean scholarly journal; and it is only to be lamented that the Chindan Hakpo is hard to come by in the United States, and that even in Korea old issues are scarce. Vol. XII (1940) is the only issue that has an index of previous issues. In the issues since 1945, there are reports of the activities of the Chindan Hakoe which include information about Korean scholars and lists of their works since 1945.

The Chindan Hakhoe was disbanded in 1941. It was reorganized in 1945 and continues to exist although its journal was stopped by the Korean War.

(50)   Hakp'ung 學風 학풍 [monthly]. Seoul: Ŭryu Munhwa-sa, 1948-1950. Articles on history and allied subjects.

(51)   Hyangt'o 鄉土 향토 [irregular]. Seoul: Chong-ŭm-sa, 1946-1950. Emphasizes history, linguistics, and ethnology.

(52)   Yŏksa Hakpo 歷史學報 역사학보 [irregular]. Pusan: Yŏksa Hakhoe, 1952- . Four issues as of April, 1953. Book reviews and excellent scholarly articles.

   Japanese

(53)   Chōsen 朝鮮 [monthly]. Keijō: Chōsen Sōtokufu, 1911-1945. Called Chōsen Sōtokufu Geppō 朝鮮總督府月報 1911-1915, and Chōsen Ihō 朝鮮彙報 1915-1920. Emphasizes laws, policies, and reforms of the Government General, but also has some significant articles on Korean history, economics, and related subjects. Sōkan Irai no Sōmokuji Benran 創刊以來の總目次便覽 (1935) is a supplementary volume with an index to the preceding issues.

(54)   Chōsen Gakuhō 朝鮮學報 [bi-annual]. Tambaichi: Chōsen Gakkai, 1951- . The journal of the Academic Association of Koreanology. Contains excellent, carefully documented articles, selected lists of recent Japanese and Korean publications about Korea, and reviews of the most important of them. Beginning with the third issue there is a supplement giving an English resume of the articles.

(55)   Chōsen oyobi Manshū 朝鮮及滿洲 [monthly]. Keijō: Chōsen Zasshi-sha, 1908-1938. Published under title Chōsen until 1920. Emphasized current affairs but had also some good articles on Korean history.

(56)   Man-Sen Chiri Rekishi Kenkyū 滿鮮地理歷史研究 [irregular]. Tōkyō: Tōkyō Teikoku Daigaku, 1915- . Published annually, 1915-1926. Journal of the Faculty of Literature. Articles of consistently high quality on the history of medieval Korea and Manchuria.

(57)   Rekishi Chiri 歷史地理 [monthly]. Tōkyō: Nihon Rekishi Chiri Gakkai, 1899- . Devoted to studies of history and geography. Issues to 1936 contained forty-four articles on Korea (see index volume, 1936, under classification kokubetsu sakuin 國別索引).

(58)   Rekishigaku Kenkyū 歷史學研究 [bi-monthly]. Tōkyō: Iwanami Shoten, 1933- . A scholarly historical journal. A special supplement (July, 1953) has a bibliography of more than 800 items of articles from Japanese periodicals and essay collections (ronshū 論集), 1927-1953.

(59)   Seikyū Gakusō 青丘學叢 [quarterly]. Keijō: Seikyū Gakkai, 1930-1939. Journal of a society of Korean and Japanese scholars formed to study the culture of Korea and Manchuria. Its articles and book reviews are a source of scholarly information about Korea. Indices were published in nos. 6, 10, 14, 18, 22, 26, and 30. These indices are not cumulative, but no. 30 has a list in kana order of authors of important articles in preceding issues.

(60)   Shien 史苑 [semi-annual]. Tōkyō: St. Paul's University, 1928- . Published quarterly, 1928-1938. Articles on Korean

history, some of them by Korean scholars writing in Japanese.

(61)   Shigaku Zasshi 史學雜誌[monthly]. Tōkyō: Tōkyō Teikoku Daigaku, 1889- . Journal of the Shigakkai. About one-tenth of its coverage is given to Korea. Several indices have been published arranged by subject and author, the latter in kana order. Shigaku Zasshi Sōsakuin 史學雜誌總索引 (Tōkyō: Fusambō, 1940) indexes vols. 1-50.

(62)   Shirin 史林[quarterly]. Kyōtō: Kyōtō Teikoku Daigaku, 1916- Journal of the Shigaku Kenkyū-kai. Articles and reviews of important books on Korea.

(63)   Tōyō 東洋 [monthly]. Tōkyō: Tōyō Kyōkai, 1898-1940. Published under title Tōyō Jiho 東洋時報, 1898-1922. Emphasizes current affairs but has a few articles valuable for Korean studies.

(64)   Tōyō Gakuhō 東洋學報[irregular]. Tōkyō: Tōyō Kyōkai Gakujutsu Chōsa-bu, 1911- . Published quarterly, 1911-1940. Some valuable articles on Korean history, linguistics, and ethnology, and reviews of books on Korea.

(65)   Zakkō 雜攷[annual]. Keijō, 1931-1938. Edited and privately published by Ayugai Fusanoshin 鮎貝房之進 . Specialized articles, most of them on philological studies of early Korean history.

II

Reference Materials

This chapter lists the best general reference works available on Korea in Western and Oriental languages, and particularly calls attention to books that can help with specific problems which may be encountered in reading Korean source material.

DICTIONARIES AND LANGUAGE AIDS

(66)   Gale, James S. The Unabridged Korean-English Dictionary, 3rd ed., A. A. Pieters, ed. Seoul: The Christian Literature Society of Korea, 1931. First edition: A Korean-English Dictionary. Yokohama, 1897. Second edition: A Korean-English Dictionary. Yokohama, 1911.

The 1931 edition lists about 75,000 words, and is probably the most inclusive Korean-English dictionary available. It lists many words still used in the nineteenth century which have now become obsolete, and the spelling of some current words does not conform to the unified system of spelling adopted by the Korean Language Association in 1933.

The words are listed by their han-gŭl spelling, and the Chinese characters are given after the han-gŭl for words that have characters; the English meaning is given last. The 1897 edition has a section which gives the Korean pronunciation of individual Chinese characters, with the character arranged by radical, but the later editions omit this.

The 1897 edition was based upon earlier dictionaries compiled by French Catholic priests in Korea. It has some 30,000 entries and contains a table listing the rulers of Japan, China, and Korea from legendary times to 1897. The table contains errors, particularly in its information about the earlier monarchs; for Gale apparently accepted traditional data without making an effort to check their accuracy.

Reference Materials   17

The 1911 edition has about 50,000 entries, some 10,000 of them being identifications of places and persons in Korean history. The table of rulers is given in briefer form.

The 1931 edition does not contain the place and person entries, but repeats the brief table of rulers.

(67)   Lew, Hyungki J. (Yu Hyŏng-gi 柳瀅基 류형기). <u>New Life Korean-English Dictionary</u> and <u>New Life English-Korean Dictionary</u>. Seoul: Sinsaeng-sa, 1947. Reprinted in 1950.   Plates were destroyed during the Korean War, but Educational Services, Washington, D. C., has reproduced the books by photolithography.

The most modern Korean-English dictionary, with many words not found in Gale (66) and other earlier dictionaries. It follows the orthography prescribed by the Korean Language Association. Words are listed in <u>han-gŭl</u>; Chinese characters for words that have them are given after the <u>han-gŭl</u>. The Korean pronunciation of individual Chinese characters is not given. A supplement lists verbal endings, conjunctive phrases, and prepositions that appear in old texts and poetry.

The book contains errors and omissions; but, as its author points out, it was written in haste, in response to the need created by the American occupation of South Korea in 1945.

(68)   Ch'oe Nam-sŏn 崔南善 최남선, ed. <u>Sinjajŏn</u> 新字典 신자전 5th ed. Seoul: Sinmun-gwan, 1928. Reprinted in 1947.   One of the better <u>okp'yŏn</u> (dictionaries used to look up the Korean pronunciation of Chinese characters).

(69)   Kim Hyŏk-che 金赫濟 김혁제. <u>Kukhan Myŏngmun Sinokp'yŏn</u> 國漢明文新玉篇 국한명문신옥편. Seoul: Myŏngmun-dang, 1952.   A more recent <u>okp'yŏn</u>, with a supplement in which Chinese characters may be looked up from their Korean pronunciation. Spelling conforms to the system adopted by the Korean Language Association.

(70)   <u>Chōsengo Jiten</u> 朝鮮語辭典. Keijō: Chōsen Sōtokufu, 1920. The best Korean-Japanese dictionary. It was begun in 1911 and finished after nine years of work by many Japanese and Korean

scholars, including the Japanese Ogura Shimpei 小倉進平 and the Korean Ŏ Yun-jŏk 魚允迪 어윤저.

It is particularly valuable for historical research because of its large number of Chinese-character compounds and historical terms. These were taken from government documents, historical works, official correspondence, and stone inscriptions, and include many unusual Chinese-character compounds used primarily in Korea that cannot be found in many Chinese dictionaries. The Chōsengo Jiten has idu words and phrases, but is weak on colloquial Korean.

There are 58,639 words, arranged in han-gŭl order; Chinese characters can be found either through a phonetic index or by number of strokes. The Korean is spelled according to one of the standardizations proposed by the Government General.

(71) Mun Se-yŏng 文世榮 문세영. Chosŏnŏ Sajŏn 朝鮮語辭典 조선어사전. Seoul: Chosŏnŏ Sajŏn Kanhaeng-hoe, 1938. Reprinted under the title Urimal Sajŏn 우리말辭典 우리말사전. Seoul: Sammun-sa, 1950. One of the best of the modern Korean dictionaries, the first to be published which follows the unified spelling system of the Korean Language Association, of which Mun Se-yŏng was a member. The dictionary was compiled by him and Yi Yun-jae 李允宰 이윤재.

The Chosŏnŏ Sajŏn pays particular attention to modern words and gives dialectical variations as well as standard forms. The words are listed in han-gŭl order followed by Chinese characters if the word is a Chinese-character compound. The explanations are simple and concise. For some words old or variant spellings are listed, and changes in conjugation are given. There is no etymology, but the dictionary has most of the information on historical terms given in the Chōsengo Jiten (70).

A special section gives the Korean pronunciation of individual Chinese characters and idu; it contains 4,223 separate Chinese characters, and twenty-one pages of idu arranged according to number of strokes.

(72) Chosŏn Ŏ Hakhoe 朝鮮語學會 조선어학회. Chosŏno K'ŭn Sajŏn 조선큰사전. Seoul: Ŭryu Munhwa-sa, 1947-1950. 3 vols.

An uncompleted Korean dictionary. Its compilation was begun in 1929 by the Korean Language Association and continued throughout World War II, although the Government General tried to suppress the association during the war. After the Japanese had withdrawn from Korea, the association, assisted by a grant from the Rockefeller Foundation, published about half of the planned work before the North Korean invasion. Fortunately, the unpublished portion has not been destroyed.

The Korean Language Association seeks to replace Chinese-character compounds with Korean expressions, and its dictionary reflects this. Words are listed in han-gŭl, and the characters for words that have them are given after the han-gŭl. Explanations are given in Korean. Dialectical variations and changes in conjugation are given. A key in each volume lists the symbols used to explain grammar, spelling, etymology, etc. The idu in the dictionary is taken from the Ridoku Shūsei (73), but there is no key for looking up the idu since this key was to have been in the last volume. Brief but informative data on historical persons, places, books, and ranks and titles are given.

(73)   Ridoku Shūsei 吏讀集成 (Collection of idu). Keijō: Chōsen Sōtokufu Chūsū-in, 1937. Idu and t'o words and phrases are classified under the first Chinese character in the word or phrase. Every character may be looked up by number of strokes or by Korean phonetic value; and for each idu word or phrase is given the corresponding han-gŭl, a romanization of the han-gŭl, and a translation of the idu into simple Japanese.

The dictionary contains a selected collection of idu sentences, a short description of origin and development of idu, a valuable bibliography of some of the more important books in idu, and an explanation of the system of romanization used in the Ridoku Shūsei. It is the most comprehensive book of its kind and is useful both in studying idu and in clarifying texts in idu.

(74)   McCune, George M., and E. O. Reischauer. "Romanization of the Korean Language Based Upon Its Phonetic Structure," TAKBRAS, XXIX (1939), 1-55. Generally accepted in the United States as presenting the system of romanization which most accurately translit-

erates the sound of Korean, and which is used by the <u>Harvard Journal of Asiatic Studies</u>, the United States Army Map Service, the Korean Affairs Institute, and other periodicals and organizations.

The article is rather technical and of interest primarily to linguists; but it includes easily understandable summaries of the method of transliteration of vowels, consonants, and their combinations in initial, medial, and final positions. A comparative table of other systems of romanization is given. The edition of the <u>New Life Korean-English Dictionary</u> (67) published by the Education Services in Washington includes many of the tables for the transliteration of Korean according to the McCune-Reischauer system.

BIOGRAPHICAL AIDS
Korean

(75)   Chŏng Hyŏn-jin 鄭鉉震 정현진, ed. <u>Taehan Yŏngam</u> 大韓年鑑 대한 년 감 (Great Han Yearbook). Seoul: Taehan Yŏngam-sa, 1952. Includes a special section which gives the age, residence, occupation, and present position of important South Koreans. The entries are very brief, useful only for the most superficial identification.

(76)   <u>Chosŏn Sinsa Pogam</u> 朝鮮神士寶鑑 조선 신 사 보 감 (Mirror of Korean Gentlemen). Seoul: Chosŏn Ch'ulp'an Hyŏphoe, 1912. A specialized and limited work which is, however, the only source of information on many Koreans who lived in the last years of the Yi dynasty and the first years of Japanese rule. It is arranged by family surname and is written in an old style of <u>kukhanmun</u> in which Chinese greatly predominates.

(77)   <u>Chosŏn Yŏngam</u> 朝鮮年鑑 조선 년 감 (Korea Yearbook). Seoul: Chosŏn T'ongsin-sa, 1948. Includes a description of the political parties of South Korea and brief biographies of their leaders.

Japanese

(78)   <u>Chōsen Jimmei Jisho</u> 朝鮮人名辭書 (Korean Biographical Dictionary). Keijō: Chōsen Sōtokufu Chūsū-in, 1937. Has some 13,000 detailed entries on important Koreans from legendary times to 1910. Lists 15,000 persons who passed the government literary

(civil service) examinations from 1392 to 1894, and gives essential biographical data for them. There is a special section listing Buddhist monks, and a supplement of important Koreans who died between 1910 and 1934. Sources of information are listed after each entry.

The dictionary was the product of combined Korean and Japanese scholarship. Research began in 1916, and the writing of the dictionary was finished in 1934. It is a most useful reference work, but it is arranged in a style difficult for persons unfamiliar with the system of ranks and titles in Korea before 1910. Explanations of these ranks and titles are given in the Chugyo Taejŏn Hoet'ong (473) and the Chōsengo Jiten (70).

Tables of alternate names of offices and districts under the Yi dynasty are given. There are two indices, one by number of strokes, the other by style (ho 號 호) or courtesy name (cha 字 자). A kana index was published separately: Chōsen Jimmei Jisho Sakuin 朝鮮人名辭書索引 (Index of the Biographical Dictionary). Keijō: Chōsen Sōtokufu Chūsū-in, 1939.

(79)   Chōsen Jimmei-roku 朝鮮人名錄 (Who's Who in Korea). Keijō: Keijō Nippō-sha, 1944. Lists Koreans and Japanese residing in Korea, with brief data on their occupations, official positions, dates of birth, schools attended, and places or residence.

(80)   Chōsen no Seimei Shizoku ni Kansuru Kenkyū Chōsa 朝鮮の姓名氏族に關する研究調査 (Investigation and Research on Korean Names and Surnames and Clans and Families). Keijō: Chōsen Sōtokufu Chūsū-in, 1934. The book was not intended as a biographical dictionary, but as a detailed study of family names and clans in Korea both before and after the advent of Chinese civilization. Because of the relatively few surnames in Korea and the persistence of clans, historians need to pay special attention to their relationships.[1] The relation between names and class differentiations, and the family-clan distinctions of immigrants into Korea are discussed. The sources of information, many of them private genealogical records, are given.

[1] According to the Chōsen no Seimei Shizoku ni Kansuru Kenkyū Chōsa, pp. 40-50, there are only 326 surnames now used in Korea, although in earlier periods, according to written records, as many as 486 were employed.

(81)   Gendai Tōa Jimmei Kan 現代東亞人名鑑 (Register of Persons in Present-Day East Asia). Tōkyō: Tōhō Kenkyū-kai, 1950. Compiled by the Japanese Ministry of Foreign Affairs. Contains biographical sketches of important Koreans in both North and South Korea. Lists of North and South Korean cabinet members and political leaders are also given.

(82)   Shinsen Jimmei Daijiten 新撰人名大辭典 (Newly Compiled Great Biographical Dictionary). Tōkyō: Heibon-sha, 1937-1941. 9 vols. Volume VII lists living Japanese of note. Koreans were included because they were Japanese subjects when the book was written. The coverage for Koreans, though, is rather inadequate, and Korean revolutionary leaders such as Kim Ku 金九 김구, Rhee Syngman (Yi Sŭng-man 李承晩 이승만), or Kim Il-sŏng 金日成 김일성 are not listed. The book is arranged in the kana order of an individual's surname and given name. Volume IX is an index.

HISTORICAL DICTIONARIES
Korean

(83)   Chŭngbo Munhŏn Pigo 增補文獻備考 증보문헌비고 (Revised Encyclopedia). Seoul, 1907. 150 books in 50 fascicles. A revised and enlarged edition of the Tongguk Munhŏn Pigo 東國文獻備考 동국문헌비고 (Korean Encyclopedia)—100 books in 40 fascicles—written in 1770 on the order of King Yŏngjo. Because the king wished to have a Korean encyclopedia compiled on the pattern of the famous thirteenth-century Chinese encyclopedia by Ma Tuan-lin 馬端臨, Wen-hsien T'ung-k'ao 文獻通考, he gave scholars access to all official and private papers, documents, histories, and other records. Consequently, the encyclopedia is remarkably accurate, and often quotes passages from sources no longer extant. It is not so exhaustive in its treatment of subjects as the Wen-hsien T'ung-k'ao, but generally follows the pattern of the Chinese work in recording historical information on a subject, and then quoting opinions and offering criticisms of the information.

The first revision of the Tongguk Munhŏn Pigo was made about 1790 by Yi Man-un 李萬運 이만운 at the command of King Chŏngjo, but was never published. In 1907, King Kojong (Yi Taewang 李大王

이대왕) ordered the original Tongguk Munhŏn Pigo re-edited and brought up to date. Yi Man-un's revisions were included. All revisions and additions in the Chŭngbo Munhŏn Pigo are indicated by the characters po 補 보 or sok 續 속 placed before a phrase or passage.

The encyclopedia is written in classical Chinese, and is divided into sixteen broad topics: astronomy, geography, genealogy, rites, music, military affairs, justice, land taxes, expenditures, household population, rice sales, exchange of gifts, choosing of officials, schools, official ranks, and the fine arts. Each of these topics is subdivided into sections on specific matters, and an attempt is made to trace the history and development of every category from earliest times to 1907. Unfortunately, it is often impossible to determine under what topic or section a subject is classified, and a subject may be scattered over several different sections. This scattering came about largely from the radical change in concepts of government organization and classification of knowledge. A careful indexing of the encyclopedia would make the vast amount of information it contains more readily available.

"A Korean Cyclopedia," Korean Review, IV (1906), 217-223, 244-248, gives the history of the Tongguk Munhŏn Pigo and translates its table of contents (substantially the same table is in the Chŭngbo Munhŏn Pigo). The translation is of doubtful merit.

(84)   Yi Chŏng-gu, 李定求 이정구. Sach'ŏnnyŏn Munhŏn T'onggo 四千年文獻通考 사 천 년 문 헌 통 고 (Encyclopedia of Four Thousand Years). Seoul: Tongmyŏng-sa, 1926. An abbreviated encyclopedia of Korea, derived largely from the Chŭngbo Munhŏn Pigo (83), but written in kukhanmun.

(85)   Yu Chi-ok 柳志玉 유지옥, ed. Kich'o Kuksa Sajŏn 基礎 國史辭典 기초 국 사 사전 (Basic Korean Historical Dictionary). Seoul: Kongŏp Munhwa-sa, 1950. A reference book primarily for high schools which gives in relatively easy Korean much useful information on places, persons, and events in Korean history. The data are arranged by han-gŭl, and Chinese characters are given in parentheses to help clarify and identify the material. An English translation of this book would provide a good basis for a Western-language Korean historical dictionary.

Japanese

(86)　**Kokushi Jiten** 國史辭典 (Dictionary of National History). Tōkyō: Fuzam-bō, 1940-1943. 4 vols. Not completed in the scope originally planned because of the war, but nevertheless one of the most detailed and accurate reference works on Japanese history. Because Korea was part of the Japanese Empire when the book was written, Korean historical materials were included, so that the work is also a good reference book of Korean history. Many articles about Korea are by Yi Hong-jik 李弘植 이홍직, a Korean historian. The subjects are arranged in kana order.

(87)　Satō Taneji 佐藤種治. **Saishin Chōsen Rekishi Chiri Jiten** 最新朝鮮歷史地理辭典 (New Historical and Geographical Dictionary of Korea). Tōkyō: Fuzam-bō, 1933. Descriptions of important Korean historical events, persons, places, government offices, administration, books, and geography, from earliest times to the present. It was written expressly for beginners in Korean historical research. The materials are in general well chosen and well organized; they are arranged in kana order.

The work contains errors. Many of the Chinese characters for books and names are misprinted; there are mistakes in the kana transliteration of the names of persons and places; and some descriptions contain errors of fact. See Seikyū Gakusō, XII (1953), 190-191, for a detailed review.

(88)　**Tōyō Rekishi Daijiten** 東洋歷史大辭典 (Great Dictionary of Oriental History). Tōkyō: Heibon-sha, 1937-1939. 9 vols. A historical dictionary for Asia, completed by historians from Tōkyō and Kyōto Imperial universities, and other specialists throughout Japan. It is less thorough than the Kokushi Jiten (86), but it contains information on important persons, places, books, events, institutions, and similar historical material that is not readily available elsewhere. The coverage on Korea is quite good, extending from ancient times to the present. Many articles are by outstanding scholars of Korean studies, such as Suematsu Yasukazu 末松保和, Nakamura Eikō 中村榮孝, Marugame Kinsaku 丸亀金作, Hatada Takashi 旗田巍, and Yi Hong-jik. Subjects are arranged in kana order, and in Vol. IX are three indices: one in

Reference Materials 25

Chinese characters, one in the kana transliteration of foreign words and names, and one in romanizations of foreign words and names.

GEOGRAPHICAL NAMES

Here are listed the important reference works on geographical names since the founding of Yi dynasty. For place names before the fourteenth century see the index to Sinjŭng Tongguk Yŏji Sŭngnam (118).

Western

(89)   Katō, Bunjirō, and S. Kanazawa. A Catalogue of the Romanized Geographical Names of Korea. Tōkyō: Imperial University, 1903. Gives the romanized Korean and Japanese names, Chinese characters, and an English translation.

(90)   Gazetter to Maps of Korea. Washington, 1950. 3 vols. Locates place names which appear on issues of Army Map Service maps, series L 751-Korea, 1:50,000; and several sheets of L 542-Manchuria, 1:250,000. Incorporates the work of the Korea Names Survey of the Far East Command. Romanization follows the McCune-Reischauer system.

(91)   A Manual of Korean Geographical and Other Proper Names Romanized. Yokohama: Japan Mail Office, 1883. Compiled for the British legation in Korea. It is divided into two parts: the first locates and identifies Korean geographical names; the second lists a selection of Chinese characters used by Koreans for proper names and places, with their more common pronunciations. The first part can be used as a modified historical atlas of Korea under the Yi dynasty. Geographical names were taken principally from the Taejŏn Hoet'ong (473) and a map of Korea published by the Japanese General Staff. Coverage is by no means complete, but the manual is one of the few books of its kind in a Western language.

(92)   Map of Korea. Washington: Korean Affairs Institute, 1945. One of the better maps of modern Korea. It is a thirteen-sheet sectional map of Korea which shows the details of administrative

boundaries, rivers, cities, roads and railroads, and important mountains. Supplemental maps bound with it show the distribution of natural resources and industries, the physiography of the country, and Korea's position in the Far East. There is a good index. McCune-Reischauer romanization is used.

(93)   Place Name Index for Korea (Chōsen). Washington: War Department, 1943.   Comprises two main indices, one transcribing place names in romanized Japanese-Korean, and the other in romanized Korean-Japanese. Korean romanization is according to the McCune-Reischauer system. Names in both indices are listed in English alphabetical order. In the Japanese-Korean index, the Chinese characters and han-gŭl are given for each place name. Both indices have location symbols by which names can be found on the map of Korea (1:1,500,000) which is bound in the book. The book also contains a glossary of common Japanese and Korean geographical terms. Despite errors, this book is a basic reference work for Korea since 1910.

MISCELLANEOUS REFERENCE WORKS
Western

(94)   Gardner, Charles S. Chinese Traditional Historiography. Cambridge: Harvard University Press, 1938.   Probably the best work in a Western language for understanding the complex process of writing history in China and how historical composition there differed from Western methods. Korean historians used the Chinese method.

(95)   Landis, E. B. "Numerical Categories of Korea," The Korean Repository, III, (1896), 431-438; 463-468.   A survey of Korean numerical categories in which some of the unique characteristics of these categories are described.

   Although Korea borrowed most of her major artistic and scientific ideas from China, it is dangerous to say that there have been no Korean survivals even in spheres where the influence of Chinese civilization was especially strong. Numerical categories provide a good example of the persistence and development of the Korean element, for although similar in many ways to the Chinese, they are unmistakably different.

(96)　McCune, George M. "The Yi Dynasty Annals of Korea," <u>TAKBRAS</u>, XXIX (1939), 57-82. Gives valuable information about the Korean method of writing history. The article deals mainly with the compilation and preservation of the <u>Yijo Sillok</u> (289), but is also has general information on the tradition of compilation and the motivation of Korean historians.

(97)　Mayers, William F. <u>The Chinese Reader's Manual</u>. London: Probsthain and Co., 1910. Reprint of 1874 edition. Helpful for general information on China needed by the student of Korea.

Korean

(98)　Ch'oe Nam-sŏn. <u>Yŏksa Ilgam</u> 歷史日鑑 역사일감 (Daily Mirror of History). Seoul: Tongmyŏng-sa, 1947. 2 vols. A day-by-day record of important events in Korean history which follows the lunar calendar—the official calendar in Korea until January 1, 1896. Lists brief biographies of important men; the dates of the completion of law codes or the promulgation of significant edicts, of influential political or military developments, of major festivals and popular celebrations, and of the establishment of various institutions, often including notes on their history, development, and importance in Korean life. There are brief discussions of each month's major festivals, their origins and historical background. There is no index. One must know the approximate date of an event to look it up.

(99)　<u>Taedong Unbu Kunok</u> 大東韻府群玉 대동운부군옥 (Korean Dictionary of Rhymes). Seoul, 1798. A very important reference book for early Korean literature. It was compiled by Kwŏn Mun-hae 權文海 권문해 in 1588 as an encyclopedia of things Korean from the time of Tan-gun to the reign of King Sŏnjo (1568-1608). The material was divided into twenty books and arranged according to the standard Chinese rhyme scheme which included eleven categories—geography, names of dynasties, family names, personal names, filial sons, virtuous wives, district magistrates, spirits, trees, plants, and birds. The preface says the book was patterned after the Yüan 元 dynasty rhyming encyclopedia, Yün-fu Ch'ün-yü 韻府群玉 by Yin Shih-fu 陰時夫 , and used 15 Chinese and 175 Korean sources. Maurice Courant in his Bibliographie Coréene (7), calls the Taedong Unbu Kunok the most valuable source he found on Korean literature.

Japanese

(100)   Chōsen Sōtokufu Tōkei Nempō 朝鮮總督府統計年報 (Statistical Yearbook of the Korean Government General, [1910-1944]). Keijō, 1911-1945. The most complete source of statistical information on Korea during the Japanese occupation. Although some of the figures seem questionable, for most purposes they may be accepted as presenting an accurate picture of economic, social, and other activities in Korea susceptible to statistical analysis.

Extracts (yōran 要覧) from the statistical tables were published for several of the yearbooks.

(101)   Kitagawa Sajin 北川左人 . Chōsen Koyūshoku Jiten 朝鮮固有色辭典 (Dictionary of Unique Characteristics of Korea). Keijō: Seiko Hakkō-sho, 1932. Contains much information on unusual Korean customs and manners, and some historical data. It has an index in kana order.

(102)   O Ch'ŏng 吳晴 오청 . Chōsen no Nenjū Gyōji 朝鮮の年中行事 (Annual Festivals of Korea). 7th ed. Keijō: Chōsen Sōtokufu, 1937. A complete and yet easily understandable description of each celebration and popular festival; songs, pictures, and stories help explain them. Arranged chronologically according to the lunar calendar. Historical sources often cited.

Geography

Korea's geographic position in the heart of the Far East has had a profound effect on its history. The peninsula of Korea has served as a bridge between the continent and Japan; along this bridge numerous invading forces have spent themselves. Despite these invasions, the Korean people have been able to develop and maintain a national consciousness and a distinctive Korean culture.

The peninsula, which stretches some 600 miles from 43°N to 34°N, has a broad mountainous base and an area of 85,328 miles. Its width varies from 120 to 160 miles, and its southern end is a maze of islands and inlets. Some fifty miles off the south coast is volcanic Cheju-do 濟州島 제주도 (Quelpart Island).

The peninsular character of Korea modifies the humid continental climate. The northern interior has bitterly cold winters; the southern coast relatively mild ones, with average January temperatures above freezing. Both sections have heavy rainfall in the hot summer months.

The largest rivers flow either west or south; some have etched out flood plains and developed alluvial plains in their lower courses. Along the shores of the Yellow Sea are extensive tidal flats, some of which have been reclaimed. Most of Korea, however, is a land of small valleys, abrupt hills, and high mountains. The northern interior is a mountainous land with narrow valleys formed by the tributaries of the Yalu (Amnok 鴨綠 암록) and Tumen (Tuman 豆滿 두만) rivers, which are Korea's northern boundary. Paektu-san 白頭山 백두산 , a volcanic massif, forms the drainage divide between these two river systems; its widespread lava flows have capped some of the summits of the northern interior. From this mountainous heartland, a major mountain chain, the T'aebaek 太白 태백 , extends southward, roughly parallelling the east coast. It is broken by passes, notably the trough between Seoul and Wŏnsan. In south Korea, from the central portion of the T'aebaek range an offshoot trends diagonally to the southwest. This range, the Sobaek 小白 소백 , culminates in the massive Chii-san 智異山 지이산 .

Some 80 per cent of the population (25,900,142 in 1944, the date of the last complete census) are farmers, although only about one-fifth of Korea, because of its rugged terrain, is suitable for agriculture. In the north they are limited generally to one crop a year; in the south they may grow two crops on some of their fields. Thus, population densities, which reflect the carrying capacities of the land, are much greater in the south than in the north. Coal, iron ore, minor minerals, and water for the production of hydroelectric power are much more abundant in the north, so that most of the Japanese industrial exploitation took place there. Korea's geographic character, essential geographic unity, and its geographic position in the Far East, need careful study and analysis.

The early Western writers of general works on Korea such as Dallet (379), Griffis (168), and Hulbert (169), included much geographic information in their writings. Numerous books of travel and description are listed in Underwood-Gompertz (15) and other bibliographies. However, the most useful works in Western languages on Korean geography have been relatively recent. These books are described in the selected titles. In addition, there are many recent publications by the American government on Korean geography, most of which are not available for general use.

The early Korean writers made little distinction between geography and history; they felt that the two subjects were closely intertwined. Thus most general works on Korean history and society have sections on the geography of Korea. Notable among such writings are the Munhŏn Pigo (83), Samguk Sagi (225), Koryŏ-sa (240), Haedong Yŏksa (241), and Sejong Sillok (289).

Some Korean writings are more definitely geographic in character, describing provinces, major routes of travel, notable sights, and cities. Courant has an interesting discussion and bibliography of these; an English translation of extracts from Courant's work was prepared by Shannon McCune (105). Unfortunately, in the postwar period Korean scholars have had little opportunity for geographic studies and little work of a scholarly character has been published in Korean. There are some simple texts and atlases prepared for school use, but major works based on field research remain to be written.

Before and during their control of Korea the Japanese developed a vast literature on Korean geography. They needed basic data, and one of their first tasks was the thorough mapping of the peninsula at a scale of 1:50,000. These topographic sheets are the basis for the United States Army Map Service maps of Korea at various scales. Shannon McCune has written a note on this subject (104). Much of the Japanese research in natural and social science is of value for geographic studies; for example, the bibliography of Korean geologic literature up to 1933 (106) lists some 547 references. However, no attempt is made to survey that Japanese research here; the basic works are listed in Lautensach's bibliography (107).

BIBLIOGRAPHIES

(103)   Lautensach, Hermann. "Korea (1926-36) mit Nachtragen aus alterer Zeit," Geographisches Jahrbuck, LIII (1938), 1:255-274.

(104)   McCune, Shannon. "Maps of Korea"; "Geographic Publications of Hermann Lautensach on Korea"; and "Recent Geographical Works on Korea," Far Eastern Quarterly, V (1946), 326-329; 330-332; XII (1953), 222-225.

(105)   McCune, Shannon. Old Korean Geographical Works: a Bibliography. Seattle: Korean Research Associates, 1939. (Mimeographed).

(106)   Chōsen ni okeru Chishitsu oyobi Kōbutsu no Chōsa Enkaku narabi ni Bunken 朝鮮に於ける地質及鑛物の調査沿革並に文献 (History and Bibliography of the Investigation of Geology and Minerals in Korea). Keijō: Chōsen Kōgyō-kai, 1933.

GEOGRAPHICAL WORKS
Western

(107)   Lautensach, Hermann. <u>Korea, eine Landeskunde auf Grund eigener Reisen und der Literatur.</u> Leipzig: K. F. Koehler, 1945. A large book, the most definitive work yet to appear on Korean geography. A section on the physical and human geography of Korea is followed by a treatment of Korean <u>landschaften</u>, or regions, and the final third of the book discusses the effect of the Japanese occupation, particularly on the economic life of Korea. The bibliography is excellent.

(108)   Lautensach, Hermann. <u>Korea: Land, Volk, Schicksal.</u> Stuttgart: K. F. Koehler, 1950. Prepared because his earlier work was out of print. This short geography brings some of the material of the larger work up to date.

(109)   McCune, Shannon. "Climate of Korea" and "Climatic Regions," <u>Research Monographs on Korea</u>, Series B, nos. 1-4; Series E, nos. 1-9 (1945). Drawn from McCune's unpublished doctoral dissertation, <u>The Climatic Regions of Korea</u> (Clark University, 1939).

A book by the same author, <u>Korea: A Regional Geography</u>, is being prepared for publication. It will be a detailed study of regional variations in Korea, intended to provide in English a readily accessible survey of Korea's geographic character, physical and human.

(110)   Zaichikov, V. T. <u>Koreia</u>. Moscow: National Institute of Geographical Literature, 1947. Second edition, Moscow, 1951. Depends greatly on the work of Dr. Lautensach (107, 108) and work of the Japanese geographers listed below. The first edition was translated by Dr. Albert Perry, of Colgate University, as <u>Geography of Korea</u> (New York: Institute of Pacific Relations, 1952). In an introduction to the translation, Shannon McCune discusses the background of Korean geographical studies and quotes some Russian comments on the book.

The second edition adds introductory chapters dealing with historical background, recent political developments, and the work of Russian explorers and geographers in Korea, and contains maps showing the political boundaries determined by North Korea.

Korean

(111) Chŏng Yag-yong 丁若鏞 정약용. <u>Taehan Kang-yŏk-ko</u> 大韓疆域攷 대한강역고 (Treatise on Korean Borders). Keijō: Chōsen Kenkyū-kai, 1915. 2 vols. An edition with a Japanese translation of a work by the Korean geographer Chŏng (1762-1836). The original, compiled in ten books in three fascicles, describes the boundaries of the states of ancient Korea and contains, in addition, much general information on the geography of old Korea. A revision, compiled in nine books in two fascicles, added a map and a description of the border markers on Paektu-san. The 1915 edition was made from the revision but does not have the map.

(112) Hong Kyŏng-mo 洪敬謨 홍경모. <u>Chungjŏng Namhan-ji</u> 重訂南漢志 중정남한지 (Re-edited Monograph on Namhan). Keijō: Chōsen Kosho Kankō-kai, 1916. An edition of the revised version (1846?) by Sŏ Myŏng-ŭng 徐命膺 서명응 of the eighteenth-century <u>Namhan-ji</u> (Monograph on Namhan). The monograph describes the area around Namhan-san 南漢山 남한산, the site of the capital of Paekche built by King Onjo (18 B.C.-28 A.D.) and of the fort completed in 1636 by King Injo to defend Korea against the Manchus.

The 1916 edition does not contain the colored map of the area which is in Sŏ Myŏng-ŭng's revision. A manuscript of his revision, in six books in four fascicles, with the map, is in the East Asiatic Library of the University of California.

(113) Kim Chŏng-ho 金正浩 김정호. <u>Taedong Yŏjido</u> 大東輿地圖 대동여지도 (Maps of Korea). Keijō: Keijō Teikoku Daigaku, 1936. Twenty-one folding sectional maps which can be fitted together and which show physical and human geography of the late Yi dynasty period. This edition has a separately bound index by Suematsu Yasukazu.

Kim, unlike many Oriental scholars of his time, did not rely upon books for his information but travelled throughout Korea to make his own observations. He published the maps, after some hesitation, in 1861 and again in 1864. Kim was imprisoned, charged with having prepared the maps to help the Japanese invade Korea.

(114)　　Kim No-gyu 金魯奎 김로규 . <u>Pugyŏ Yosŏn</u> 北輿要選 북여요선 (Essential Selections on Northern Geography). 1903. 2 books in 1 fascicle. A border marker was set up in 1712 to indicate the boundary between Korea and China, but there were continual disputes about its proper location. Kim No-gyu, a Korean government inspector, reviewed all available sources for a study of the subject and extracted important quotations for this compilation.

(115)　　Min Chu-myŏn 閔周冕 민주면 and Sŏng Wŏn-muk 成原默 성원묵 . <u>Tonggyŏng Chapki</u> 東京雜記 동경잡기 (Miscellany of the Eastern Capital). 1845. 3 books in 3 fascicles. First printed in 1669. Compiled from the extant geographies of Kyŏngju 慶州 경주 . Supplemented and given its present title by Sŏng Wŏn-muk in 1845.

Kyŏngju, the seat of the kings of Silla for several centuries, was popularly known as the Eastern Capital. Min Chu-myŏn received the degree of <u>chinsa</u> in 1648, and was later an official in the city.

This work contains much to interest the archaeologist and sociologist as well as the historically minded geographer under such topical subdivisions as "History of Official Titles," "Village Names," "Customs," "Famous Places," "Storehouses," "Schools," "Way-stations," "Bridges," "Buddhist Houses," "Monuments," "Forests," "Number of Households," "Famous Officials," "Mausolea," "Arts," and "Books."

(116)　　Pak No-sik 朴魯植 박로식 . <u>Sin Chosŏn Chiri</u> 新朝鮮地理 신조선지리(New Geography of Korea). Seoul: Tongji-sa, 1947. One of few modern Korean works in geography. Written, the author states in his preface, for teachers in elementary and secondary schools, for university students, and for specialists. It is in three sections: physical geography (location, land, weather);

human geography (industry, communications, villages); and regional divisions (dialectical and geographical regionalism, local peculiarities). The bibliography lists Japanese and Korean works.

(117)   Sŏng-nŭng 聖能 성능 (Sŏk Sŏng-nŭng 釋聖能 석성능). Pukhan-ji 北漢志 북한지 (Monograph on Pukhan). 1745. 1 fascicle. Describes the topography of Pukhan, its look-out towers, bridges, and moats; gives the history of the castle.

According to the Samguk Sagi (225), the first fortification at Pukhan was built by King Kaeru of Paekche in 132. Sŏk Sŏng-nŭng was a bonze resident at the mountain fortress after its renovation in 1711.

(118)   Yang Sŏng-ji 梁誠之 양성지 and No Sa-jin 盧思愼 로사진. Sinjŭng Tongguk Yŏji Sŭngnam 新增東國輿地勝覽 신증동국여지승람 (Revised Survey of Korean Geography). Keijō: Chōsen Shigak-kai, 1930. 4 vols. The most important early Korean work on geography; written for early Yi dynasty administrators. It contains data on place names, important shrines, halls, palaces, tombs, and monuments; on the changes in administrative divisions of Korea; on the natural products of several areas; on important families, family seats, and government officials; and on folklore and legends.

The book was begun in 1455 by Yang Sŏng-ji and completed in 1481 by No Sa-jin. The first revision was ordered in 1486 by King Sŏngjong, who wanted to pattern the geography after the Chinese Ta Ming I T'ung Chih 大明一統志 (Record of the Realm of the Great Ming), 1461. Revised again in 1499 and 1530. The geographical sections of the Munhŏn Pigo (83) depend on the Sinjŭng Tongguk Yŏji Sŭngnam for much information about the period before 1530.

There are several modern reprints, but often these do not reproduce the cartography of the earlier Korean editions. The Shidehara edition (Tōkyō, 1905-1906) has many errors and omissions. The East Asiatic Library at the University of California has one of the rare early editions.

A description of the contents and the story of the compilation of the work was given by H. B. Hulbert in his "An Ancient Gazetteer of Korea," Korean Repository, IV (1897), 407-416.

(118a)   Suematsu Yasukazu. Shinzō Tōkoku Yochi Shōran Sakuin 新増東國輿地勝覽索引 (Index to the Revised Survey of Korean Geography). Keijō: Chōsen Sōtokufu, 1937-1940. 2 vols. A detailed breakdown of the contents of the work.

Japanese

(119)   Nihon Chiri Taikei 日本地理大系 (Outline Geography of Japan). Tōkyō: Kaizōsha, 1930. 12 vols. Each volume covers a particular region of the Japanese Empire. The work has hundreds of maps and photographs, many in colors, and much of the text is commentary on the pictures.

Volume XII deals with the Korean peninsula. It contains a general description of the country, sections on physical geography (including topography, climatology, oceanography, botany, zoology, and endemic diseases); human geography (including government, defense, industry, agriculture, forestry, marine science, mining, engineering, trade, communications, population, education, and religion); ethnology; language; customs; general history; and a history of art. The treatises on specialized subjects were written by well-known Japanese scholars.

(120)   Tsuda Sōkichi 津田左右吉 . Chōsen Rekishi Chiri 朝鮮歷史地理(Korean Historical Geography). Tōkyō: Minami Manshū Tetsudō Kabushiki Kaisha, 1913. 2 vols. Deals with the geographical aspects of Korean history from the time of the Sam Han period through the first hundred years of the Yi dynasty. The work discusses the changing boundaries of Korea and the historical events related to these changes; the establishment of towns, fortresses, garrisons, and the intricacies of their constantly changing names. Both volumes contain many detailed colored maps on which the old names of places are printed in red and the new names in black. The maps thoroughly illustrate the discussions in the text, e.g., wakō raids, military advances of Silla, and the southward expansion of Koguryō.

Geography 37

Chinese

(121) Hu Huan-yung 胡煥庸. Ch'ao-hsien Ti-li 朝鮮地理 (Geography of Korea). Chungking: Ching-hua Yin shu kuan, 1945. Gives a brief description of the various provinces, and information on topography, rivers, coasts, weather, agriculture, mining, communications, trade, and population.

Note: For further information on geography see 83, 87, 89, 90, 91, 92, 93, 185, 191, 208, 222, 344, 346.

IV

Art and Archaeology

When the plan for the <u>Guide</u> was drawn up, art and archaeology were each given separate chapters. The chapter on archaeology was placed here, the first of the chapters on history, because many archaeological studies give information on Korea's early political history. The chapter on art was placed with the chapters on music and literature. This arrangement created a serious difficulty: the two bibliographies overlapped. Some books on Korean art began with archaeological artifacts; some books on Korean archaeology were also studies of art. Separate bibliographies involved either repeating many titles or giving so many cross-references that the bibliographies became unwieldy; they were therefore combined.

Archaeology

From 1902, when Sekino Tadashi 關野貞 made a survey of Korean antiquities, until 1945, the Japanese conducted the investigations into ancient Korea on which all Korean archaeology is based. The work was done by a small group of men, most of them members of the Service of Antiquities for the Government General and later, of the Society for the Study of Korean Antiquities, which was formed in 1931 and which after 1935 took over most of the archaeological activity.

They made many important discoveries: the site of the Han 漢 Chinese colony of Lo-lang 樂浪 락 낭 (Nangnang) near modern P'yŏng-yang 平壤 평양, by Sekino; tumuli of Paekche, Silla, and Mimana 任那 in South Korea, by Hamada; the Kŭmhae 金海 금해 shell mounds, by Umehara and Hamada; Koguryŏ remains in North Korea and Manchuria. Studies of these and other findings were published by the Service or the Society.

After 1945 Korean archaeologists continued the work of the

Japanese—e.g., the publications of Kim Chae-wŏn 金載元 김재원, of the National Museum of Korea—until the Korean war. There is still much work to be done, both new research and the editing and publication of Japanese material that has remained in manuscript.

Conclusive evidence of a paleolithic culture in Korea has not been found, but neolithic remains are abundant, especially in river basins and on sea shores. Kitchen middens are widely scattered. A very few chipped stones have been uncovered in northeastern Korea. Polished stones are much more numerous throughout the peninsula, as in China and Japan. Bone tools have been found in early neolithic sites on the northeast coast and near Pusan, and are numerous in later neolithic sites.

There are five types of neolithic tombs: dolmen, cyst, cairn, urn, wooden chamber. Menhirs and two types of dolmens exist throughout Korea. Northern dolmens resemble those found in Europe. No dolmens have been found in Japan. Most dolmens seem to date from the third century B.C. Cyst graves were apparently more popular than dolmens in the later neolithic period. Stone cairns cover stone cyst tombs. The cairns of central Korea are of the late stone age. Most of the burial urns are near the shell mounds around Pusan. In urn burials the body was laid in two urns, whose mouths were sealed together. Bronze weapons were found in one urn burial site. Similar urns, dating apparently from the first century B.C. to the first century A.D., are in northern Kyūshū 九州, Japan. The wooden chambers seem to predate the Lo-lang colony. They are subterranean, like those in North China, and contain bronze implements.

There are three types of stone-age pottery in Korea: comb-marked, unfigured, and red figured. Comb-marked pottery, which resembles the kamm keramics of northern Europe and central Siberia, has been found in Korea with stone implements (never with metal objects) and only near river mouths. Unmarked pottery exists throughout the peninsula and in Japan; this suggests a migration from China through Korea to Japan. Red pottery has been found in neolithic burial sites, occasionally with unmarked pottery.

After Chinese metal culture entered Korea, metal and stone

implements existed together for a long time. Chou 周 bronze culture came into Korea during the time of the Warring Kingdoms (403-221 B.C.). Bronze knife money minted in the Chinese state of Yen 燕 has been found in north Korea along with metal tools and polished stones.

During the Han dynasty (202 B.C.-220 A.D.) Chinese colonists settled in Korea, and this encouraged Korean trade with China and Japan. This period is rich in archaeological finds, especially around P'yŏng-yang. In the tombs of Lo-lang (c. 108 B.C.-313 A.D.) have been found bronze and iron weapons and implements, horse trappings, jewelry, pottery, lacquerware, and fragments of silk and leather. Some coins found were minted in 60 B.C. Coins struck by Wang Mang 王莽 (9-23) have been uncovered in the Kŭmhae shell mounds together with stone and deer-horn artifacts. On Cheju-do, bronze mirrors, daggers, and Wang Mang coins were found under deep volcanic ash. Some Korean bronzes, especially some types of bells not found in China, show Scytho-Siberian influence in design.

Tombs of the Three Kingdoms, especially Silla tombs of Kyŏngju, yielded numerous kinds of implements, jewelry, and pottery; and there are notable wall paintings in some Koguryŏ tombs. Paekche tombs are less fruitful; they were looted by T'ang 唐 Chinese troops in 660, when Paekche was destroyed by the coalition of T'ang and Silla.

Stone monuments of the Three Kingdoms and of later Korean states are valuable for the light they throw on political activities, national boundaries, and disputed historical points.

Art

The Three Kingdoms period was notable for its Buddhist art, which, in Chinese forms from Indian inspiration, flowed into Korea and on to Japan. Huge bronze bells, icons after the manner of Sui 隋 and T'ang, carved stupas, and especially the stone reliefs of the Sŏkkuram 石窟庵 석굴암 cave temple, are some of the major achievements in the art of the Three Kingdoms.

In the Koryŏ period, Buddhist inspiration continued. The outstanding new development was the delicately cracked celadons, some of them incised with black and white clays to form unique designs. In the tenth century Buddhism encouraged the cutting of wooden printing blocks after the manner of those invented shortly before in China; and in the thirteenth century Koreans began to use movable wooden type.

The Yi dynasty supported the philosophy of Confucius instead of the theology of Buddha. The Yi kings confiscated the wealth of the temples and regulated the number of priests. With this persecution Buddhist art gradually declined, and the great period of sculpture and architecture ended. At the same time, the ceramic industry of Koryŏ, already badly impaired by Mongol despoilment, fell off in the quality of its product.

On the other hand, Confucian scholarship furthered the development of typography and paper-making. By 1403, fifty years before Gutenberg, the Koreans were using movable metal type, and magnificent books were printed at royal expense. Copying Chinese classics in preparation for the Confucian examinations created a new interest in calligraphy and a dexterity in the use of the brush. This dexterity greatly affected Korean painting, which still shows the calligraphic influence in its dignity, breadth of execution, simplicity of form, and refinement of taste.

BIBLIOGRAPHIES

(122)   Gerow, Bert A. Publications in Japanese on Korean Anthropology. Stanford University, 1952. (Mimeographed.) Compiled from uncatalogued material in the professional library of Professor Kanaseki, formerly of Taihoku Imperial University, Taiwan, purchased by the Far Eastern Library Committee of Stanford University in 1949. Lists 225 items which include many Korean anthropological studies previously unavailable to Western scholars in a single library or collection.

(123)   Hewes, G. W. "Archaeology of Korea: A Selected Bibliography." Research Monographs on Korea, Series F, no. 1 (1947). A list of books and articles in Western languages, and some Japanese publications.

WORKS ON ART AND ARCHAEOLOGY
Western

(124) Carter, Thomas Francis. The Invention of Printing in China and Its Spread Westward. New York: Columbia University Press, 1925. Does not state whether printing came from China and Korea to Europe, but it does point out "the parallelism in the working of the human mind on the two sides of the world, a parallelism that has been manifest at every stage in the history of printing." Part four deals with printing in movable type, and chapter xxiii describes the invention and development of metal movable type by the Koreans. Carter used Oriental sources, but rarely from Korea. Unfortunately, he did not use the Tongguk Yi Sangguk-chip (245).

(125) Courant, Maurice. "Stèle chinoise du royaume du Ko Kou Rye," Journal asiatique, IX (1899), 210-239. Describes the Hot'ae-wang-bi好太王碑호태왕비, a stele dedicated to King Kwanggaet'o (391-413) of Koguryŏ, in Manchuria near the Korean border—its authenticity, place names on it, etc. This stele gives important information about Japanese-Korean relations in the fourth century. Courant gives a reproduction and a translation of the inscription. The article is based on the work of Yokoi, Tsuboi, Suge, and Naka.

(126) DuPont, Maurice. Décoration Coréene. Paris: Libraire des Arts Décoratifs, 1927. Forty-eight admirable plates in portfolio, some in color, with a brief preface and a descriptive table by M. Dupont, librarian of the Musée Guimet. The illustrations show tomb frescoes, paintings on silk, sculpture, metal mirrors, ceramics, lacquerware, inlaid work, embroidery, and woodblock prints.

(127) Eckhardt, Andreas. A History of Korean Art. Translated from the German by J. M. Kindersley. London: E. Goldston, 1929. The first general history of Korean art in any European language. Gives special attention to architecture, sculpture, painting, and pottery; but also discusses bronze articles, bells, silver and gold work, lacquer, woodcarving, and embroidery. Over 500

well-chosen illustrations support the thesis of the book: that "we
are . . . fully justified in speaking of a Korean art, an art which
differs in manifold respects from the art of China and Japan."

(128)   Honey, W. B. Corean Pottery. London: Faber and Faber,
1947. Regards Korean pottery as "one of the summits of all
ceramic achievement," outstanding for its distinctive beauty of
form and sombre decoration, inferior to the Chinese wares only
in range of technical resources and variety of colored glazes.
Gives a brief description of surviving pottery in chronological
sequence, showing the progression from incised and inlaid patterns to the painted simplicity of the late Koryŏ and early Yi
celadons. Numerous illustrations.

(129)   Kümmel, Otto. Die Kunst Chinas, Japans und Koreas. Wild-
park-Potsdam: Academische Verlagsgesellschaft Athenaion, 1929.
A scholarly survey of Far Eastern art, with many beautiful illustrations. Korean art, as an independent subject, is treated in
five pages, but the work as a whole distinguishes the position of
Korea, midway between China and Japan, in the historical development of artistic forms.

(130)   Rackham, Bernard. Catalogue of the Le Blond Collection of
Corean Pottery. London: Victoria and Albert Museum, 1918.
Describes the collection of Korean pottery formed by Aubrey Le
Blond during a visit to Korea in 1913, one of the largest collections in Europe. The catalogue has a general introduction, a bibliography, and many illustrations. Rackham was Assistant Keeper
of the Department of Ceramics of the Museum.

(131)   Szczesniak, Boleslaw. "The Kōtaiō Monument," Monumenta
Nipponica, VII½ (1951), 242-268. Discusses the Hot'ae-wang-
bi erected in 414—the significance of the stele and previous
studies. It has a transcription of the inscription, an annotated
translation, and photographs of the stele.

Korean

(132)   Han Hŭng-su 韓興洙 한흥수 "Chosŏn ŭi Kŏsŏk Munhwa Yŏn-
gu" 朝鮮의 巨石文化硏究 조선의 거석문화 연구 (Studies

on Megalithic Culture of Korea), Chindan Hakpo, III (1935), 132 ff. Classifies Korean megalithic remains as (1) standing stones (menhirs), (2) supported stones (dolmens), and (3) stone piles and fences. These Han describes in detail. For a resume, see James Hoyt's "Some Points of Interest from Han Hŭng-su's 'Studies on Megalithic Culture of Korea,'" American Anthropologist, L (1948), 573-574.

(133)   Kim Chae-wŏn. Ho-u Ch'ong kwa Ŭnnyong Ch'ong 壺杅塚과 銀鈴塚 호우총과 은령총 (Ho-u Tomb and Silver Bell Tomb). Kungnip Pangmulgwan Kojŏk Chosa Pogo Che-ilch'aek 國立博物館古蹟調査報告第一册 국립박물관고적조사보고 제일책 (Report of the Research of Antiquities of the National Museum of Korea, Vol. 1). Seoul: Ŭryu Munhwa-sa, 1948. Describes two tombs excavated at Kyŏngju, with an English summary. One of these tombs contained a bronze vessel dated 415. 44 plates.

(134)   Kim Yŏng-gi 金永基 김영기. Chosŏn Misul-sa 朝鮮美術史 조선미술사 (History of Korean Art). Seoul: Kŭmnyong Tosŏ Chusik Hoesa, 1947. A complete outline of Korean art, suitable as a college text or as a reference work. Essential information about architecture, sculpture, crafts, calligraphy, and painting from the Lo-lang period through the Yi dynasty.

(135)   Ko Yu-sŏp 高裕燮 고유섭. Chosŏn T'app'a ŭi Yŏn-gu 朝鮮塔婆의硏究 조선탑파의 연구 (Study of Korean Stupas). Seoul: Ŭryu Munhwa-sa, 1948. A comparative study of Chinese, Korean, and Japanese stupas—their history, aesthetic value, and methods of construction. The stupas of China were usually of brick; those of Korea, of stone; and those of Japan, of wood. Partly because of the material used, Korea has some of the oldest examples of pagoda art.

(136)   Sŏng Hyŏn 成俔 성현. Yongjae Ch'onghwa 慵齋叢話 용재총화 (Collected Essays of Yongjae). N.p., 1909. (Mimeographed). 3 books in 3 fascicles. These 15th-century essays are important in the history of Korean belles-lettres, and are valuable to the student of Korean art for their critical remarks on calligraphy and painting. Sŏng wrote them under his style Yongjae. There is no known printed edition.

(137)   Yun Hi-sun 尹喜淳 윤희순. Chosŏn Misul-sa Yŏn-gu 朝鮮美術史研究 조선미술사연구 (Research on the History of Korean Art). Seoul: Sŏul Sinmun-sa, 1946. A collection of brief subjective essays on the history and philosophy of Korean art. Most of them are about painting and calligraphy.

Japanese

(138)   Chōsen Bijutsu Taikan 朝鮮美術大觀 (Survey of Korean Art). Keijō: Chōsen Kosho Kankō-kai, 1910. A brief history of Korean art introduces the photographic illustrations of art objects of all periods—paintings, sculptures, ceramics, lacquerware, costumes, jewelry, swords and armor. These are briefly described in the book's appendix. 82 plates.

(139)   Chōsen Hōbutsu Koseki Zuroku 朝鮮寶物古蹟圖錄 (Illustrated Catalogue of Korean Treasures and Relics). Kyōto: Chōsen Sōtokufu, 1938-1940. 2 vols.

   Vol. I. "Bukkoku-ji to Sekkutsu-an" 佛國寺と石窟庵 (Pulguk-sa and Sŏkkuram). A folio of plates with a short introduction in Japanese giving the history of the Pulguk-sa, a Buddhist temple, and the Sŏkkuram, a cave containing many beautifully carved Buddhist images, both of the Silla period. They are near Kyŏngju. The plates consist of diagrams, sketches, and detailed photographs of both sites and their sculpture, and each is accompanied by a brief description. There is a list of plate titles in English. 76 plates.

   Vol. II. "Keishū Nanzan no Busseki" 慶州南山の佛蹟 (Buddhist Remains on Nam-san at Kyŏngju). Discusses the remains of several Buddhist temples and stupas built during the Silla period, and numerous Buddhist images and statues carved out of the rocks. Panoramic photographs of Nam-san and its vicinity; and photographs and sketches of the remains, both distant views and details. 111 plates.

(140)   Chōsen Kinseki Sōran 朝鮮金石總覽 (A Complete Survey of Korean Stone Monuments). Keijō: Chōsen Sōtokufu, 1919. 2 vols. Contains the text of inscriptions on stone monuments, grave stones, decrees engraved on stone, inscriptions on Buddhist statues, bells, incense burners, etc., collected by the

Government General from 1913 to 1916. The inscriptions are grouped chronologically by periods from the Three Kingdoms to the Yi dynasty. Nearly all the extant inscriptions of the Three Kingdoms and United Silla periods, and selected ones from the later periods, are reproduced. The earliest is dated 85 and the latest 1910.

(141)　　Chōsen Kofun Hekiga-shū 朝鮮古墳壁畫集 (Collection of Old Korean Tomb Wall Paintings). Keijō: Ri-ō-shoku, 1917. A collection of 105 fine photographs and sketches, many in color, of Koguryŏ tombs, tomb sites, tomb interiors, and details of tomb wall paintings. Sketches illustrate the various forms of tomb construction. There is a one-page introduction in English as well as an introduction in Japanese.

(142)　　Chōsen Koseki Zufu 朝鮮古蹟圖譜 (Album of Korean Antiquities). Keijō: Chōsen Sōtokufu, 1915-1935. 15 vols. A record of historical remains with examples of the arts, crafts, and architecture of each period. The collection is based on the archaeological survey that began before the Japanese annexation of Korea and continued through 1914. The first five volumes cover the period from before the Han Chinese invasion to the end of United Silla. Vols. VI-IX concern the Koryŏ period, and the rest cover the Yi dynasty. There is no explanatory text. It was planned to issue a commentary on each volume; but commentaries on only the first five volumes were published:

(142a)　　Chōsen Koseki Zufu Kaisetsu 朝鮮古蹟圖譜解說 (Commentary on the Album of Korean Antiquities). Keijō: Chōsen Sōtokufu, 1915-1917. 5 vols.

(143)　　Fujita Ryōsaku 藤田亮策. Chōsen Kōkogaku Kenkyū 朝鮮考古學研究 (Studies in Korean Archaeology). Kyōto: Takagiri Shoin, 1948. Nine studies of stone-age culture, Chinese knife money, Lo-lang tombs, Koguryŏ tombs, etc. 20 plates.

(144)　　Fujita Ryōsaku. Sugihara Chōtarō-shi Shūshū Kōkohin Zuroku 杉原長太郎氏蒐集考古品圖錄 (Illustrated List of Sugihara Chōtarō's Collection of Archaeological Articles). Kyōto: Chōsen Kōkogak-kai, 1944. Contains plates and descriptions of selected items from the collection of Sugihara. These items, ranging from Lo-lang to the end of Koryŏ, include weapons, bronze mirrors and vessels, gold earrings, tiles, ceramics, Buddhist metal objects, and statuary. 30 plates.

(145)　Hamada Kōsaku 濱田耕作 and Umehara Sueji 梅原末治. <u>Shiragi Koga no Kenkyū</u> 新羅古瓦の研究 (Study on the Ancient Tiles of the Silla), Kyōto Teikoku Daigaku Bungaku-bu Kōkogaku Kenkyū Hōkoku 京都帝國大學文學部考古學研究報告 (Report on Archaeological Research in the Department of Literature, Kyōto Imperial University, Vol. XIII). Tōkyō, 1934. A thorough description and discussion of tiles from the Silla period, tracing their development and the influences upon them from China and other lands. 119 plates.

(146)　Harada Yoshito 原田淑人 and Tazawa Kingo 田澤金吾. <u>Rakurō</u> 樂浪 (Lo-lang). Tōkyō: Tōkō Shoin, Tōkyō Teikoku Daigaku Bungaku-bu, 1930. A report of the excavation of the tomb of Wang Hsü 王旴. The site, excavation, and contents are described in detail and beautifully illustrated. Appended is an important discussion by Kiyono Kenji 清野謙次, Kaneseki Takeo 金關丈夫 and Hirai Takashi 平井隆 of the human remains in the tomb. The authors argue that the teeth found there show a closer resemblance to those of modern Koreans than to either Japanese or Chinese. English resume of the text, German resume of the appendix. 128 plates.

(147)　Ikeuchi Hiroshi 池内宏 and Umehara Sueji. <u>Tsūkō</u> 通溝 (Tung-kou [ancient Koguryŏ site in Chi-an 輯安 District, T'ung-hua 通化 Province, Manchuria]). Tōkyō: Nichi-Man Bunka Kyōkai, 1940, 2 vols. Vol. I describes an ancient capital of Koguryŏ, stelae including that of King Kwanggaet'o, and the dating of the tombs. Vol. II describes the tombs and their contents with particular attention to the wall paintings. Resumes in English and Chinese. 165 plates.

(148)　Karube Jion 輕部慈恩. <u>Kudara Bijutsu</u> 百濟美術 (Art of Paekche). Tōkyō: Hōun-sha, 1946. A survey of Paekche architecture, sculpture, metal work, pottery, and painting, and a history of Paekche, written by a resident of many years in Kongju 公州 공주, the ancient capital.

(149) Katsuragi Sueji 葛城末治. Chōsen Kinseki-kō 朝鮮金石攷 (Notes on Korean Stone Monuments). Keijō: Ōsaka-yago Shoten, 1935. Discusses inscriptions in general, the types and kinds of inscriptions found in Korea, both metal and stone, and the problems involved in their study. Major inscriptions are grouped by Korean historical periods and described at considerable length. 29 plates.

(150) Koizumi Akio 小泉顯夫. Rakurō Saikyō-zuka 樂浪彩篋塚 (Tomb of the Painted Basket of Lo-lang). Keijō: Chōsen Koseki Kenkyū-kai, 1934. Describes the excavation of Han Chinese tombs near P'yŏng-yang. Contents of the tombs are minutely described. 28-page English resume. 133 superb plates, some in color. Two maps and 50 illustrations. Plates have English and Japanese captions.

(151) Koseki Chōsa Gaihō 古蹟調査概報 (Brief Report of Investigation of Ancient Remains). Keijō: Chōsen Koseki Kenkyū-kai, 1934-1936. 3 vols. Three reports of excavations of Lo-lang tombs. Each has a descriptive title, and the last two contain a progress report for the year of the society's activities. They are listed by the year for which the report was made. (See also entry 152)

1933. Rakurō Kofun 樂浪古墳 (Lo-lang Tombs). Describes the excavation of eight Lo-lang tombs. 28 plates.

1934. Rakurō Kofun 樂浪古墳 Describes the excavation of four Lo-lang tombs. 21 plates.

1935. Rakurō Iseki 樂浪遺蹟 (Lo-lang Remains). Describes the excavation of five Lo-lang tombs and the site of an earth fort. 31 plates.

(152) Koseki Chōsa Hōkoku 古蹟調査報告 (Report of Investigation of Ancient Remains). Keijō: Chōsen Sōtokufu, 1917-1937; Keijō: Chōsen Koseki Kenkyū-kai, 1937-1940. 16 vols. The annual reports of the Service of Antiquities for the Government General for 1916-1934, and of the Society for the Study of Korean Antiquities for 1936-1938. The reports of the society may be con-

Art and Archaeology, 49

sidered as continuing the reports of the service, since all of them were published under the same title. In Japanese these are dated by the year of reign of the Emperor, e.g., Taishō Go-nendo Koseki Chōsa Hōkoku [Report for 1916]; Shōwa Roku-nendo Koseki Chōsa Hōkoku [Report for 1931]. They are listed by the year for which the report was made.

1916. Published in 1917. Contains the regulations of the committee for archaeological investigation. Describes (1) old forts and temples, (2) remains of Koryŏ, Silla, and Paekche, (3) royal graves of Koryŏ and Silla, (4) the excavation of Lo-lang tombs near P'yŏng-yang, (5) dolmens in Hwanghae-do 黄海道 황해도, and (6) shell mounds in P'yongan Namdo 平安南道 평안남도. 151 plates and 490 photographs.

1917. Published in 1920. Describes (1) remains of forts, temples, tombs, stelae, stupas, stone Buddhas, etc. found in Kyŏngsang Namdo 慶尚南道 경상남도, Kyŏngsang Pukto 慶尚北道 경상북도, P'yŏng-an-do 平安道 평안도, Hwanghae-do, and Kyŏnggi-do 京畿道 경기도; and (2) finds of Koguryŏ and of the Han Chinese colony in Hwanghae-do. 102 plates and 261 photographs.

1918. Published in 1922. By Hamada Kōsaku and Umehara Sueji. Describes the excavation of tombs in Kyŏngsang Pukto. A report on temples, forts, stelae, and stupas of Kyŏngsang Pukto is appended. 181 plates.

1919. Published in 1922. By Ikeuchi Hiroshi. Describes the remains of Koryŏ forts in Hamgyŏng Namdo 咸鏡南道 함경남도.

1920. Published in 1923. By Umehara Sueji and Hamada Kōsaku. Describes the excavation of the important Kŭmhae shell mounds in which were found Chinese coins. 24 plates and 14 maps.

1921. None issued.

1922. Published in 1924-1929. 2 vols. Vol. I, by Umehara Sueji and Hamada Kōsaku, has supplementary material on the Kŭmhae shell mounds. Vol. II, by Fujita Ryōsaku, Umehara Sueji, and Koizumi Akio, describes Han Chinese remains (largely bronze artifacts) in southern Korea. It has a supplement on bronze weapons excavated in northern Korea.

1923. Published in 1931. By Koizumi Akio and Nomori Takeshi 野守健 . Describes tombs (fifth or sixth century) excavated in Kyŏngsang Pukto. Pottery, swords, jewelry, and horse trappings were in the tombs. 152 plates.

1924. Published in 1932. Describes the excavation of the Kinsuzu-tsuka 金鈴塚(Golden-bell tomb) and the Shokuri-tsuka 飾履塚(Ornamental-shoe tomb) in Kyŏngju. These sixth-century Silla tombs contained harness, weapons, pottery, jewelry, glassware, bronze pots, and a clay wine pot in the shape of a mounted warrior. 214 plates separately bound.

1925. None issued.

1926. None issued.

1927. Published in 1929-1935. 2 vols. Vol. I, by Kanda Sōzō 神田惣藏 and Nomori Takeshi, is an excellent study of a Koryŏ kiln site at Kyeryong-san 鷄龍山 계룡산 . Vol. II describes Paekche tombs and their contents excavated at Kongju. 98 plates.

1930. Published in 1935. By Nomori Takeshi, Kayamoto Kamejirō 榧本龜次郎, and Kanda Sōzō. Describes the excavation of four Lo-lang tombs near P'yŏng-yang, notable for their wooden coffins and wooden statuary. 119 plates.

1931. Published in 1935. By Arimitsu Kyōichi 有光教一 . Describes the excavation of two Silla tombs at Kyŏngju.

1932. Published in 1937. 2 vols. Vol. I, by Kayamoto Kamejirō and Nomori Takeshi, describes the excavation of a grave in P'yŏng-yang dated the ninth year of Yung Ho 永和 of the Emperor Mu 穆 of the Eastern Chin 晉 dynasty. An appendix lists inscriptions of thirty-seven tombs whose dates of construction are known. The earliest is dated the ninth year of Chien Wu 建武 of the Han Emperor Kuang Mu 光武 (c. 33); the latest is reckoned either as 288 or 408 by the Christian calendar. 15 plates. Vol II, by Arimitsu Kyōichi, describes the excavation of ten Silla tombs near Kyŏngju. 54 plates of excellent sketches and photographs of details.

1933. None issued.
1934. Published in 1937. By Saitō Tadashi 齊藤忠. Describes the excavation of two tombs of the Three Kingdoms period near Kyŏngju. They contained pottery, iron weapons, jewelry, and harness. Many sketches and photographs. 53 plates.
1935. None issued.
1936. Published in 1937. The first of these reports issued by the Society for the Study of Ancient Remains. Describes (1) Koguryŏ tombs near P'yŏng-yang, (2) a tomb of the Three Kingdoms period in Kyŏngju, and (3) the site of a Paekche temple. 28 plates.
1937. Published in 1938. Describes (1) Koguryŏ tombs near P'yŏng-yang, (2) Silla stone Buddhas in Kyŏngju, (3) temple sites, (4) a Lo-lang tomb, and (5) foundations of the Unified Silla period in Kyŏngju. Has a progress report for 1937. 21 plates.
1938. Published in 1940. Describes (1) the site of a Koguryŏ temple, (2) six tombs of the Three Kingdoms period at Taegu 大邱 대구, and (3) a Silla temple site and restored stupa in Kyŏngju. Has a progress report for 1938. 31 plates.
See also entry 151.

(153)　Koseki Chōsa Tokubetsu Hōkoku 古蹟調査特別報告 (Special Report of Investigation of Ancient Remains). Keijō: Chōsen Sōtokufu, 1919-1929. 6 vols. Vols. II-VI have also descriptive titles. These reports are listed by volume, with date of publication immediately following.

　Vol. I. 1919. By Sekino Tadashi and others. Describes types of Lo-lang tombs. 63 illustrations.

　Vol. II. 1922. Hoku-Manshū oyobi Tōbu Shiberiya Chōsa Hōkoku 北滿洲及び東部西伯利亞調査報告 (Report of Investigation of Northern Manchuria and Eastern Siberia). By Torii Ryūzō 鳥居龍藏. A brief account of his observations of the people and the areas made during a trip in 1919.

　Vol. III. 1924-1927. Two parts. Keishū Kinkan-tsuka to Sono Ihō 慶州金冠塚と其遺寶 (The Gold Crown Tomb at Kyŏngju and Its Treasures). By Hamada Kōsaku and Umehara Sueji. Describes an early Silla tomb, and compares its contents with similar items found in other parts of Asia and in Europe. English titles and resume. 156 plates.

Vol. IV. 1927. Four parts. Rakurō-gun Jidai no Iseki 樂浪郡時代の遺蹟(Remains of the Lo-lang period). By Sekino Tadashi and others. Part one describes the administrative remains determined from archaeological evidence. Part two describes the history of the investigation of tombs, and the findings of an investigation of ten tombs. Part three describes Nien Ch'an Hsien 粘蟬縣 from stone monuments and other evidence. Part four describes art objects—stone, tile, clay, bronze; weapons, mirrors, jewels, lacquerware, and harness. 250 plates and 1,334 illustrations.

Vol. V. 1927. Two parts. (1) Ryōsan Fufu-tsuka to Sono Ibutsu 梁山夫婦塚と其遺物 (The Tomb of the Couple of Yangsan and Its Remains). By Ogawa Keikichi 小川敬吉 and Baba Koreichirō 馬場是一郎. A critical discussion of an early Silla tomb. (2) Kōkuri Jidai no Iseki 高句麗時代の遺蹟 (Remains of Koguryŏ period). By Sekino Tadashi and others. 222 plates and 662 illustrations of art objects and other remains. These pictures have no relation to the text of part one.

Vol. VI. 1929. Shinkō Ō no Boshi Junkyō-hi to Shiragi no Tōhoku-kyō 眞興王の戊子巡境碑と新羅の東北境 (King Chinhung's Border Marker o. 568 and the Northeast Boundary of Silla). By Ikeuchi Hiroshi. Describes Silla border markers in general as well as the marker named in the title. 11 plates and a map.

(154)   Nomori Takeshi. Kōrai Tōji no Kenkyū 高麗陶磁の研究 (Research on Koryŏ Pottery). Tōkyō: Seikan-sha, 1944. Describes in detail the wares of the Koryŏ period, classified by color, glaze, crackle, pattern and from. Discusses identifying descriptions such as reign titles, temple names, cyclical designations, Cites contemporary references to ceramics, e.g., the Koryŏ-sa (240) and the Tongguk Yi Sangguk-chip (245). Discusses remains of

Koryŏ kilns, with accounts of their sites; the operation of the kilns; and the tools of the craft. A color chart shows more than sixty-five tints used on this pottery. A chronological chart shows ceramic products of China, Japan, and Korea during the Koryŏ period. The 175 illustrations include several maps of historic kilns.

(155)   Oba Tsuneyoshi 小場恒吉 and Kayamoto Kamejirō. <u>Rakurō Ōkō-bo</u> 樂浪王光塚 (Tomb of Wang Kuang of Lo-Lang). Keijō: Chōsen Koseki Kenkyū-kai, 1935. Describes excavations made in 1932. The tomb contained a Han Chinese crossbow lock. 8-page English resume. 99 plates, some in color. 12 illustrations.

(156)   <u>Ri-ō-ke Hakubutsukan Shozō Shashin-chō</u> 李王家博物館所藏寫真帖 (Albums of Photographs of Art Objects Held by the Museum of the Yi Royal House). Keijō: Ri-ō-shoku, 1929. 3 vols. Three large folios of photographs, many in colors, of the art treasures from the museum of the royal family, classified as sculpture, ceramics, and painting. Each illustration is annotated, and there are general historical remarks in each volume.

(157)   Saitō Tadashi. <u>Chōsen Kodai Bunka no Kenkyū</u> 朝鮮古代文化の研究 (Study of Korean Ancient Culture). Tōkyō: Chijin Shokan, 1943. A discussion of Korean culture from the stone age through the Three Kingdoms period, comparing it with that of Japan. The basis of the book is the archaeological finds in Korea and Japan. The index is quite extensive.

(158)   Sekino Tadashi. <u>Chōsen Bijutsu-shi</u> 朝鮮美術史 (History of Korean Art). Kyōto: Chōsen Shigak-kai,. 1932. A survey history from the earliest time through the Yi dynasty. Concise statements on painting, sculpture, architecture, ceramics, lacquer, metalware, and archaeological remains. Sekino points out the importance of Korea to any study of Far Eastern art because copper bells, stone stupas, and other relics once common to China and Japan as well as Korea are now best preserved in the peninsula. 111 plates.

(159)   Sekino Tadashi. **Chōsen no Kenchiku to Geijutsu** 朝鮮の建築と藝術 (Korean Architecture and Art). Tōkyō: Iwanami Shoten, 1941. Contains the text of the **Chōsen Bijutsu-shi** (155) and twenty-three essays on specialized topics about the remains of the Three Kingdoms and earlier eras.

(160)   Sugihara Sadakichi 杉原定吉. **Chōsen Kokuhō Taikan** 朝鮮國寶大觀 (Survey of the National Treasures of Korea). Tōkyō: Dōbun-kan, 1911. Fifty beautiful plates selected to present a panoramic view of the best in Korean art from the Three Kingdoms period through the Yi dynasty—sculpture, metalwork, calligraphy, ceramics, embroidery, painting, and mother-of-pearl inlaid work. The illustrations accompanied by brief descriptions.

(161)   Sugiyama Shinzō 杉山信三. **Nippon Chōsen Hikaku Kenchiku-shi** 日本朝鮮比較建築史 (A History of the Comparative Architecture of Japan and Korea). Kyōto: Ōyashima Shuppan-sha, 1946. Examines the art of building in Korea and Japan in ancient and modern times to discover resemblances and differences in methods and techniques. The indebtedness of the early Japanese to Korean artisans is noted, but Japanese modifications and independent contributions are emphasized.

(162)   Umehara Sueji. **Chōsen Kodai no Bosei** 朝鮮古代の墓制 (Funerary Practices of Ancient Korea). Tōkyō: Zauhō Kankō-kai, 1947. Describes burial customs from the stone age through the Three Kingdoms period. 32 plates. It is reviewed by Sidney Kaplan in the **Harvard Journal of Asiatic Studies**, XI (1948), 223-227.

(163)   Umehara Sueji. **Chōsen Kodai no Bunka** 朝鮮古代の文化 (Ancient Culture of Korea). Kyōto: Takagiri Shoin, 1946. Reviews Korean culture from the stone age to the introduction of Buddhism in the Three Kingdoms period. A good summary of the archaeological work in Korea. The thorough documentation functions as an excellent bibliography. 32 plates.

(164)   Umehara Sueji and Fujita Ryōsaku. **Chōsen Kobunka Sōkan** 朝鮮古文化綜鑑 (A survey of the Ancient Culture of Korea). Kyōto: Yōtoku-sha, 1947-1948. 2 vols. The first two

volumes of a planned series of twelve. This series is intended to supplement the Chōsen Koseki Zufu (142). Vol. I, "Rakurō Zenki" (Pre-Lo-lang), concentrates on Chinese remains in Korea prior to the establishment of the Lo-lang prefecture, but does not include neolithic remains. Vol. II, "Rakurō" (Lo-lang), is devoted to materials from the Han Chinese colony Lo-lang tombs. The 100 plates are superb.

(165)   Yanagi Sōetsu 柳宗悦. Chōsen to Sono Geijutsu 朝鮮とその藝術 (Korea and Her Art). Tōkyō: Sōbun-kaku, 1922. A journalist's reaction to the Korean independence movement of 1919. Sensitive to the aesthetic values of the Korean people, the author desired a rapprochement of the Japanese and Koreans through a Japanese appreciation of peninsular art. His work is frankly sympathetic to the Korean point of view to a degree unusual in the writings of Japanese. Because of the writer's refreshing perspicacity, it is a good statement on the nature and value of Korean art.

(166)   Yoshida Eizaburō 吉田英三郎. Chōsen Shogaka Retsuden 朝鮮書畫家列傳 (Biographies of Korean Painters and Calligraphers). Keijō: Keijō Nippō-sha, 1915. Five hundred brief biographies of painters and calligraphers of the Three Kingdoms period. Entries are listed under surnames and also, by cross-reference, under all styles and courtesy names. There is a chronology from 47 B.C. to 1915 in the Korean, Japanese, Chinese and Western calendars. Based partly on the Samguk Sagi (225) and the Haedong Yŏksa (241).

Note: For further information on art and archaeology see 83, 185, 205, 212, 428.

V

General History

Ancient Korea.—According to legend the Korean nation was founded by Tan-gun, a semidivine figure, in 2333 B.C. Another tradition says that in 1122 B.C. Kija, the uncle of the last monarch of the Chinese Shang 商 dynasty, fled to Korea when the Shang were deposed by the Chou and built a capital at P'yŏngyang. The historicity of these figures has been severely challenged by many modern scholars. However, the legends tend to confirm very early contact between China and the peninsula.

Anthropological studies show that the earliest known inhabitants of the peninsula were a proto-caucasoid or paleo-asiatic people similar to the Ainu of northern Japan. During several millenia these people were submerged by migrations of Tungusic peoples from Manchuria.

The first actual records of Chinese contacts come from about 500 B.C., when Chou refugees founded a short-lived colony in northern Korea; the next from about 300 B.C., when exiles from the Kingdom of Yen in North China settled briefly in Korea. In 108 B.C. the Han Wu emperor invaded Korea and set up four prefectures. Of these, Lo-lang, centered on the Taedong 大同 대동 River, lasted until 313, when the Kingdom of Koguryŏ overran it.

Three Kingdoms.—The Chinese noted three tribes in southern Korea, usually referred to as the Sam 三 삼 (Three) Han 韓 한: the Ma Han 馬韓 마한 in the southwest; the Pyŏn Han 弁韓 변한 in the Naktong River basin; and the Chin Han 辰韓 진한 in the southeast. From the loose confederacy of these tribes emerged, in about the fourth century, two of the three Korean kingdoms that give the period its name—Silla and Paekche. Koguryŏ, the third kingdom, was formed a few years earlier north

56

of the Lo-lang colony from the Puyŏ 扶餘부여 and related tribes.

The two fundamental themes of the Three Kingdoms period are the struggle between Silla and Koguryŏ for dominance and the beginnings of Buddhist culture in the peninsula. From about 313 to about 550 Koguryŏ was the chief power in Korea. It defeated Chinese attempts to conquer it; it overran Lo-lang; it gradually expanded both northward and southward. Silla, during these years, was harassed by Japanese raids. Paekche, which sent scholars and artisans to bring Buddhist culture to Japan, was in turn sustained by an alliance with Japan. About 560, Silla began to eliminate the Japanese influence in the peninsula, first by absorbing the tiny state of Karak,[1] and later by uniting with T'ang China to destroy Paekche and Koguryŏ.

Unified Silla.—This period is usually considered to have existed from 661 to 935. Silla was then the prevailing power throughout the peninsula; its northern boundary, however, was quite short of the present Korean boundary. The influence of Buddhism, which had become the state religion of Silla in 528, led to a flourishing culture. The first hundred years were marked by strong, capable government; the next hundred by a gradual decline under weaker monarchs; the last century or so by rebellions and factional strife. In 918, Wang Kŏn, a lieutenant of one of the rebel warlords, usurped his chief's position, carved out an independent state and in 935 deposed the king of Silla.

Koryŏ.—This kingdom existed from 918 (or 935) to 1392, under the rule of the Wang dynasty, with two usurpers at the end. Korean Buddhist culture rose to its supreme accomplishments and fell into decline during the Koryŏ period. The first century or so was marked by vigorous expansion and the repulse of the Khitan, a Manchurian tribe who thrice tried to invade Koryŏ. Between 1033 and 1044 a wall was built across the northern end of the peninsula to keep out Manchurian raiders. The era from 1047 to 1122 is known as the "In-law" period because the royal authority was often

---

[1] Called also Kaya or Imna in Korean, and Mimana or Kara in Japanese. Its capital was Kŭmhae (near Pusan). Little is known of its history, but it has yielded valuable archaeological finds.

in the hands of the kings' fathers-in-law. In 1107, the Jürchen, another Manchurian people, sought unsuccessfully to overrun Koryŏ, but in 1127 the king of Koryŏ acknowledged himself vassal to the Chin dynasty, which the Jürchen had founded in North China.

The "In-law" regency was followed by a troubled period, when Koryŏ was in effect ruled by generals and the court split among military cliques. There were frequent revolts. Then, in 1231, the Mongols overran the peninsula and in 1259 divided it into military districts. Thereafter the Koryŏ king was a feeble vassal of the Great Khan, his court a petty imitation of the Mongols'. Mongol dress and customs were introduced, and Mongol princesses married Koryŏ kings.

Koryŏ was impoverished under its Mongol vassalage. It was taxed mercilessly to prepare for the attempted invasions of Japan which the Khan undertook in 1274 and again in 1281. In the next century it was further ruined by the Japanese pirate raiders (wakō 倭寇; Korean: waegu 倭寇 왜 구); who roamed over large areas of the country.

Yi Dynasty.—In 1392, the general Yi Sŏng-ge (Yi T'ae-jo), who had been a leader of the pro-Ming party at court and who had been successful in his campaign against the wakō, deposed the feeble Koryŏ monarch he had served. He founded a new dynasty which lasted until 1910. The Yi revolution deposed Buddhism as the state religion for the Yi were patrons of Confucianism. Under Yi Sŏng-ge and his immediate successors the administration was reformed and the country strengthened. In 1419, Tsushima 對馬 Island, which the wakō used for a base of operations, was overrun; this diverted Japanese raids from Korea for more than a century.

In 1576, from a complex of causes, the royal court split into two parties—generally known as the East and West parties—from which came centuries of intrigue and dissension that gradually sapped the strength of the Yi government. In 1592, the Japanese invaded Korea, under the generalship of Hideyoshi, who directed the invasions from Japan. On land, the Koreans were generally helpless against Hideyoshi, on sea, their fleets, especially under the naval genius Yi Sun-sin 李舜臣 이순신, frequently defeated the Japanese. In 1598, Hideyoshi died and the invaders were recalled.

In 1627, the Manchus invaded Korea, and in 1637 reduced it to vassalage under the Ch'ing (Manchu dynasty). Korean troops were sent in 1654 to the Amur River to help the Manchus repel a Russian advance.

In 1777, Catholicism was introduced from China, but Korea remained hostile to Western missionaries and merchants: ports were closed to ships; missionaries and their converts were persecuted. In 1839, French Catholic priests were killed; in 1866, French warships bombarded Kanghwa 江華 강화 Island, and the USS General Sherman was burned on the Taedong River; in 1871, American naval units seized the forts on Kanghwa Island.

The Western threat remained, however, remote and nebulous, even if occasionally destructive. However, much closer to home a new power was rising—Westernized Japan. In 1876, Japan obtained a Western-style treaty from Korea, and from the embassy thereby established began a gradual but relentless intrusion. In 1894, Japan won a quick war against China, and eliminated Korea's ancient nominal vassalage to the Chinese throne; in 1895, the Japanese minister was a collaborator in the plot to murder Queen Min; in 1905, the Japanese defeated Russia, their chief Western rival for influence in Korea. In 1910 they annexed the country.

There are only a few Western survey histories of Korea, most of them written at the turn of the century and most of them outdated by later Japanese and Korean research.

There are comparatively few modern general histories of Korea in Korean. The Japanese discouraged Korean scholars from publishing in their native language between 1910 and 1945, although they allowed and, in fact, encouraged Koreans to contribute to Japanese publications. The five-year interval between Korea's liberation and the Korean War was too short for much to be published.

Japanese histories of Korea are numerous, for from the mid-nineteenth century to the present Japanese historians have carried out meticulous research in the affairs of the peninsula. Unfortunately, many of these books interpret Korean history to suit Japan's imperialistic policy toward the peninsula. Some are outright distortions. The Japanese historian Hatada, writing after 1945, made the following statement about five Japanese histories of Korea:

> These are all inclined to record political events and do not meet modern requirements; moreover, since they were written during the period of Japanese rule of Korea, there was a conscious or unconscious expression of Japanese superiority toward Korea, and much of the truth could not be written; when viewed from the present, there are many points that naturally require revision. [2]

SURVEY HISTORIES
Western

(167)   Gale, James S. A History of the Korean People. Seoul: The Christian Literature Society, 1927. From the legendary period to 1919. Based on Korean books and first-hand observations. Gale was a missionary in Korea. Published serially in Korean Mission Field, XX-XXIII (1924-1927).

(168)   Griffis, William E. Corea, the Hermit Nation. 9th ed., rev. and enl. New York: Scribner's Sons, 1911. First printed in 1882. Divided into three parts: ancient and medieval Korea; political and social Korea; modern and recent Korea. Griffis, who lived in Japan, used Japanese sources and the Korean histories known to the Japanese.

(169)   Hulbert, Homer B. The History of Korea. Seoul: The Methodist Publishing House, 1905. 2 vols. Legendary period to 1904. It is the most detailed account of Korea in English, but its account of a few important events is much too brief. Most of the book is based on the Tong-sa Kangmok (238), for the periods before the Yi dynasty, and the Taedong Kinyŏn (267), for the Yi dynasty. It was published serially in the Korea Review, I-IV

---
[2]Hatada Takashi. Chōsen-shi (190), pp. 253-254.

(1901-1905), and there is a resume of it in Koreans and Their Culture (351).

(170)   Hulbert, Homer B. The Passing of Korea. New York: Doubleday, Page, 1906. A brief cultural and social survey, and an outline history. Hulbert's account of events after 1882, when Korea was opened to the West, is especially good, for he lived in Seoul during this period and had the confidence of the king. An excellent book to begin a study of old Korea.

(171)   Kuno, Yoshi S. Japanese Expansion on the Asiatic Continent. Berkeley: University of California Press, 1937-1940. 2 vols. Vol. I begins with the third century and ends with Hideyoshi's activities in the sixteenth century. Vol. II begins with Ieyasu's 家康 activities in the seventeenth century and ends with the opening of Japan in the 1850's. The work is particularly valuable for information about early Japanese contacts with Korea, for translations of documents, and for a correct chronology of early Japanese history

(172)   Longford, Joseph H. The Story of Korea. New York: Scribner's Sons, 1911. A popular history, valuable chiefly as a brief survey of Korea. Based on Western sources.

(173)   Ross, John. History of Corea, Ancient and Modern, with Manners and Customs, Language and Geography. London: Eliot Stock, 1891. First printed in 1880. Covers the years 1122 B.C. to 1876, and contains a good account of customs and conditions in Korea in the mid-nineteenth century with comparisons to Chinese customs. Based on Chinese sources. This is the first history of Korea in English.

Korean

(174)   Ch'oe Nam-sŏn. Chosŏn Yŏksa 朝鮮歷史 조선 역사 (History of Korea). Keijō: Tongmyŏng-sa, 1931. A short survey, about half of it on events since the beginning of the Yi dynasty. Ch'oe is a specialist on early Korean history.

(175)　　Ch'oe Nam-sŏn. **Kungmin Chosŏn Yŏksa** 國民朝鮮歷史 국민조선역사(People's History of Korea). Seoul: Tongmyŏng-sa, 1947. From Tan-gun to 1945 in 127 short chapters, each about an incident, trend, or person. Valuable mainly as a topical outline of events. Difficult Chinese characters have han-gŭl equivalents beside them.

(176)　　Kang Hyo-sŏk 姜斅錫 강효석. **Tongguk Chŏllan-sa** 東國戰亂史 동국전란사(History of Korean Wars). Keijō: Hanyang Sŏwŏn, 1927. 6 books in 1 fascicle. An account of the wars, rebellions, and invasions from the Three Kingdoms period to the end of the Yi dynasty. Contains information on the wakō raids, on old place names and their modern equivalents, and has a table of kings which gives the reign, parents, and manner of death of each king. Compiled from standard histories of the periods covered. Written in hanmun with han-gŭl reading aids.

(177)　　Sŏul Taehak Kuksa Yŏn-gu Sil 서울大學國史研究室 서울대학국사연구실 (Seoul National University National History Research Room). **Chosŏn-sa Kaesŏl** 朝鮮史概說 조선사개설 (Outline of Korean History). Seoul: Hongmun Sŏgwan, 1949. Compiled by scholars at Seoul National University under the direction of Yi In-yŏng 李仁榮 이인영.

　　A critical history covering earliest times to 1910, which emphasizes social, political, and economic trends and forces rather than events and persons and is divided by topics rather than by dynastic divisions. This emphasis and arrangement result in a new interpretation of Korean history. New and valuable material is given, e.g., the criticism by Japanese and Korean scholars of the Tan-gun legend.

　　The book contains three bibliographies: (1) Korean, Chinese, and Japanese primary sources; (2) secondary sources divided by topics—government, art, religion, archaeology, and others—which includes periodicals and a few Western titles; (3) books and collections of primary sources in hanmun reproduced by the Chōsen-shi Henshū-kai, the Chōsen Kosho Kankō-kai, and other societies.

　　There are also genealogical tables of Korean dynasties and

of Po-hai kings, and a chronology table from 194 B.C. to 1910,
in which dates are given by the Western calendar; by the Korean
calendar, which reckons from Tan-gun; by a Japanese calendar
which reckons from Jimmu Tennō 神武天皇 (660 B.C.); and by
the Chinese cyclical stems and reign names.

(178)   Sŏul Taehak Kuksa Yŏn-gu-hoe 서울大學國史硏究會
서울대학국사연구회 (Seoul National University National
History Research Association). Kuksa Kaesŏl 國史槪說 국사
개설 (Outline of National History), Seoul: Hongmun Sŏgwan, 1950.
A slightly revised version of the Chosŏn-sa Kaesŏl (177), the
principal revision being perhaps the elimination or reduction of
material critical of the authenticity of the Tan-gun legend.

(179)   Sin Chŏng-ŏn 申鼎言 신정언. Sangsik Kuksa 常識國史
상식국사 (Common Sense National History). Seoul: Kyemong
Kurakpu, 1945. From Tan-gun to 1945. Emphasizes the three
independence movements during the Japanese occupation. Brief
and very condensed, but contains many items of interest; for
example, a chart of Shintō shrines in Japan in which the principal deity is a Korean king or noble, and a chart of bureaus and
ministries of the Yi dynasty. Chronology table from 57 B.C. to
1907. Tan-gun and Kija are treated as historical.

(180)   Yi In-yŏng. Kuksa Yoron 國史要論 국사요론 (Essentials
of National History). Seoul: Kŭmnyong Tosŏ Chusik Hoesa, 1950.
From the earliest times to Dr. Rhee's inauguration. A mature,
scholarly account, even though the book was intended as a secondary school text.

(181)   Yi Pyŏng-do 李丙燾 이병도. Kuksa Taegwan 國史大觀
국사대관 (General Survey of National History). 5th rev. ed.
Seoul: Tongji-sa, 1949. The earlier editions are called Chosŏn-
sa Taegwan 朝鮮史大觀 조선사대관. From the neolithic
period to 1945. A critical, dispassionate analysis of the significant social and political trends of Korean history. Many valuable
charts and tables show ministries and bureaus of the Koryŏ and
Yi dynasties, the provinces of the Koryŏ period, ranks and titles
during the Yi dynasty, and factionalism in the Yi court. The

chart of social and government changes is particularly good, especially for the periods before the tenth century.

Japanese: Encyclopedic Histories

(182)   Chōsen-shi 朝鮮史 (History of Korea). Keijō: Chōsen Sōtokufu, 1932-1940. 37 vols.   A detailed account of Korea from the earliest times to 1894 related in extracts from books, diaries, reports, rubbings, letters, and other primary sources. Information is arranged chronologically; all entries are carefully dated. Each year is designated by its cyclical character, the name of the Korean king and the year of his reign, the names of the Chinese and Japanese emperors, and the year of the era; each month is designated by its cyclical characters; the day, if known, is also given in cyclical characters.

In Vols. I-III the extracts are given in their original language. In Vols. IV-XXXV the extracts are given in a kanamajiri paraphrase which often uses obsolete characters and archaic phrasing in an effort to retain the style of the original. This method creates a reading problem for anyone unacquainted with obsolete Chinese characters. Short passages are quoted whole; longer passages are abstracted.

The thirty-five volumes of text are divided into six series, each corresponding to a traditional division of Korean history. Series One (3 vols.) covers the origins of Korea to the triumph of Silla (668), and is based chiefly on the Samguk Sagi (225), Nihon Shoki 日本書紀 (Chronicles of Japan), and other Japanese histories, Chinese histories, and archaeological evidence. Series Two (1 vol.), which covers Unified Silla, is based chiefly on the Samguk Sagi. There are errors in the dates of this series. Series Three (7 vols.) covers the Koryŏ period, chiefly from the Koryŏ-sa (240) and Koryŏ-sa Chŏr-yo (242). Series Four (10 vols.) covers the Yi dynasty until 1608, largely from the Yijo Sillok (289) and other official records. Diaries and other contemporary accounts of the Hideyoshi invasion are cited. Series Five (10 vols.) covers the middle years (1608-1800) of the Yi dynasty. Series Six (4 vols.) brings the account to 1894, and includes extracts from Western source material.

Vol. XXXVI gives the history of the compilation of the work, describes its organization, and lists its compilers. It contains also a table of contents in the form of a chronology, and a list of the 377 plates in the work (mostly photographs of source materials), a list which makes a good bibliography. Appended is a description of the content and size of each volume, and a list of publications in the Chōsen Shiryō Sōkan (183).

Vol. XXXVII is a kana index of more than 850 pages, with a four-page supplement of Western names. Two keys, one according to the on 音 reading of characters, the other according to 214 radicals, are given.

The Chōsen-shi is the most ambitious Japanese history of Korea. Research toward its compilation began in 1915, soon after the Japanese occupied Korea, first under the direction of the Chūsū-in, which was superseded in 1921 by the Chōsen-shi Hensan Iin-kai (Korean History Compilation Committee), and finally in 1925 by the Chōsen-shi Henshū-kai (Korean History Compilation Society). Each group was more comprehensive than its predecessor, and encouraged more Korean scholars to assist in the project. Local research groups were established throughout the provinces of Korea; and all available materials in Japan, China, and other countries were collected. From the outset the compilers attempted to follow a policy of respectful impartiality toward their subject: they would seek only facts, weigh all the evidence on debatable issues, suppress nothing and distort nothing.

The Chōsen-shi has some defects. There is no attempt to interpret or synthesize its mass of material. Its chronological arrangement makes it hard to find information by topics. (The extensive index helps only partly to overcome this difficulty.) The abstracted passages do not indicate what has been omitted. Sources are cited only by title. Nevertheless it is still the most valuable single work for the student of Korean history.

(182a)　Chōsen-shi Henshū-kai Jigyō Gaiyō 朝鮮史編修會事業概要 (Outline of the Work of the Korean Compilation Society). Keijō, 1937. Contains a detailed account of the compilation of the Chōsen-shi.

(183)   Chōsen Shiryō Sōkan 朝鮮史料叢刊(Korean Historical Materials Series). Keijō: Chōsen Sōtokufu, 1932-1942. Twenty-one re-issues of rare source materials (some printed, some photo-offset, some reproduced by other means) used in compiling the Chōsen-shi (182). The society planned to publish all of the source materials, but reduction of funds and other difficulties forced them to give up this plan.

These materials, except item nineteen, which was unavailable, are listed under their titles in the appropriate chapters. See entries 242, 243, 263, 265, 271, 273, 276, 277, 278, 282, 283, 284, 288, 290, 292, 293, 294, 303, 466, 491. Most of the items contain a table of contents and a kanamajiri commentary.

(184)   Chōsen Shiryō Shūshin 朝鮮史料集真(Korean Historical Materials, Photographic Reproductions). Keijō: Chōsen Sōtokufu, 1935-1937. 3 vols. Another collection of rare source materials. Reproduced by collotype. Each volume consists of a box of 75 plates and 3 pamphlets of commentary. Most of the materials are brief documents—citations, autographs, etc.—and have not been listed in the Guide. They are quoted in the Chōsen-shi (182). The collection also contains photographs of portraits of famous persons.

(185)   Chōsen-shi Kōza 朝鮮史講座(Symposium on Korean History). Keijō: Chōsen Shigak-kai, 1923-1924. 3 vols. Lectures and other studies are collected under three headings:

Vol. I, Chōsen Ippan-shi 朝鮮一般史(General History of Korea). Six parts. The first four survey Korean history to 1910; the fifth surveys Korean geography until about 1900, with emphasis upon political boundaries and changes in administrative districts; the sixth reviews historical types of administrative systems and the creation of the Korean national state, and notes the Chinese influence in Korea's development.

Vol. II, Bunrui-shi 分類史(Topical History). Contains twelve studies of various aspects of Korean culture—legal systems, social systems, finance, taxes, literature, Buddhism, etc. Two of the studies are in kukhanmun with kana paraphrase.

Vol. III, Tokubetsu Kōgi 特別講義(Special Lectures). Contains twenty-seven studies of Korean culture: Sekino's history of Korean art; Korean philology; coins, weights, and measures; ceramics; stelae; block printing; selected historical bibliography; intellectual currents in Korea; geomancy; archaeology; dynastic genealogies from Silla to 1776 (unusually informative; includes ministers of state and other data rarely found in such tables); Korean trade with Ch'ing China; naval battle in 1597; genealogy of the Sŏl 偰 설 family; comparative history of the Far East; ocean currents and their effects upon population distribution in Korea and Japan; the Ulsan fort (1597-1598); Confucianism.

A good basic history of Korea, containing the work of some of the best Japanese and Korean scholars. Its organization, however, is poor, its pagination is chaotic, it lacks a complete table of contents, and it has no index.

(186)　Chōsen-shi Taikei 朝鮮史大系 (Outline History of Korea). Keijō: Chōsen Shigak-kai, 1927. 5 vols. Prepared by some of the men who had contributed to the Chōsen-shi Kōza (185). Persons are identified, incidents are explained, and sources are cited by passages in reduced type in the text. Lacks an index and a table of contents for the work as a whole.

Vols. I-IV cover respectively ancient Korea (stone age to 935), the Koryŏ period, early modern Korea (1392 to 1863), and recent history (to 1920). Emphasis throughout is on foreign relations, invasions, and party strife, but other matters are also adequately treated. Vol. I contains an appendix of extracts from Chinese chronicles and histories; Vols. II-III have sections on Buddhism and Confucianism; Vol. IV contains an appendix on the Government General.

Vol. V contains a chronology that begins with 1154 B.C. and becomes a year-by-year citing after 57 B.C. Events are dated by the Western calendar and by the year of the reigns of the Korean, Chinese, and Japanese monarchs. There are charts of dynastic changes and royal genealogies, and tables of the Korean kings with elaborate data—surnames, titles, consorts, capitals, etc. The author discusses the unreliability of Japanese chronology, although he uses it as a convenience. He ignores Tan-gun and Kija.

Japanese: Shorter Survey Histories

(187)　　Aoyagi Tsunatarō 青柳綱太郎. <u>Chōsen Bunka-shi</u> 朝鮮文化史 (Korean Cultural History). By Aoyagi Nammei 青柳南冥 [pseud.] Keijō: Chōsen Kenkyū-kai, 1924. From Tan-gun to 1919. Arranged topically: political history, history of Confucianism, vignettes of important Korean families, history of education and religion, Korean culture by periods, history of Korean government and administrative organization, military history, military organization, music, land system, medicine, economics, currency, foreign invasions, cultural exchanges with Korea's neighbors, Yi dynasty party factionalism, rites, foreign affairs and foreign intercourse, communications, art history, popular literature, and royal genealogy.

(188)　　Aoyagi Tsunatarō. <u>Chōsen Yonsen-nen-shi</u> 朝鮮四千年史 (Korea's Four Thousand Years of History). By Aoyagi Nammei [pseud.] Keijō: Chōsen Kenkyū-kai, 1917. From Tan-gun to 1910. A political history divided by reigns. To the account of each dynastic period is appended a chapter on Confucianism, Buddhism, art, and other cultural matters. (The account of the Yi dynasty does not discuss art.) The style is difficult, strongly influenced by its original sources. The work is not objective but reflects the "period of assimilation" mood of the annexation. The detailed table of contents serves as an index.

(189)　　<u>Chōsen-shi no Shirube</u> 朝鮮史のしるべ (Introduction to Korean History). Keijō: Chōsen Sōtokufu, 1936. From legendary times to 1910. A popular survey designed to acquaint the Japanese with Korean history. Interesting chapters on "Buddhism and Confucianism," "The Organization of Documents," and "The New Trends in Learning." Folding colored map of Korea and a chart of the administrative machinery of the Government General, national and local.

(190)　　Hatada Takashi. <u>Chōsen-shi</u> 朝鮮史 (History of Korea). Tōkyō: Iwanami Shoten, 1951. From ancient times to the Korean War. Emphasis is upon social and economic developments, and events are interpreted in the light of these developments. The eight chapters are subdivided topically. Each chapter lists works for suggested reading. An annotated bibliography of 75 secondary sources is topically organized.

This is the first postwar Japanese account of Korea written according to modern methods of interpreting history. It gives a picture of Korea notably different from the traditional dynastic accounts and older political histories. It also assesses frankly Japan's occupation, showing how Korea was exploited to benefit Japan.

There is a detailed analytical review by three Japanese scholars in Rekishigaku Kenkyū, No. 156 (1952), 41-49, and a review by a Korean scholar in Yŏksa Hakpo I (1952), 123-128.

(191)　　Hayashi Taisuke 林泰輔. Chōsen-shi 朝鮮史 (History of Korea). Tōkyō: Yoshikawa Hanshichi, 1901. First published in 1892. From legendary times to the foundation of the Yi dynasty. Divided into five books: (1) geography, tables of kings (these name the clan, father, family, position, mother, reign, age, and consort of each king) and capitals, and discussion of the traditional founding of Korea and the Sam Han, and the cultural and political history of the period; (2) the Three Kingdoms, Unified Silla, and Po-hai, with discussions of customs, art, literature, and economics; (3) administration, and further information on culture (particularly good for an account of the development of court, government, and military organization throughout Korean history); (4) and (5) Koryŏ, with many good charts and tables.

(192)　　Hayashi Taisuke. Chōsen Kinsei-shi 朝鮮近世史 (Modern History of Korea). Tōkyō: Yoshikawa Hanshichi, 1901. A companion work to his Chōsen-shi (191). Surveys the Yi dynasty to 1895, with some information about later years. Excellent charts of bureaus and ministries, court parties, and royal genealogy. Chronological table from 1392 to 1901, dated by the year from the legendary founding of Japan, cyclical character, Japanese era name and reign year, year of the shogun, year from the founding of the Yi dynasty, reign year of the Korean king, Chinese era name and reign year, and the Western date. Well documented.

(192a)   A popularized version of the book, which lacks the charts, chronology, and documentation, is called: Kinsei Chōsen-shi 近世朝鮮史. Rev. and enl. [!] Tōkyō: Waseda Daigaku Shuppan-bu, 1904.

(193)   Hayashi Taisuke. Chōsen Tsūshi 朝鮮通史 (General History of Korea). Rev. ed. Okazaki: Shinkō-sha, 1944. First edition published in 1912. Based upon his Chōsen-shi (191) and Chōsen Kinsei-shi (192). Covers Korea from legendary times to 1910, with emphasis on political and military events. It does not include the valuable charts of the two other books, but it does analyze four Korean primary sources at some length. The book has been widely praised in Japan as one of the most concise and accurate general histories of Korea. The late Imanishi Ryū 今西龍, one of the foremost authorities on Korea, recommended the book to his students.

(193a)   There is a Chinese translation by Ch'en Ch'ing-ch'üan 陳清泉, Ch'ao-hsien Tung-shih 朝鮮通史. Shanghai: Shang-wu Yin-shu-kuan, 1934.

(194)   Higasa Mamoru 日笠護. Nis-Sen Kankei no Shiteki Kōsatsu to Sono Kenkyū 日鮮關係の史的考察と其の研究 (Historical Consideration and Research on the Relations between Japan and Korea). Tōkyō: Yonkai Shobō, 1930. Legendary period to 1910. Uncritically accepts the thesis that linguistically, racially, and historically Korea and Japan had the same origin. Despite this bias, much of the study is well done. Particularly valuable are the bibliographies to each chapter and the general bibliography, which lists Japanese, Korean, and Chinese books, monographs, and articles.

(195)   Hong I-sŏp 洪以燮 희섭. Chōsen Kagaku-shi 朝鮮科學史 (History of Korean Science). Tōkyō: Sansei-dō, 1944. A review of Korean scientific and technological development from ancient to recent times. Discusses fire-making, hunting and fishing instruments, pottery, and other ancient artifacts. Reviews development of astronomy, geography, medicine, agriculture, and other sciences and crafts from the Three Kingdoms

period to modern times. Concludes with an account of the Western influence on Korean science. Well documented with Oriental and Western sources.

(195a) There is a Korean translation containing minor changes, Chosŏn Kwahak-sa 朝鮮科學史 조선 과학 사. Seoul: Chŏngŭm-sa, 1946.

(196) Hosoi Hajime 細井肇. Chōsen Bunka Shiron 朝鮮文化史論 (Essays on Korean Cultural History). Keijō: Chōsen Kenkyū-kai, 1911. Traces the development of Korean literature and religion from the legendary period through the Yi dynasty. Particular attention is given to the introduction of Buddhism and Confucianism, and to their subsequent vicissitudes. Much attention is given to factionalism in the Yi court. Brief biographies of Buddhist priests and Confucian scholars, and extracts from outstanding literary works. Concludes with a section on the Korean novel. Lacks an index, but the detailed table of contents partly serves as one.

(197) Im Kwang-ch'ŏl 林光澈 임 광철 Chōsen Rekishi Tokuhon 朝鮮歷史讀本 (A Textbook of Korean History). Tōkyō: Hakuyō-sha, 1949. From pre-historic times to 1949. The author is an avowed Marxist, and the work emphasizes ideological and class struggles.

(198) Imanishi Ryū. Chōsen-shi no Shiori 朝鮮史の栞 (A Guide to Korean History). Keijō: Chikazawa Shoten, 1935. A posthumous publication, divided into three parts. The first deals with source materials; contains a valuable discussion of historical geographies, and much information on political history, customs, and economies. The second is an outline of Korean history from prehistoric times through the Yi period. The last is a survey of Korean culture from the Three Kingdoms through the Yi dynasty.

(199) Inaba Iwakichi 稻葉岩吉. Chōsen Bunka-shi Kenkyū 朝鮮文化史研究 (Studies in the History of Korean Culture). By Inaba Kunzan 稻葉君山 [pseud.] Tōkyō: Yūzan-kaku, 1925. A collection of articles on various aspects of Korean cultural history. Among them are studies of the three historical divi-

sions of the Korean government; Korean social history; the origin of Korean surnames; Korean legends and intellectual activity; historical differences in Korean and Japanese cultures; Korean cultural history; Korean and Manchurian relations with China; Korean, Chinese, and Manchurian relations with Japan; and Lo-lang culture.

(200)   Inaba Iwakichi, Yano Jin'ichi 矢野仁一, et al. <u>Chōsen-Manshū-shi</u> 朝鮮満洲史 (History of Korea and Manchuria). Vol. XI of <u>Sekai Rekishi Taikei</u> 世界歷史大系 (Outline History of the World). Tōkyō: Heibon-sha, 1938. The first 201 pages, by Inaba, contain a brief but useful outline of Korean history; the rest of the book is about Manchuria. Inaba is interested chiefly in the period from the Lo-lang culture to the Yi dynasty. Deals briefly with social and economic aspects of history; for example, the major changes in the land-distribution system, and the problem of the succession of natural children in the Yi dynasty. Concludes with a chapter sketching the development of Korean historiography in Japan from the Tokugawa 徳川 period on. The section on Manchurian history also contains considerable information about Korea.

(201)   Kubo Tenzui 久保天隨. <u>Chōsen-shi</u> 朝鮮史 (History of Korea). Tōkyō: Hakubun-kan, 1909. Legendary period to 1904. A political history with the emphasis on foreign relations.

(202)   Mishina Akihide 三品彰英. <u>Chōsen-shi Gaisetsu</u> 朝鮮史概説 (Outline of Korean History). Rev. ed. Tōkyō: Kōbun-dō, 1952. From the stone age to the Korean War. Considers basic trends and significant developments of economic and social factors. A chapter added to the revised edition, "Present Time," contains a section on the Government General and liberation and a section on the postliberation period.

(203)   Miyazaki Isogi 宮崎五十騎. <u>Gaikan Chōsen-shi</u> 概観朝鮮史 (Survey History of Korea). Tōkyō: Yonkai Shobō, 1937. From the stone age to 1910. A political and cultural history. A brief chronological chart compares Korea, Japan, and China. Another chart lists Korean, Chinese, and Japanese dynasties and periods. Numerous photographs.

General History

(204)   Oda Shōgo. <u>Chōsen Shōshi</u> 朝鮮小史 (A Short History of Korea). Rev. ed. Keijō: Ōsaka-yago Shoten, 1938. First printed in 1931 in Tōkyō. A popular outline of political history from the stone age to 1936 stressing foreign affairs and invasions. Contains a list of kings with the lengths of their reigns; genealogical charts by dynasties; comparative chronology of Korea, China, and Japan (including Western dates); eight maps of the various Korean kingdoms, giving old and modern place names. The 1931 edition has less material on the Yi dynasty and concludes with 1910.

(205)   Oda Sensei Shōju Kinen-kai 小田先生頌壽記念會 (Society to Honor Professor Oda), <u>Oda Sensei Shōju Kinen Chōsen Ronshū</u> 小田先生頌壽記念朝鮮集 (A Collection of Essays Concerning Korea in Honor of Professor Oda), Keijō: Ōsaka-yago Shoten, 1934. Contains twenty-six studies by outstanding Japanese scholars of Korean history, language, anthropology, religion, and archaeology; the archaeological studies are illustrated. There are articles on bronze mirrors, clay seals, the romanization of Korean script, the Mimana question, ancient Korean currency, and many other subjects.

(206)   Shidehara Taira 幣原坦. <u>Chōsen Shiwa</u> 朝鮮史話 (Essays on Korean History). Tōkyō: Fuzam-bō, 1924. Twenty-one papers on the history of Korea, some of which are: "An Outline of the Development of Japanese-Korean Relations"; "Records and Relics in Korea of Kija"; "First Experience of Chinese Rule in Korea"; "Japanese Pirates in Korea"; and "Tsushima Viewed from Japanese-Korean Relations." There are also papers on Korean personalities, places, and books.

(207)   Tsuneya Morifuku 小豆屋盛服. <u>Chōsen Kaika-shi</u> 朝鮮開化史 (History of Korean Civilization). Tōkyō: Hakubun-kan, 1900. Reflects Japanese views current at the turn of the century but has, nevertheless, some interesting material to offer. Divided into four parts: historical geography (thirteen chapters), demography (nine chapters), culture (fifteen chapters), and foreign relations (thirteen chapters).

VI

Ancient Korea

Ancient Korea is here defined as that period in Korean history from the earliest known times to 313, when Koguryŏ overran the Lo-Lang colony. According to legendary and traditional reckoning, the period begins with Tan-gun (2333 B.C.) and ends with the supposed founding of the Three Kingdoms in the first century B.C. The books listed below deal, for the most part, with events prior to the Three Kingdoms; a few extend their accounts of ancient Korea into the Three Kingdoms period.

The best primary sources are the early parts of the Korean Samguk Sagi (225) and Samguk Yusa (226), and the early Chinese dynastic histories, especially the Shih-chi 史記 (Historical Record), the Han Shu 漢書 (History of the Han), the Hou Han Shu 後漢書 (History of the Later Han), the San Kuo Chih 三國志 (History of the Three States), and the Chin Shu 晉書 (History of the Chin). The Shih-chi, for example, which was compiled by Ssu-ma Ch'ien 司馬遷 (c. 145-?86 B.C.), describes the conquest of Ch'ao Hsien 朝鮮 (Korea) by the Han Wu Emperor. The section Wei Chih 魏志 in the San Kuo Chih gives one of the earliest extended accounts of Korea. The Chin Shu, completed in 646 under the T'ang dynasty, contains details of the Chinese withdrawal from their Lo-Lang and Tai-fang prefectures in 313, and has information on the Three Kingdoms that cannot be found in Korean sources.

Extracts from these and other sources are given in Vols. I-III of the Chōsen-shi (182), and the appendix to Vol. III lists the early Chinese records of Korea. Further information about them is in Ogiyama and Sugano "Chōsen-shi Kankei Tosho Kaidai" 朝鮮史關係圖書解題 (An Annotated Bibliography of Korean History) in Vol. III of the Chōsen-shi Kōza (185).

Archaeological studies (see chapter iv) are another very important source of information about this period.

HISTORIES OF ANCIENT KOREA
Western

(209)   Ikeuchi Hiroshi. "A Study of the Fu-yu," Memoirs... of the Toyo Bunko (214), Series B, no. 6 (1932) 23-60. Describes the Puyŏ tribes from their legendary beginnings until their disappearance from history in the sixth century. Based on Chinese dynastic histories, especially the Wei-Chih, stellae, and the Samguk Sagi (225).

(210)   Ikeuchi Hiroshi. "A Study on Lo-lang and Tai-fang, Ancient Chinese Prefectures in the Korean Peninsula," Memoirs... of the Toyo Bunko (214), Series B, no. 5 (1930), 79-96. Describes these colonies from the last years of the Later Han dynasty through the first years of the Chinese Three Kingdoms period—that is, the first half of the third century—including their relations with the Korean Han tribes and Korean states to the south. Based on Chinese sources.

(211)   Kim Che-won (Kim Chae-wŏn). "Han Dynasty Mythology and the Korean Legend of Tangun," Archives of the Chinese Art Society of America, III (1948-1949), 43-48. An article by the Director of the National Museum of the Republic of Korea which summarizes his theories about the relationship of the Han dynasty myths found in the Wu tombs to the legend of Tan-gun.

(212)   McCune, Evelyn B. History of Lo-lang, with Special Attention to the Ways in which Chinese Institutions Were Adopted by Surrounding Korean Tribes. Unpublished M.A. thesis. University of California, 1950. The history of the Koreans from their first recorded contacts with the Chinese down to 313. The extensively annotated bibliography is a valuable guide to the Oriental-language literature of the period and to a limited number of Western sources.

(213)   McCune, George M. "Notes on the History of Korea: Early Korea," Research Monographs on Korea, Series I, no. 1 (1952).

A posthumous publication of the drafts of the first three chapters of a Short History of Korea, which McCune was preparing. Chapter i is a general description of the country and its people. Chapter ii is perhaps the best summary of information on the early Koreans in English. One would be wise to read this chapter before reading Korean history in Oriental-language sources, since some writers, especially Koreans, do not critically examine early material and often give legend as fact. Chapter iii is a brief description of the Three Kingdoms and Karak during their first four or five hundred years of existence.

(214)   Memoirs of the Research Department of the Toyo Bunko [irregular]. Tōkyō: Tōyō Bunko, 1925- . Monographs published in various languages. Five series: A, Japanese language, some with English resumes; B, Western languages, C, primarily Japanese, with some reprints of Chinese works; D, Western (including Sanskrit); E, various languages, (catalogues and similar material). The Memoirs contain studies of various Oriental subjects. A few are about Korea, especially ancient Korea. See 209, 210, 216, 224, 247.

(215)   Parker, E. H. "On Race Struggles in Korea," Transactions of the Asiatic Society of Japan, XVIII (1890), 137-228. A translation of the sections of the Han Shu and the Hou Han Shu that describe the tribes and states in Korea from 200 B.C. to about 200 A.D. The translation is not always accurate. Added is the translator's account of the rivalry of various groups to dominate Korea in more recent times, an account which becomes increasingly sketchy after the fourth century.

(216)   Shiratori Kurakichi 白鳥庫吉. "The Legend of the King Tun-ming, the Founder of Fu-yu-kuo," Memoirs... of the Toyo Bunko (214), Series B, no. 10 (1938), 1-39. A study of a legend regarding their origin common to the Puyŏ and to Koguryŏ. Drawing upon philological and geographical data, as well as early Chinese and Korean records, the author concludes that the Koguryŏ version was borrowed from the Puyŏ when Koguryŏ conquered them to create a closer bond. The legend was then engraved on the Hot'ae-wang-bi.

Korean

(217) An Chae-hong 安在鴻 안 재홍. Chosŏn Sanggosagam 朝鮮上古史鑑 조선 상고사 감 (Mirror of Korean Ancient History). Seoul: Minu-sa, 1947. 2 vols. Discusses Tan-gun, Kija, the Sam Han and other early tribes, and each of the Three Kingdoms.

(218) Kim Chae-wŏn. Tan-gun Sinhwa ŭi Sinyŏn-gu 檀君神話의 新研究 단군 신화 의 신 연구 (Recent Research on the Tan-gun Legend). Seoul: Chong-um-sa, 1947. An examination of the Tan-gun legend as it appears in Korean texts, in Han Chinese mythology, and in ancient art.

Japanese

(219) Ikeuchi Hiroshi. Man-Sen-shi Kenkyū Jōsei-hen 滿鮮史研究上世編 (Studies in the History of Manchuria and Korea: Ancient History). Kyōto: Sōkoku-sha, 1951. Sixteen studies originally planned as part of a series on ancient and medieval Korea, two volumes of which were published. (See entry 248). Contains information on the Chinese colonies in Korea, the history of Koguryŏ, and the tribes in northern Korea and Manchuria. Based on Chinese sources, archaeological finds, and linguistic analyses.

(220) Imanishi Ryū. Chōsen Koshi no Kenkyū 朝鮮古史の研究 (Studies in Ancient Korean History). Keijō: Chikazawa Shoten, 1937. Eleven studies which had been published in various scholarly journals, collected and published posthumously. Contains studies of Tan-gun and Kija, Lo-lang, early Koguryŏ, the boundaries of Karak, and the Hot'ae-wang-bi.

(221) Ōta Akira 大田亮. Nik-Kan Kodai-shi Shiryō 日韓古代史資料 (Japanese-Korean Ancient Source Material). Tōkyō: Isobe Kōyō-dō, 1928. Extracts about Korean and Japanese history and geography from Chinese and Korean primary sources. Each is printed in the original Chinese or in hanmun with a brief in kanamajiri; the Chinese texts include kunten. A convenient, compact work, but Vols. I-III of the Chōsen-shi (182) contain more authoritative versions of the same material.

(222)　　Shiratori Kurakichi, ed.-in-chief. **Manshū Rekishi-chiri** 滿洲歷史地理 (Historical Geography of Manchuria). Tōkyō: Maruzen, 1913. 2 vols. and a box of maps. The chapter "Kandai no Chōsen" 漢代の朝鮮 (Korea of the Han Period), of which Shiratori was co-author, is particularly valuable. It describes Han Chinese activities in Korea based on Chinese records, and gives considerable attention to the boundaries of the Chinese administrative units. There is an excellent map entitled "Zen-kan Jidai Chōsen-zu" 前漢時代朝鮮圖 (Map of Korea During the Former Han Period).

Note: For further information on ancient Korea see 83, 120, 146 150, 151, 152, 153, 157, 162, 163, 177, 185, 224, 225, 226, 227, 228, 231, 234, 235, 237, 238, 241.

VII

Three Kingdoms and Unified Silla

This period is defined by modern reckoning as 313 to 935—that is, from the overthrow of the Lo-lang colony by Koguryŏ to the deposition of the last king of Silla. By traditional dating, it begins in 57 B.C., with the supposed founding of Silla. The period is known in considerable detail, although the source materials on it are comparatively few. Archaeological evidence, particularly various stelae and especially the Hot'ae-wang-bi, is an important source of information.

Korean primary sources are limited to the Samguk Sagi (225) and the Samguk Yusa (226). There is, however, little doubt that the extant Samguk Sagi was based upon an earlier work of a very similar title. Yi Kyu-bo 李奎報 이 규 보 (1168-1241) in the preface to the Tongmyŏng P'yŏn-sŏ 東明篇序 동 명 편 서 (Introduction to the Eastern Brightness Section), which is part of his Collected Works (see entry 245), quotes long sections from the older Samguk Sagi. This lost Samguk Sagi may have been the history which King Yejong (1106-1122) commanded Hong Kwŏn 洪灌 홍 관 to compile, an event recorded in the biography of Hong Kwŏn in the Koryŏ-sa (240).

Chinese dynastic histories, especially the Wei Chih section of the San Kuo Chih, the Sui Shu 隋書, the T'ang Shu 唐書, and Japanese chronicles, especially the Nihon Shoki, are also important sources. Parts of the Samguk Sagi are based on these works.

HISTORIES OF THE THREE KINGDOMS AND OF SILLA
Western

(223)   Courant, Maurice. "La Corée jusqu'au IXe siècle (ses rapports avec le Japon et son influence sur les origines de la civilization japonaise)," T'oung Pao 通報, IX (1898), 1-27. Traces

Korean-Japanese relations from the origins through the ninth century. Based chiefly on the Nihon Shoki and the Samguk Sagi (225). Contains errors, but is nonetheless a useful work.

(224)　Ikeuchi Hiroshi. "The Chinese Expedition to Manchuria Under the Wei Dynasty," Memoirs... of the Toyo Bunko (214), Series B, no. 4 (1929), 71-120. A study of the Chinese expedition into Manchuria and northern Korea in 244. One of the objects of this expedition was to chastise Koguryŏ and its subject tribes; therefore, this study has valuable information on Koguryŏ in its formative years.

Korean: Primary Sources

(225)　Kim Pu-sik 金富軾 김부식 . Samguk Sagi 三國史記 삼국사기 (Historical Record of the Three Kingdoms). Keijō: Chōsen Kenkyū-kai, 1914. 2 vols. This edition contains the original text and a kanamajiri translation. An edition by the Chōsen Shigak-kai (1928) lacks the kanamajiri translation. In 1948, the Pangmun Sŏgwan published an edition with commentaries and revisions by Yi Pyŏng-do. There have been many other reprints.

In 1145, King Injong commanded Kim Pu-sik (1075-1151), a noted warrior, statesman, and scholar, to compile an account of the Three Kingdoms. Kim used the traditional annals-and-biography form. The annals of Silla comprise twelve books; of Koguryŏ, ten; of Paekche, six. In addition there are three books of tables, nine of monographs, and ten of biography—a total of fifty books in ten fascicles. The books are brief, and the history is not a large one. Kim used various Korean records no longer extant. He also used Chinese histories, both to beautify his style and to supplement his information.

Besides being the oldest extant Korean history, the book is valuable for its information on old place names, many of which give some clue to the vernacular of the times. Its chronology is inaccurate for the early period—for Paekche and Koguryŏ until the late fourth century, for Silla until the end of the fifth century.

(226)　Il-yŏn 一然 일연 (Sŏk 釋 석 Il-yŏn). Samguk Yusa (Remains of the Three Kingdoms). Keijō: Chōsen Shigak-kai, 1928. Contains a chronology of the Three Kingdoms which includes Tan-gun, Kija, Wei-man, the Sam Han, the four Chinese prefectures, Po-hai, and Karak. Among its other information, the book has a detailed account of Buddhism, and Silla folk songs. The compiler Il-yŏn (1206-1289) was a Buddhist priest.

All modern editions are based upon the 1512 reprint, 5 books in 3 fascicles. An edition in modern kukhanmun is: Sasŏ Yŏnyŏk-hoe (Association for the Translation of Historical Materials). Samguk Yusa. Seoul: Koryŏ Munhwa-sa, 1946.

Korean: Secondary Sources

(227)   Chŏng In-bo 鄭寅普 정인보. Chosŏn-sa Yŏn-gu 朝鮮史研究 조선사연구 (Studies in Korean History). Seoul: Sŏul Sinmun-sa, 1946-1947. 2 vols. Begins with Tan-gun and continues through the early tribal period and the Han Chinese colonies. The greater part of the two volumes concerns the Three Kingdoms.

(228)   Sin Ch'ae-ho 申采浩 신채호. Chosŏn-sa Yŏn-gu-ch'o 朝鮮史研究草 조선사연구초 (Some Studies on Korean History). Seoul: Yŏnhak-sa, 1946. Six studies on early Korean history. The first is on rules for interpreting nouns in old historical texts. The second is a short article on the interchange of the characters "east" and "west" in the Samguk Sagi (225). The third is on corrections of those parts concerning Korea in the San Kuo Chih, that is, the Minor Han, Wei, and Wu of the third century. The fourth is on the P'aesu 浿水 패수, the old name for the Taedong River at P'yŏng-yang. The fifth is on the Sam Han tribes and their fate. The last is the author's interpretation of the development of the Chinese orientation of Korea.

(229)   Yi Sŏn-gŭn 李瑄根 이선근. Hwarang-do Yŏn-gu 花郎道研究 화랑도연구 (Study of the Way of Hwarang). Seoul: Haedong Munhwa-sa, 1949. Reviews the origin and nature of hwarang, and its effect on the successful rise of Silla, its subsequent decline in Koryŏ and Yi dynasty. The author believes the Tonghak 東學 동학 movement of the nineteenth century and the independence movement of the twentieth century to be extensions of the hwarang spirit.

Japanese

(230) Fukuda Yoshinosuke 福田芳之助. Shiragi-shi 新羅史 (History of Silla). Kyōto: Wakabayashi Shunwa-dō, 1913. Based upon the Samguk Sagi (225), and on Chinese and Japanese materials. Reviews the entire history of Silla. Has some information on China's influence in Silla's culture, the geography of Silla, and official titles. Royal genealogies and tables of kings of Silla, Paekche, and Koguryŏ. The tables contain the king's name, posthumous name, consort's name and family, father's name, mother's name, reign, age at death, and pertinent remarks.

(231) Imanishi Ryū. Shiragi-shi Kenkyū 新羅史研究 (Study of the History of Silla). Keijō: Chikazawa Shoten, 1933. A posthumous collection of thirteen studies which had previously been published separately, and one study which had not. These studies cover a wide variety of subjects—history, geography, archaeology, art, and philology. The general survey of Silla and the paper on Ch'oe Ch'i-wŏn, the leading scholar of late ninth-century Silla, are especially good.

(232) Imanshi Ryū. Kudara-shi Kenkyū 百濟史研究 (Study of the History of Paekche). Keijō: Chikazawa Shoten, 1934. Another posthumous collection compiled from published and unpublished articles and lecture notes. It comprises seven studies and a supplement containing Imanishi's notes on a trip he made through Chŏlla Pukto 全羅北道 전라북도, the province in Korea where most Paekche ruins are found. Imanishi based these studies on primary sources.

(233) Mishina Akihide. Chōsen Kodai Kenkyū Dai-ichi-bu: Shiragi Karō no Kenkyū 朝鮮古代研究第一部新羅花郎の研究 (Study of Ancient Korea. Part One: Study of Hwarang of Silla). Tōkyō: Sansei-dō, 1943. A comparative study of hwarang. The appendix contains material on similar institutions in Japan, Formosa, and among the Amerinds of the United States.

(234) Paek Nam-un 白南雲 백남운. Chōsen Shakai Keizai-shi 朝鮮社會經濟史 (Social and Economic History of Korea).

Keizai-gaku Zenshū 經濟學全集 (Complete Collection on Economics), Vol. LXI. Tōkyō: Kaizō-sha, 1933. Begins with a summary of the economic interpretation of history and a criticism of the Tan-gun myth. The body of the work treats early Korean society and its structure—the Han tribes, their culture and economic activity, and the Puyŏ and other tribes of northern Korea. The economic organization of each of the Three Kingdoms is dealt with at length with emphasis on the class structure and the development of slave institutions. Paik has been reported to be Minister of Education for North Korea, and the book reflects its author's Marxist leanings.

(235)   Shiikawa Kamegorō 椎川龜五郎, ed. Nik-Kan Jōko-shi no Rimen 日韓上古史の裏面 (The Background of Japanese-Korean Ancient History). Tōkyō: Kaikō-sha (The Military Club), 1910. 3 vols. A political history of early Korea based on Japanese, Chinese, and Korean primary sources. From Kija through the Three Kingdoms period, with considerable emphasis on Japanese and Chinese policy and activity in Korea. Many folding maps showing political boundaries, trade routes, and campaigns.

(236)   Suematsu Yasukazu. Mimana Kōbō-shi 任那興亡史 (The Rise and Fall of Mimana). Tōkyō: Ōyashima Shuppan Kabushiki Kaisha, 1949. A study of the little-known state of the Naktong River basin which is known in Japanese as Mimana, Kara, or Mimana-kara, and in Korean as Imna, Karak, or Kaya. Reviews the studies on Mimana from 1893 onwards, and presents the tools necessary to examine the problem—the archaeological, linguistic, and critical examinations of early texts. This is a valuable study of early Japanese-Korean contacts, and of the struggles of the Three Kingdoms and Japan relative to this small state.

A summary in English by the author is in The Japan Science Review: Literature, Philosophy and History, Abstracts and Reviews of Dissertations, III (1952), 157-161.

(237)   Yoshida Tōgo 吉田東伍. Nik-Kan Koshi Dan 日韓古史斷 (Fragments of Old Japanese-Korean History). Tōkyō:

Fuzam-bō, 1911. An old but stimulating volume based on Japanese, Korean, and Chinese texts. From the prehistoric period through Unified Silla. Includes numerous sketches of archaeological finds and several maps. The last one shows many of the names the West gave Korean islands, bays, and capes about the turn of the century.

Note: For further information on the Three Kingdoms see 83, 87, 88, 115, 120, 125, 131, 133, 139, 140, 141, 142, 143, 145, 148, 152, 153, 157, 158, 162, 163, 166, 167, 168, 169, 171, 176, 177, 182, 185, 186, 191, 206, 213, 216, 217, 219, 220, 241, 244, 246, 326, 352, 354, 366, 370, 371, 432, 444, 459, 461, 469, 474, 475, 477.

VIII

Koryŏ Period

The Koryŏ period extends from 918 to 1392. Koryŏ was the name which the Wang dynasty finally gave the kingdom which they founded and ruled. Its capital was Songdo 松都 송도 (modern Kaesŏng 開城 개성).

Primary sources for the Koryŏ period are quite numerous. The most important Korean book is the Koryŏ-sa (240); and, in addition, there are several contemporary Japanese and Chinese accounts. Koryŏ is referred to in Mongolian chronicles such as the Altan Tobči .[1]

HISTORIES OF KORYŎ
Korean: Primary Sources

(238)　An Chŏng-bok 安鼎福 안정복. Tongsa Kangmok 東史綱目 동사강목 (Outline History of the East). Keijō: Chōsen Kosho Kankō-kai, 1915. 4 vols. From Tan-gun and Kija to the end of Koryŏ. Two kings at the end of the Koryŏ period, who were considered usurpers, are left out. Compiled in 20 books by An Chŏng-bok (1712-1786) from Korean and Chinese sources, and patterned after the T'ungchien Kangmu 通鑑綱目 (Outline of the Complete Mirror) of Chu Hsi 朱熹 (1130-1200).

(239)　Aoyagi Tsunatarō 青柳綱太郎, ed. Chosŏn Oegu-sa 朝鮮外寇史 조선외구사 (History of Foreign Invasions of Korea). Keijō: Chōsen Kenkyū-kai, 1915. A reprint of the original Chosŏn Oegu-sa with a kanamajiri translation. The work was compiled by scholars from Chinese and Korean sources in 1452 at the command of King Munjong. It covers Chinese invasions be-

---
[1] The most available edition is Altan Tobči: A Brief History of the Mongols. Cambridge: Harvard University Press, 1952. Contains the Mongolian text and a French commentary.

ginning with the Han, and also the Khitan, Jurchen, and Mongol invasions. The greatest part of the narrative concerns the Koryŏ period. This edition adds material on the Hideyoshi and Manshu invasions.

(240)　　Chŏng In-ji 鄭麟趾 정인지. Koryŏ-sa 高麗史 고려사 (History of Koryŏ). Tōkyō: Kokusho Kankō-kai, 1909. 3 vols. A reprint of the principal source of information about Koryŏ. In its original form consisted of forty-six books of annals, thirty-nine books of monographs, two books of tables, fifty books of biography, and two books of table of contents.

　　It was written in 1395 and revised several times within a few years to correct errors or reinterpret events. The earilest extant version, here reprinted, was begun in 1445 by royal command at the Ch'unch'u-gwan under the direction of Chŏng In-ji (d. 1468) and completed in 1451. It was patterned after the Shih-chi of Ssu-ma Chien. The original Koryŏ-sa and its lost revisions were based upon annals (sillok) of the reigns of the Koryŏ kings which no longer exist.

(240a)　　"Kōrai-shi Retsu-den Jimmei Sakuin" 高麗史列傳人名索引 (Index to the Biographies of the Koryŏ-sa), Seikyū Gakusō. Appendix to Vol. 16 (1934). A kana index helpful for locating biographical information in the Koryŏ-sa. Lists each name with the book and Chinese character for the category (i.e., royal, noble, official, etc.) in which the biography appears and gives the page number of each biography in the 1909 edition.

(241)　　Han Ch'i-yun 韓致奫 한치윤. Haedong Yŏksa 海東繹史 해동역사 and Sok 續 속 (History of the Eastern Sea) and (Supplement). Keijō: Chōsen Kosho Kankō-kai, 1911. 4 vols. Compiled by Han Ch'i-yun (b. 1765) from Chinese and Japanese sources. From Tan-gun through Koryŏ. Its subjects include music, military organization, customs, art, officials, priests, poetry, official correspondence, and bibliography. The supplement is devoted to historical geography, and contains eleven old maps and a section on the names of the provinces in various eras.

(242)   Nam Su-mun 南秀文 남수쿤. **Koryŏ-sa Chŏryo** 高麗史節要 고려사절요 (Summary of the History of Koryŏ). Item 1 of the Chōsen Shiryō Sokan (183). Keijō, 1932. 25 fascicles.
A photo-offset reprint of part of a fifteenth-century chronological history of Koryŏ. The original was written in 35 books in 25 fascicles at the Ch'unch'u-gwan by order of King Munjong (1451-1452). It was based upon versions of the Koryŏ-sa (240) no longer extant. It often condenses information given at greater length in the Koryŏ-sa, but also contains some information not found in the latter. Until this edition was published the work was virtually unknown.

(243)   **Koryŏ-sa Chŏryo Pogan** 高麗史節要補刊 고려사절요보간 (Supplement to the Summary of the History of Koryŏ). Item 18 of the Chōsen Shiryō Sōkan (183). Keijō, 1938. 4 fascicles.
A photo-offset edition of the portions of the Koryŏ-sa Chŏryo (242) lacking in the 1932 edition. Taken from a copy found in 1935 in the Tokugawa Library, Tōkyō.

(244)   Sŏ Kŏ-jŏng 徐居正 서거정. **Tongguk T'onggam** 東國通鑑 동국통감 (Complete Mirror of the Eastern Country). Keijō: Chōsen Kenkyū-kai, 1915. 6 vols. Compiled in 56 books in 28 fascicles by Sŏ Kŏ-jŏng (b. 1420) and others, and completed in 1484. Based on the Samguk Sagi (225), Samguk Yusa (226), Koryŏ-sa (240), and several Chinese sources. Covers the Three Kingdoms, Unified Silla, and Koryŏ periods.

(245)   Yi Kyu-bo. **Tongguk Yi Sangguk-chip**. 東國李相國集 동국이상국집 (Collected Works of Minister Yi of the Eastern Country). Keijō: Chōsen Kosho Kankō-kai, 1913. 2 vols. The collected works of a great scholar who was an official at the court of King Kojong (1214-1259). It contains essays, poems, commentaries, state papers, etc., and is particularly useful for official documents dealing with the Mongols and material about printing. Originally written in 53 books in 14 fascicles.

Japanese: Primary Sources

(246)　　Gaikō-bu 外文部 (Foreign Relations Section). Vol. XXVII of the Koji Ruien 古事類苑 (Enclyopedia of Ancient Matters). 2d ed. Tōkyō: Koji Ruien Kankō-kai, 1931-1936. From the Sam Han to the mid-seventeenth century. A convenient source of extracts of much original material about Japanese-Korean relations. Particularly valuable for Japanese relations with Koryŏ and the early Yi dynasty. The entries are in the languages of the original texts.

The Koji Ruien, in sixty volumes, was originally compiled between 1898 and 1914 in fifty-one volumes for the Jingu Shichō 神宮司廳 (Office of the Great Shrine). It extracts original documents and indicates its sources.

Japanese: Secondary Sources

(247)　　Ikeuchi Hiroshi. Genkō no Shin-Kenkyū 元寇の新研究 (New Studies of the Mongol Invasions). 2 vols. Memoirs... of the Toyo Bunko (214), Series A, no. 15 (1931). A study of the attempted Mongol invasion of Japan. Based on Japanese, Korean, and Chinese sources which had not previously been adequately studied. Vol. I has twelve chapters, six of which deal primarily with Koryŏ-Mongol relations, including the Mongol conquest of Koryŏ. The other chapters contain considerable information about Koryŏ's part in the attempted invasions of Japan by the Mongols. Vol. II consists of plates of the beautifully illustrated Ōyano-hon 大矢野本 (The Ōyano Book), a contemporary account of the Mongol invasion by the Ōyano brothers, who fought against the Mongols.

(248)　　Ikeuchi Hiroshi. Man-Sen-shi Kenkyū Chūsei 満鮮史研究中世 (Studies in Manchurian and Korean History: the Middle Ages). Tōkyō: Ogiwara Sei Bunkan, 1943; Zauhō Kankō-kai, 1937. 2 vols. Vol. I is primarily about Manchuria. Vol. II contains much material on early Koryŏ and Koryŏ's relations with the Khitan and Jürchen.

(249)　　Imanishi Ryū. Kōrai-shi Kenkyū 高麗史研究 (Studies in the History of Koryŏ). Keijō: Chikazawa Shoten, 1944. A posthumous publication of thirteen studies of Koryŏ. The first is an outline of Koryŏ's history; the others are studies on special subjects, e.g., the so-called "ten-article testament" of the founder of the dynasty, the author of the Samguk Yusa (226), and the court office of historical compilation during the Wang dynasty.

(250)   Nakamura Eikō. "Muromachi Jidai no Nis-Sen Kankei" 室町時代の日鮮關係(Japanese-Korean Relations in the Muromachi Period). Iwanami Kōza: Nihon Rekishi 岩波講座 日本歷史 (Iwanami Lectures: Japanese History), No. 5, Item 2 (1934). Tōkyō: Iwanami Shoten, 1933-1935.   Describes Japan's diplomatic, commercial, and piratical relations with Korea from about 1350 to about 1550.

Chinese

(251)   Sŭ Ching 徐兢. Hsüan Ho Feng Shih Kao Li T'u Ching 宣和奉使高麗圖經(An Envoy's Illustrated Account of Koryŏ). Rev. ed. Keijō: Chikasawa Shoten, 1932.   A record in 40 books of Sŭ's visit as envoy to Koryŏ in 1123. Gives a contemporary picture of customs, foods, towns, and many other matters. It is significant that Sŭ mentions several things that are not in official histories of Koryŏ, e.g., he speaks of the legends of the founding of Korea but does not mention Tan-gun. This edition contains a brief description of the book in kanamajiri by Imanishi Ryū.

Mongolian

(252)   Inzenaşi ᠴᠠᠩᠬᠤᠯᠠᠨ. Jeke Juvan Ulus Un Mandŏsan Tŏry Jin Kŏke Sudar ᠶᠡᠬᠡ ᠶᠤᠸᠠᠨ ᠤᠯᠤᠰ ᠤᠨ ᠮᠠᠨᠳᠤᠭᠰᠠᠨ ᠲᠥᠷᠥ ᠵᠢᠨ ᠬᠥᠬᠡ ᠰᠤᠳᠤᠷ (Blue Book on the Flowering of the Great Yüan). K'ai-lu: Mongŏul Udx-a Jin Xorij-a, 1940. 13 fascicles. Inzenşi's (b. 1838) history of the Mongols from the time of Genghis Khan contains considerable information about Korean-Mongol relations.

Note: For further information on Koryŏ see 83, 87, 88, 111, 120, 140, 152, 154, 158, 167, 168, 169, 171, 176, 177, 181, 182, 185, 186, 191, 271, 311, 326, 339, 352, 369, 370, 371, 420, 432, 442, 443, 444, 447, 450, 459, 467, 469, 488.

Yi Dynasty

The Yi dynasty (1392-1910) ruled Korea throughout the longest and perhaps the most complex period of Korean history. It is a period abundant in primary sources, both Oriental and, after 1850, Western. Only the most important or most available are listed here. Notable among Western materials are the Horace Allen and George C. Foulk collections at the New York Public Library. A very important Oriental source is the collection at Stanford University Library of 349 glass negatives of photographs of Japanese state papers on Korean affairs.

Secondary sources are abundant, but there are few survey histories of the period, and most of them are inadequate. Japanese and Korean historians have given undue attention to a few events, notably the Hideyoshi invasions. Students of nineteenth-century Korea have stressed foreign affairs or the Western influence to the neglect of other topics.

HISTORIES OF THE YI PERIOD
Western: Primary Sources

(253) Carnegie Endowment for International Peace. <u>Korea: Treaties and Agreements</u>. Washington, 1921. Contains copies of 22 treaties and proclamations by China, Great Britain, Japan, and Russia, from 1882 to 1910. A good collection, but it lacks many important treaties.

(254) Chung, Henry, comp. <u>Korean Treaties.</u> New York: H. S. Nichols, 1919. Contains 41 treaties and agreements with references to Korea by Austria-Hungary, Belgium, China, Denmark, France, Germany, Great Britain, Italy, Japan, and the United States from 1876 to 1910. Arranged chronologically under each nation. Incomplete, but together with entry 253 gives most of the important treaties and agreements.

(255) Hamel, Hendrick. "An Account of the Shipwreck of a Dutch Vessel on the Coast of the Isle of Quelpart, together with a Description of the Kingdom of Korea," TAKBRAS, IX (1918), 91-148. A reprint of an early English translation (undated) of the first extended description of Korea by a Westerner. Hamel was captured by the Koreans in 1653 and lived among them for thirteen years. See also entry 287.

(256) Hulbert, Homer B., trans. "Korean Relations with Japan: a Translation of the Cheung-jong Kyorin-ji," Korea Review, III and IV (1903-1904), [various paging]. A fragmentary translation and abstraction of a work which describes Korean relations with Japan, Manchuria, and Tsushima during the period after the Hideyoshi invasions. Hulbert used a copy edited in 1862 by Kim Kŏn-sŏ 金健瑞 김건서 at Seoul. See also entry 266.

(257) McCune, George M., ed. Korean-American Relations: Documents Pertaining to the Far Eastern Diplomacy of the United States. Vol. 1, The Initial Period, 1883-1886. Berkeley: University of California Press, 1951. The first volume of a projected three-volume series on Korean-American relations from 1883 to 1903. Made up of documents from the archives of the American legation in Seoul. The book is edited, with an introduction, by McCune and John Harrison. It is reviewed in the Far Eastern Quarterly, XI (1952), 252-254.

(258) Sands, William F. Undiplomatic Memories: The Far East, 1896-1904. New York: McGraw-Hill, 1930. The records and recollections of the author's role in Korean politics from 1896-1904, when he was Secretary to the United States Legation in Seoul, and later, Advisor to the Emperor. He gives a valuable description of the Korean government and of the international rivalries engulfing Korea.

(259) Winkler, Robin L. "The Horace Allen Manuscript Collection at the New York Public Library," Research Monographs on Korea, Series H., no. 1 (1950). A summary of the contents of the collected private and public papers of Horace Allen. The collection contains letters, official missionary documents, pho-

tographs, translations from Korean newspapers, and a file of the Seoul Daily Independent.

Western: Secondary Sources

(260)   Aston, W. G. "Hideyoshi's Invasions of Korea," Transactions of the Asiatic Society of Japan, VI (1878), 227-245; IX (1881), 87-93, 213-222; XI (1883), 117-125. A comprehensive account. Sources are listed at the end of the last article. There are many quotations, apparently translations from Japanese and Korean works, which are not documented.

(261)   Harrington, Fred Harvey. God, Mammon, and the Japanese. Dr. Horace M. Allen and Korean-American Relations, 1884-1905. Madison: University of Wisconsin Press, 1944. Covers missionary activity, economic imperialism, and political intrigue in Korea, especially as these concerned Dr. Allen, who from 1884 to 1905 played an important role in the struggle between the conservative Min clan and the pro-Japanese clique to control the court. Excellent bibliography, with a few annotations. The book was written after careful research into the available pertinent documents, especially the Horace Allen Collection.

(262)   McCune, George M. Korean Relations with China and Japan 1800-1864. Unpublished Ph.D. Thesis. University of California, 1941. A good account of the two fundamental themes of Korean foreign affairs: her tributary status to China and her relationship with Japan. Emphasizes Korean source materials. The bibliography, which contains materials available in Korea to McCune during 1937 and 1938, is useful for the study of the Yi dynasty as a whole as well as for the topic of the thesis.

Two parts have been published:

(262a)   "The Exchange of Envoys between Korea and Japan during the Tokugawa Period," Far Eastern Quarterly, V (1946), 308-325.
(262b)   "The Japanese Trading Post at Pusan," Korea Review, I (1948), 11-15.

Korean: Primary Sources

(263)   Chin-gwan Kwanbyŏng P'yŏn-o Ch'aek Chan-gwŏn 鎭管官 兵編伍冊殘卷 진관 관 병편 오 책 잔 전 (Remnants of a Military Garrison Register). Item 10 of the Chōsen Shiryō Sōkan (183). Keijō, 1936. 2 fascicles. A photo-offset reproduction of the remains of a military register remitted in 1596 by Yun Sŭng-gil 尹承吉 윤 승 길, an administrative inspector of P'yŏng-an province. Valuable for a study of Korean military reorganization in the face of aggression from Japan and Manchuria.

(264)   Chŏng To-jŏn 鄭道傳 정 도 전 . Sambong-jip 三峯集 삼 봉 집 (Collected Works of Sambong). Keijō: Chōsen Kosho Kankō-kai, 1916. First printed at Andong, Kyŏngsang province, in 1464. Reprinted in 1487. Chŏng To-jŏn, style Sambong, was a poet, scholar, and politician who helped Yi T'ae-jo to gain the throne and who was involved in the intrigue over Yi's successor. His poems are full of political comments and satirical portraits of persons and factions at Court.

(265)   Chŏng-wŏn Chŏn-gyo 政院傳敎 정 원 전 교 (Relayed Commands from the Office of Royal Secretaries). Item 5 of the Chōsen Shiryō Sōkan (183). Keijō, 1934. 3 fascicles. The first two fascicles contain collotypes of 77 royal commands from the Sŭngjŏng-wŏn 承政院 승 정 원 (Office of Royal Secretaries) to Yu Sŏng-nyong 柳成龍 유 성 룡 , the chief minister, from 1592 to 1607. The third fascicle contains other royal commands.

They are part of the Sŭngjŏng-wŏn Ilgi 承政院日記 승 정 원 일 기 (Daily Records of the Office of Royal Secretaries), the 3047 fascicles of which, except for this excerpt, have remained in manuscript in the archives of the Korean government. It contains accounts of court affairs, memorials, edicts, ministerial meetings, etc. It was begun in 1392, but all records were destroyed in 1592 by the Japanese invaders. The unpublished portion covers the years 1623 to 1894, and a few months of 1894.

(266)   Chŭngjŏng Kyorinji 增正交隣志 증 정 교 린 지 (Revised History of Foreign Relations). Keijō: Keijō Teikoku Daigaku

Hōbungaku-bu, 1940. A printing with a brief kanamajiri commentary of an important document of the early seventeenth century. See entry 256.

(267)   Hulbert, Homer B., et al. Taedong Kinyŏn 大東紀年 대동기년 (A Chronicle of Korea), by Hŭlbŏp 紇法[pseud.] Shanghai. n.p., 1905. 5 books. A chronological account of Korea from 1392 to 1896 extracted from various primary sources. Compiled by Hulbert under his Korean pen-name with the aid of Korean scholars.

(268)   Hwang Sin 黃愼 황신. "Ilbon Wanghwan Ilgi" 日本往還日記 일본왕환일기 (Diary of a Trip to Japan), Seikyū Gakusō, Supplement to Vol. 11 (1933). Records the author's experiences as envoy to Japan in 1596 in his unsuccessful effort to see Hideyoshi and to bring about peace.

(269)   Kosa Ch'waryo 攷事撮要 고사촬요 (Outline of Events). Keijō: Keijō Teikoku Daigaku Hōbungaku-bu, 1941. A reprint of a chronological outline of major events between 1368 and 1554 intended as a reference book for officials. Compiled in 1554 by Ŏ Suk-kwŏn 魚叔權 어숙권; revised and extended to 1585. Particularly useful for Korean relations with China and Japan.

(270)   Kukcho Pogam 國朝寶鑑 국조보감 (Dynastic Mirror). Keijō: Chōsen Kenkyū-kai, 1917. 5 vols. The hanmun text, with a kanamajiri translation, of the official Yi dynasty history compiled under the auspices of the court. Begun by Kwŏn Nam 權擥 권남 at the command of King Sejo (1456-1468). Each year was treated as an entity so that the account could be continued in later reigns. The work was continued to the reign of Ch'ŏl-jong (1850-1863), and earlier entries were revised. The history is, of course, entirely sympathetic to the Yi dynasty.

(271)   Kwŏn Kŭn 權近 권근. Yangch'on-jip 陽村集 양촌집 (Anthology of Yangch'on). Item 13 of the Chōsen Shiryō Sōkan (183). Keijō, 1937. 8 fascicles. A photo-offset reproduction of the collected writings in 7 fascicles of Kwŏn Kŭn, style

Yangch'on, (1352-1409). Kwŏn was an intellectual, courtier, and man of affairs at the Wang court who, in 1392, gave his allegiance to the Yi. His writings contain important information on the emergence of Confucianism as the dominant philosophy under Yi T'ae-jo. The eighth fascicle contains a printed kanamajiri commentary.

(272) Ri Shun-shin Zenshū 李舜臣全集 (Complete Works of Yi Sun-sin). Keijō: Chōsen Kenkyū-kai, 1916. 2 vols. A printing of the original documents, with a kanamajiri translation. Korean scholars refer to the work as Ch'ungmukong Chŏnsŏ 忠武公全書 충무공전서 (The Complete Works of Ch'ungmukong [Yi Sun-sin]). The book, despite its title, is actually not the complete works of Korea's naval genius. Additional material in the possession of the Yi family has since come to light. See also entry 288.

(273) Sadae Mun-gwe 事大文軌 사대문제 (Documents Concerning the Serving of the Great). Item 7 of the Chōsen Shiryō Sōkan (183). Keijō, 1935. 24 fascicles. Photo-offset reproductions of seventeenth-century copies of the official records of Korea's tributary relations with China. Only the records from 1593 to 1608 are extant, and these are not complete. Contains an account of Korea's obedience to the Ming, of the rise of the Manchu, of diplomatic relations with Japan and the Ryūkyū Islands, and of Hideyoshi's invasions as reflected in diplomatic exchanges with China.

The missing portions may have been destroyed because of their sympathetic attitude toward Kwanghae-gun (1609-1623). He is often regarded by Korean historians as a usurper and was forced to abdicate when a rival clique gained power. He was, however, recognized by the Ming, and Chinese accounts of him are usually laudatory.

(274) Samban Resik 三班禮式 삼반례식 (Rites of the Three Classes). [Seoul] 1868. 2 books in 1 fascicle. A manual of court etiquette compiled and printed in 1868 which defines the court rites and ceremonies then current in the Yi court for

the three ranks or classes of nobles—the military, the civil, and the hereditary.

(275)   Simyang Changgye 瀋陽狀啓 심양장계 (The Shen-yang Papers). Keijō: Keijō Teikoku Daigaku, 1935. A modern printing of one of the most important collections on Korea's relations with the Manchu during their rise to power. In 1636-1637, Manchu troops invaded Korea, defeated the Korean army, captured Seoul, and surrounded King Injo in his fortress at Namhan-san. The King was obliged to humiliate himself before the Manchu leader, to give tribute, and to promise to cease his obedience to the Ming. To bind the King to his promises, the Manchu took hostage the Crown Prince, another royal prince, and 190 other persons. The hostages were marched to Shen-yang (Mukden), the Manchu capital. Here the Crown Prince was allowed considerable freedom within his compound, and through him negotiations between Korea and the Manchu were conducted until 1643, when the Manchu felt themselves strong enough to release the hostages.

The collection consists of memorials, letters, orders, instructions, and other documents that passed between the hostages and the Korean court, and a few papers written after 1643. They are particularly valuable for a description of the Manchu during their war against the Ming. They were secreted in the vaults of the royal library during the period when Korea was a vassal of the Manchu.

The papers are a complex mixture of Chinese and idu. This edition punctuates the text, underscores the idu, and gives an idu glossary with kukhanmun and kanamajiri translations.

(276)   Sin Suk-ju 申叔舟 신숙주. Haedong Chŏgukki 海東諸國記 해동저국기 (Record of the Countries of the Eastern Sea). Item 2 of the Chōsen Shiryō Sōkan (183). Keijō, 1933. A photo-offset reproduction of a book written in 1471 at the command of King Sŏngjong. Sin Suk-ju was head of the Ŭijŏngbu, Korea's highest political office, when he wrote the book. It is particularly informative about Korean relations with Japan, Tsushima, and the Ryūkyū Islands. It contains a survey of relations with

Japan, an account of Japanese history and geography, state papers exchanged between Korea and Japan, and descriptions of several Korean missions to the island powers.

(277)   Sin Suk-ju. Pohanjae-jip 保閑齋集 보한재 집 (Anthology of Pohanjae). Item 14 of the Chōsen Shiryō Sōkan (183). Keijō, 1937. 8 fascicles. A photo-offset reproduction of the collected poetry and prose of Sin Suk-ju, style Pohanjae. Contains information about the violent political struggles in fifteenth-century Korea. There is also some information on foreign relations, for Sin was envoy to China and Japan.

(278)   Sok Mujŏng Pogam 續武定寶鑑 속무정보감 (Supplement to the Mirror of Military Events). Item 16 of the Chōsen Shiryō Sōkan (183). Keijō, 1937. 2 fascicles. A photo-offset reproduction of a work written in 1548 at the command of King Myŏngjong. Deals mainly with military events from the accession of King Sŏngjong (1470). It was intended as a continuation of the lost Mujŏng Pogam, which apparently was a history of military campaigns since 1392. Sections of the last part, dealing with internal political strife, are missing; but the book is nevertheless an important source of information on the factional struggles that ended in the deposing of Yŏnsan-gun (1506). It contains important references to relationships with Japan, China, and the tribes on the northern frontier.

(279)   Song Hŭi-gyŏng 宋希璟 송희경 . Nosongdang Ilbon Haengnok 老松堂日本行錄 노송당 일본행록 (Record of Nosongdang's Trip to Japan). Tōkyō: Taiyō-sha, 1933. The diary kept by Song Hŭi-gyŏng, style Nosongdang, at King Sejong's command, of his embassy to Japan in 1420, shortly after the Koreans had attacked Tsushima, the base for Japanese pirate raids. Presumably the oldest diary of a Korean envoy to Japan.

(280)   Tabohashi Kiyoshi 田保橋潔, ed. Tongmun Hwigo 同文彙考 동문휘고 (Documents of Foreign Relations). Keijō: Keijō Teikoku Daigaku, 1936. 2 vols. Part of the documents on foreign affairs compiled in 1784 by Chŏng Ch'ang-sun 鄭昌順 정창순 at royal command. Contains papers sent to and received

from China and Japan between 1643 and 1783, classified by subject matter and arranged chronologically. The complete collection also has the title Tongmun Hwigo; its contents are extracted in the Chōsen-shi (182). Tabohashi planned to publish the complete collection in twelve volumes, but only the second and third volumes were published.

(281)　Taedong Yasŭng 大東野乘 대동야승 (Unofficial Records of Korea). Keijō: Chōsen Kosho Kankō-kai, 1909-1911. 13 vols. Fifty-seven selections from the writings of important scholars and officials from about 1392 to 1623. Valuable for comparison with official accounts. This type of collection became popular in the late Yi period, when individuals gathered selections from important or favorite authors for their private libraries. The Chōsen Tosho Kaidai (18) and the Chōsen Sōtokufu Kotosho Mokuroku (17) list the selections and their authors.

(282)　Tang Chang Sŏ Hwa Ch'ŏp 唐將書畫帖 당장서화첩 (Collections of Letters and Paintings of Chinese Generals). Item 4 of the Chōsen Shiryō Sōkan (183). Keijō, 1934. 4 fascicles. Letters, reproduced by collotype, arranged chronologically, by Ming generals sent in 1592 to Yu Sŏng-nyong, the Korean chief minister, concerning their common war effort against the Japanese. Also contains the poems and paintings on fans which the Ming generals sent to Yu.

(283)　T'ongmun-gwanji 通文館志 통문관지 (Records of the Office of Interpreters). Item 21 of the Chōsen Shiryō Sōkan (183). Keijō, 1944. 2 fascicles. A reprinting of the summaries of the records of the Office of Interpreters from 1636 to 1888, together with a detailed account of the Office of Interpreters throughout its history. The office was established in the reign of Ch'ungnyŏl (1275-1308). The first compilation of its records was made in 1720 by Kim Kyŏng-mun; later compilations were made in 1778, 1840, 1881, and 1888, each summarizing the account of the preceding compilation as well as adding new material for the intervening years. This edition contains the introduction to the 1888 compilation. There is no kanamajiri commentary.

(284)   Yi Il 李鎰이일. <u>Chesŭng Pangnyak</u> 制勝方略 제승방략 (Strategy for Victory). Item 12 of the <u>Chōsen Shiryō Sōkan</u> (183). Keijō, 1936. 1 fascicle.   A photo-offset reproduction of the records of the military legate of Hamgyŏng Pukto 咸鏡北道 함경북도 province, adjoining Manchuria. Gives a detailed account of the military strategy on the frontier, particularly during the reign of Sŏnjo (1568-1608), and much information about relations with the Jürchen. See also <u>Sok Mujŏng Pogam</u> (278).

(285)   Yi Kŏn-ch'ang 李建昌 이건창. <u>Tang-ŭi T'ongnyak</u> 黨議通略 당의통략 (Brief Survey of Factionalism). Seoul: Chosŏn Kŭmyung Chohap Yŏnhap-hoe, 1948. A brief survey of factional struggle at the Korean court from 1555 to 1755. Written in the late nineteenth century in <u>hanmun</u>. The 1948 edition contains the original text, with annotations and a <u>kukhanmun</u> translation by Yi Pyŏng-sik 李丙植 이병식 and Yi Min-su 李民樹 이민수.

(286)   Yi Kwang-sa 李匡師 이광사. <u>Yŏllyŏsil Kisul</u> 燃藜室記述 연려실기술 (Narrative of Yŏllyŏsil). Keijō: Chōsen Kosho Kankō-kai, 1912-1914. 9 vols.   A history of the Yi dynasty compiled in the latter half of the eighteenth century by Yi Kwang-sa, style Yŏllyŏsil, in 69 books. These are divided in the 1912-1914 edition into three categories: (1) the original section, 33 books (Vols. I-V), which is essentially a chronological account of the period from 1392 to 1674, together with biographies of important persons in each reign; (2) the supplementary section, 7 books (Vol. VI), which contains similar materials for the reign of King Sukchong (1675-1720); (3) the special section, 29 books (Vols. VII-IX), which is an encyclopedia arranged topically.

   The work contains extracts from some 400 sources, many of them diaries, letters, private histories, collectanea—materials that might otherwise have perished. It offers valuable information about almost every phase of life during the Yi dynasty. Sources are cited.

   There are two versions of the work. It has been argued, probably erroneously, that there were actually two independent works with the same title. Most scholars contend, however, that the later version is a revision, presumably more accurate than the original. The 1912-1914 edition is based upon the later version.

There has also been some dispute about the authorship. A minority of scholars maintain that Yi Kŭng-ik 李肯翊 이긍익, the son of Yi Kwang-sa, wrote the book. But most scholars favor Yi Kwang-sa, on evidence from the work itself and from the inscription on his grave.

(287)   Yi P'yŏng-do. Hamel P'yoryugi 하멜 漂流記 하멜표류기 (Hamel's Record of a Castaway). Seoul: Pangmun Sŏgwan, n.d. An annotated translation which lists the editions of Hamel's book (255) in several languages, and quotes Japanese and Korean sources pertinent to the subject.

(288)   Yi Sun-sin. Nanjung Ilgi-ch'o; Imjinjang-ch'o 亂中日記草 壬辰狀草 란중일기초, 임진장초   (Draft War Diary; Draft Letters of Imjin). Item 6 of the Chōsen Shiryō Sōkan (183). Keijō, 1935. An edition in hanmun, with modern punctuation and kanamajiri notes, based upon the original manuscripts, access to which was allowed by the Yi family, in whose hands they have been for more than three centuries. Earlier printings contain somewhat different versions.

The personal diary covers the years of the Hideyoshi invasions (1592-1598). The letters, which include the admiral's replies to royal orders, cover the years 1592 to 1594, but are designated by the cyclical characters for 1592 (imjin) because this year is so famous in Korean history. Yi was killed in 1598 in a naval battle.

(289)   Yijo Sillok 李朝實錄 이조실록(Yi Dynasty Annals). Keijō: Keijō Teikoku Daigaku. 1933-1934. 900 fascicles. A photolithographic reproduction of the annals from 1392 to 1864, and a printing of the annals from 1864 to 1910. These latter were prepared for publication by a board of Japanese and Korean Historians.

The Yijo Sillok is actually a collection of twenty-seven separately titled books, one for each of the twenty-seven Yi kings, e.g., Injo Sillok (The Annals of King Injo). The dignified word sillok was used to designate the annals of the kings upon whom a regal posthumous title was bestowed. Two Yi kings were denied this honor and were known simply as kun 君 군 (-gun), that is, "prince," by the Confucian historians. Their annals are designated by the less dignified word ilgi 日記 일기 (diary), viz., Yŏnsan-gun Ilgi and Kwanghae-gun Ilgi. These ilgi, however, are part of the Yijo Sillok.

The work is in effect a daily record of the Yi court. It is one of the most valuable materials of the Yi period. George McCune, who had more acquaintance with the annals than anyone else in the United States, called them "an indispensable source," both for the Yi dynasty and for general Far Eastern history.[1]

The 1933-1934 edition lacks an index. A photolithographic edition, with an index and kanamajiri supplementary material, is being prepared by the Gakushuin Institute of Oriental Culture, Tōkyō. Vol. I of this edition has been published (1953); it covers the first two reigns.

(289a)   Suematsu Yasukazu, ed. Chōsen Rekidai Jitsuroku Ichiran 朝鮮歷代實錄一覽 (Synopsis of the Chosŏn Successive Annals). Keijō: Keijō Teikoku Daigaku, 1941. A useful guide to the 1933-1934 edition of the Yijo Sillok. Describes its publication, and gives a detailed table of contents arranged in seven columns: (1) fascicle, (2) chapter, (3) reign year of the Korean king together with the cyclical characters for the day of the full moon in each month, (4) the first recorded event in the month, (5) reign year of the Chinese emperor and (6) of the Japanese emperor, (7) the date in the traditional Japanese calendar.

(289b)   Seno Umakuma 瀨野馬熊. "Richō Senso Shūsei Jitsuroku to Kensō Kaishū Jitsuroku ni tsuite" 李朝宣祖修正實錄と顯宗改修實錄に就いて (In Regard to the Corrected Annals of Sŏnjo and the Revised Annals of Hyŏnjong of the Yi Dynasty). Seikyū Gakusō, X (1932), 24-42. A discussion of revisions in the annals of Sŏnjo and Hyŏnjong made by later historians. These

---

[1] McCune, "Yi Dynasty Annals of Korea" (96), p. 59.

annals, and the annals of Kyŏngjong, were rewritten, but both versions were retained.

(290) Yu Hŭi-ch'un 柳希春 유희춘 . Miam Ilgi-ch'o 眉巖日記 草 미암일기초 (Draft of the Diary of Miam). Item 8 of the Chōsen Shiryō Sōkan (183). Keijō, 1936-1938. 5 vols. A reprint of the diary of Yu Hŭi-ch'un, style Miam, a high official at the court of King Sŏnjo. The diary, covering the years 1567-1577, is very informative about court activities, and about social and economic conditions which Yu noticed in his frequent travels. The diary was used by the compilers of the Sŏnjo Sillok (289), but many important passages were left out. The 1936 edition is punctuated, has notes, and indicates the parts cited in the Sŏnjo Sillok. Vol. V contains a genealogy of the Yu family.

(291) Yu Sŏng-nyong. Chingbirok 懲毖錄 징비록 (Record of Lessons from Misconduct). Keijō: Chōsen Kosho Kankō-kai, 1913. A reprint of Yu's observations of the sufferings caused by the Japanese invasions. Yu (1542-1607) served King Sŏnjo in several government offices, including the Bureau of History. He had official responsibilities in connection with the Hideyoshi invasions, and saw the suffering caused by them. His account, covering the years 1592 to 1598, describes the causes of the war and its developments. His purpose was apparently to warn future generations to be prepared against invasion lest they suffer also from the horrors of war. The book was well known in Tokugawa Japan, and a Japanese edition was published in Kyōto in 1695.

(292) Yu Sŏng-nyong. Ch'obon Chingbirok 草本懲毖錄 초본 징비록 (Draft of Record of Lessons from Misconduct). Item 11 of the Chōsen Shiryō Sōkan (183). Keijō, 1936. 1 fascicle. A collotype of the manuscript of the Chingbirok (291). The text differs from the 1936-1938 edition. The cursive handwriting is hard to read.

(293) Yu Sŏng-nyong. Kunmun Tŭngnok 軍門謄錄 군문등록 (Military Records). Item 3 of the Chōsen Shiryō Sōkan (183). Keijō, 1933. 1 fascicle. A photo-offset reproduction of 168

military orders from 1595 to 1598 which Yu Sŏng-nyong caused to be copied for his personal memoirs after his retirement. This book should be used in conjunction with the Chingbirok (291).

(294)   Yu Sŏng-nyong. Nanhu Chamnok 亂後雜錄 란후잡록 (Post-war Miscellany). Item 9 of the Chōsen Shiryō Sōkan (183). Keijō, 1936. 2 fascicles. A photo-offset reproduction of Yu's reflections on the Hideyoshi invasions written after his retirement. The handwriting is difficult to read.

Korean: Special Topics

(295)   Minjok ŭi T'aeyang 民族의太陽 민족의 대양 (Luminary of the People). Pusan: Yi Ch'ungmukong Kinyŏn-hoe, 1951. A patriot's biography of Yi Sun-sin based on primary sources. Passages from Yi's Ri Shun-shin Zenshu (272) and Nanjung Ilgich'o (288) are given in a kukhanmun translation.

Japanese: Primary Sources

(296)   Mutsu Munemitsu 陸奧宗光. Kenkenroku 蹇々錄 (Record of My Afflictions). Tōkyō: Iwanami Shoten, 1933. Written in 1896 by the second Minister of Foreign Affairs in the Itō cabinet but long refused publication because it contained classified information. Deals with foreign affairs between May, 1894, and May, 1895, with information about later years added in 1928 by a relative of the author. Contains important information about the Tonghak Rebellion, the reforms of 1894, and the Sino-Japanese War. It is written from the official Japanese point of view.

Japanese: Secondary Sources

(297)   Aoyagi Tsunatarō. Richō-shi Taizen 李朝史大全 (Complete History of the Yi Dynasty). By Aoyagi Nammei [pseud.] Keijō: Chōsen Kenkyū-kai, 1922. A lengthy, popular history. Valuable despite its lack of documentation and its occasional patriotic rantings. Treats each reign in a chapter, with subdivisions on the trends within the reign. Contains much information on music, economic developments, Confucianism, and

literature, as well as political activities. A chart of the Yi kings gives their titles and dates. The forty-page table of contents serves as both an outline and a topical index.

(298)　　Ikeuchi Hiroshi. <u>Bunroku Keichō no Eki</u> 文禄慶長の役 (Wars of the Bunroku and Keichō Periods). Tōkyō: Minami Manshū Tetsudō Kabushiki Kaisha, 1914; and <u>Memoirs... of the Toyo Bunko</u> (214), Series A, no. 25 (1936). Two parts of a proposed exhaustive study of the Hideyoshi invasions of Korea. The part published in 1914 gives a general account of Hideyoshi's campaigns. The part published in 1936 contains detailed studies of the operations of Japanese divisions based on Korean and Japanese primary sources. Maps and an English summary are appended to the second part. Both parts are indexed.

(299)　　Inaba Iwakichi. <u>Kōkai-kun Jidai no Man-Sen Kankei</u> 光海君時代の滿鮮關係 (Manchu-Korean Relations in the Time of Kwanghae-gun). Keijō: Osaka-yago Shoten, 1933. A study of the reign of Kwanghae-gun which emphasizes foreign relations instead of court intrigue. Contains an essay on the <u>Kwanghae-gun Ilgi</u> (289); photographs, with commentary, of passages from a diary of a Korean soldier; and an added chapter of materials supplementary to the original thesis.

(300)　　<u>Kindai Nis-Sen Kankei no Kenkyū</u> 近代の日鮮關係の研究 (Study of Japanese-Korean Relations in Modern Times). Keijō: Chōsen Sōtokufu, 1940. 2 vols. A detailed, official account, long classified as secret, of Korean-Japanese relations and a general account of Korea during the reign of King Kojong (1864-1907). Vol. 1 contains a survey of internal conditions when Korea was being forced to open to the West and an account of Japanese influence in Korea. Vol. II contains a monograph on Korean and Japanese relations with the Sō 宗 Clan of Tsushima, the historical basis of the present conflicting claims of the two countries in these islands. The bibliography lists Japanese, Korean, Chinese, and Western materials. See also entry 347.

(301)　　Sambo Hombu 參謀本部 (General Staff Office). <u>Chōsen-eki</u> 朝鮮役 (Korean War). Tōkyō: Kaikō-sha, 1924. 3 vols. Vol. I contains a general account of the Hideyoshi invasions and appendix comparing Korean, Japanese, and Ming Chinese ordnance, supplies, communications, fortifications, etc. Vol. II contains 246 military communications, most of them to or from Hideyoshi, and 191 brief extracts from primary sources about important persons in the invasions. Vol. III contains a chronology of the war, Japanese military-strength tables and twenty-two maps of land and sea campaigns and engagements. The work is well documented and contains a bibliography. Extracts are given in their original language.

(302)   Taka Kenzō 高橋三. **Kindai Chōsen Seiji-shi** 近代朝鮮政治史 (Modern Korean Political History). Tōkyō: Kōtetsu Shoin, 1930. Treats the political history of the dynasty under three headings: military rule, clique rule, and decadence.

Chinese: Primary Sources

(303)   Tung Yüeh 董越. **Ch'ao-hsien Fu** 朝鮮賦 (A Korean Idyll). Item 15 of the Chōsen Shiryō Sōkan (183). Keijō, 1937. 1 fascicle. A photo-offset reproduction of an account by the envoy Yüeh, style Shang-chü 尚矩, of his journey in 1488 to Korea to announce the accession to the throne of the Ming Emperor Hsiao Tsung 孝宗. Reproduced from a Chinese printing of 1531. With the photo-offset reproduction is a 53-page pamphlet with a reprinting of the text in clearer type and extracts from other writings by Yüeh.

Note: For further information on the Yi dynasty see 20, 21, 24, 76, 78, 83, 84, 87, 88, 96, 111, 112, 113, 114, 115, 117, 118, 136, 140, 167, 168, 169, 171, 176, 177, 179, 181, 182, 185, 186, 250, 305, 306, 309, 311, 313, 316, 320, 324, 326, 335, 336, 339, 340, 341, 342, 347, 349, 352, 357, 358, 359, 368, 370, 371, 375, 376, 377, 379, 380, 382, 389, 427, 432, 442, 443, 447, 451, 453, 462, 465, 466, 467, 472, 473, 479, 488, 491.

X

Government, Economics, and Recent History

When Korea was opened to Western influences in the last quarter of the nineteenth century, it was a monarchy founded on Confucian principles. Historical and cultural traditions, and a homogeneous people, made Korea intensely nationalistic and conservative, suspicious of foreigners and of change. The government was tyrannical, corrupt, and weak; the court was divided by the factionalism which had developed in the late sixteenth century from entangled philosophical and political issues. The monarch was the nominal vassal of the Manchu; therefore, when a faction or party was in office, it generally looked to China for support and played the conservative role. When it was out of office, a party often tried to regain control by posing as a supporter of measures to reform the government or by seeking support from Japan. At this time, the two principal rivals for the control of the court were Queen Min and the King's father, Tae-wŏn-gun 大院君 대원군 (1811-1898).

Most of the people were, in effect, serfs, living in farming villages and tilling an exhausted land. Taxation was oppressive and arbitrary, so that few peasants were able to become owners of land. Merchants were regarded with contempt in the Confucian scheme of things and occupied a low social position. The arts and crafts had never recovered from the Mongol invasions of the thirteenth century and the Japanese invasions of the sixteenth century. A small, privileged class (the yangban 兩班 양반) controlled the national wealth and dominated the government. This class alone was admitted to the Confucian civil service, although in theory this service was open to all who could pass the examinations.

After 1882, when the United States obtained entrance by treaty into Korea, some Westerners were accepted as advisers to the court, others were granted industrial and mining concessions. Some young Koreans were sent to study in Japan, where they came to respect Western technology and methods of government, but in general Korea showed few signs of Westernizing itself in a way comparable to the unique revolution-from-above that the Japanese had made under the Emperor Meiji.

Nor was Korea given the opportunity. For from 1876, when by treaty they established an embassy in Seoul, the Japanese struggled relentlessly to gain control over Korea. To achieve this, Japan had to dispose of three opponents: the anti-Japanese elements at the Yi court and among the people; the Manchu, who claimed traditional obedience from Korea; and Western powers, especially Russia, who also attempted to gain control of Korea. In 1894, Japan picked a quarrel with China over the sending of Chinese troops to suppress the Tonghak uprising. The short Sino-Japanese War eliminated the Manchu from Korea. In October, 1895, Queen Min was murdered as the result of a plot in which the Japanese envoy, Viscount Miura 三浦, was involved. The King and the Crown Prince took asylum in the Tsar's embassy, and Russian influence, which had been gradually growing as the Tsars expanded their economic penetration of Manchuria, now became a threat to Japan's interests in Korea. In 1905, over issues that directly concerned Manchuria but were also concerned with Korea, Japan went to war with Russia and broke its power in the Far East. Japan then proclaimed a protectorate over Korea, and, in 1907, forced the Korean "Emperor" to abdicate and placed his feeble-minded son on the throne. In 1910, the Japanese abolished all pretence of Korean independence, annexed the peninsula, and established what is usually called the Government General, an organization with Japanese in all policy-making positions and headed by a governor who was responsible only to the Japanese emperor. All of the governors were generals of the Japanese army, except Viscount Saitō, who was an admiral.

The Japanese ruled Korea from 1910 to 1945, sometimes with severity, other times with moderation, usually with some efficiency, and never with the thought of encouraging Korea toward emancipation or self-sufficiency. The peninsula was systematically developed—or exploited—to become part of the imperial political and economic system, to further Japan's ambitions in Asia and elsewhere, and to contribute toward whatever efforts these ambitions entailed. During their first few years in Korea the Japanese were harsh in their effort to establish themselves and to anticipate attempts to displace them. Their fears of revolt were not unrealistic. In 1919, Korea was swept by an independence movement fostered by the ideals of national self-determination that Mr. Wilson, the president of one of Japan's allies, was enunciating. In January, 1919, the deposed "Emperor" Kojong died, and his corpse became the focus for anti-Japanese sentiment. On March first, thirty-three leaders of various religions united in a declaration of independence, and their followers joined in widespread peaceful demonstrations which the Japanese ruthlessly suppressed. Later in the year, a provisional government was organized in Shanghai with Rhee Syngman (Yi Sŭng-man) as its president.

During the twenties, especially under the comparatively liberal administration of Viscount Saitō, some of the most restrictive and inequitable features of the Government General were modified or eliminated. In the thirties, as Japan made ready to embark on the creation of her "co-prosperity sphere," Korea was subject to increasing economic and political restrictions, as was Japan itself. The war economy of the forties brought acute economic distress to Korea: agriculture suffered from lack of fertilizer as chemicals were diverted toward armaments; machinery was overworked and poorly maintained; shipping losses were high; and taxes became severe.

Although Japanese rule proved ultimately disastrous to the Korean economy, the peninsula was in earlier years enormously developed by the Japanese. Japan annexed in 1910 a backward, feeble nation with a haughty, corrupt nobility, an oppressed peasantry, and an exhausted land. Under the Japanese, the government was modernized, the taxes regularized, the fields revitalized, and Korean technology greatly advanced. In the south, improved agricultural techniques caused the yields of rice and

Government, Economics, Recent History   109

other foodstuffs to rise steadily until the beginning of World War II; the denuded hills were reforested; the fishing industry modernized. In the north, mineral resources were exploited; and hydroelectric plants, steel and textile mills, fertilizer and other chemical factories were built. Roads and railroads, telephone and telegraphy systems were built, and an efficient postal system created.

Unfortunately for Korea, all this was done to make the peninsula an integral part of the Japanese economy, a base for continental expansion, and a field for credit investment. There were government monopolies on transportation and communication, on the salt, tobacco, and other industries, and the Bank of Chōsen was government affiliated. Joint stock companies were formed in Tōkyō to exploit the land and other resources of Korea. The Oriental Development Company, with Imperial blessing, became the greatest landlord in Korea. The Korean economy suffered from the abuses of absenteeism.

When Korea became politically independent of Japan in 1945, the country became at the same time economically isolated and denuded. For with the Japanese "oppressor" went also the Japanese technician and manager; and there were not enough trained Koreans to replace them. Sources of raw materials were cut off and outlets for trade closed. This is the key to Korea's present economic difficulty and was, of course, enormously aggravated by the strains of the long war economy, by the arbitrary division of the peninsula into North and South Korea, and by the Korean War.

Korea's political problems stem from much the same cause, and are aggravated by many of the same conditions. The Japanese withdrew from a country that had never known popular responsible government, that had no experience with a parliament, a free political press, suffrage, and so forth. In 1943, at the Cairo Conference, the Allied leaders had agreed that "in due course Korea shall be free and independent." Military expediency caused the Allies to divide Korea at the 38th parallel, Soviet troops occupying the north, American troops the south. In December, 1945, the Moscow Conference announced a trusteeship over Korea which was angrily denounced by the Korean people. Throughout 1946, American-Soviet conferences failed to integrate the two zones; and eventually the two powers set up interim governments in their respective spheres, each naturally encouraged along lines of the opposing ideologies of America and Russia. In July, 1948, Rhee Syngman was inaugurated president of the Republic of Korea; in September, Kim Il-sŏng became premier of the Democratic People's Republic. Russia announced that its troops would be withdrawn from Korea by the end of the year; and the American withdrawal was completed in June, 1949. On June 25, 1950, North Korean troops invaded South Korea. The Security Council of the United Nations immediately branded the attack a breach of peace and called for a cessation of hostilities. President Truman authorized American troops to engage in ground support of the South Korean armies, the American air force to conduct missions on strategic military targets in North Korea, and the American navy to blockade the coast of Korea. Russia and Communist China supported North Korea. Within a few months a war of considerable proportions was being fought on Korean soil.

Most books about Korean government, economics, or recent history contain information in all of these fields. Therefore, there has been no attempt to classify them separately. Before the twentieth century, Korean and other Oriental scholars did not distinguish "government" from political history and usually mixed economics with history or geography. Many of these early accounts are reprinted in the Munhŏn Pigo (83). Articles on the economy of old Korea can be found in TAKBRAS (46), The Korean Repository (39), Korea Review (38), Korean Review (40), Chindan Hakpo (49), Seikyū Gakusō (59), and Chōsen Gakuhō (54). There are, besides those listed here, many Government General publications on special subjects such as fishing, irrigation, rice production, etc. The bibliographies of the Library of Congress (1-3) list this and other material both for the Japanese and post-Japanese periods in Korea.

Government, Economics, Recent History   111

WORKS ON GOVERNMENT, ECONOMICS, AND RECENT
HISTORY
Western

(304)   Annual Report on the Administration of Tyosen [1907-1937].
Keijō: Chōsen Sōtokofu, 1908-1938. Called Annual Report of
Reforms and Progress in Korea, 1908-1910; . . . in Chosen,
1911-1922; Annual Report on the Administration of Chosen,
1923-1936. Reports of the Government General. Contains articles and statistical tables on the history, organization, and
administration of the Government General, and on finance, industry, communications, education, religion, and social work.
The report for 1937 contains a chart of the organization of the
Government General. See also entry 334.

(305)   Bank of Chōsen. Economic History of Chosen. Keijō: Hoshino Tokuji, 1920. Compiled and published in commemoration of the decennial of the Bank of Chōsen by the Manager of
the Research Department. The book contains (1) an introduction,
which scans Korean geography and history; (2) a section called
"Economic Reconstruction of Chosen," which deals with financial, monetary, commercial, and industrial reforms and innovations prior to 1910, and a brief history of currency; (3) a section
called "Economic Development of Chosen," which covers the development of agriculture, industry, commerce, and finance after
1910; (4) appendices which contain the Bank of Chōsen act and
the bylaws of the Bank of Chōsen. See also entry 327, which contains similar material in addition to an account of the economy
of Manchuria.

(306)   Crémazy, Laurent. La code pénal de la Corée. Seoul: The
Seoul Press, 1904. A translation and analysis of the penal
code of Korea in 1901, with notes comparing it to the Ch'ing
legal code Ta-Ching Lu-li 大清律例 and the Annamite penal
code Hoang-Viet Luat-lê 皇越律例.

(307)   Grajdanzev, Andrew J. Modern Korea. New York: International Secretariat, Institute of Pacific Relations, 1944. Contains a brief description of Korean geography and history and a

detailed account of Korean economy under the Japanese—agriculture, population, industry, transportation, communication, commerce, finance, administration, health, education, religion, and also problems of Korean independence. The author employs Japanese statistics. Five appendices: "Agricultural Statistics of Korea," "Reliability of Korean Agricultural Statistics," "Some Industrial Statistics," "External Trade of Korea," and "List of Equivalents of Geographical Names in Korea in Japanese and Korean Languages."

(308)   McCune, George M., and Arthur L. Grey, Jr. Korea Today. Cambridge: Harvard University Press, 1950. Issued under the auspices of the International Secretariat, Institute of Pacific Relations. Summarizes the history and economy of old Korea; studies Korea as a Japanese colony; and considers the post-World War II political, economic, and social problems in North and South Korea. South Korea, for which there were more data, is given the longer account. Three appendices—"Selected Documents Relating to Korean Relations," "A Note on Korean Demography," and "Tables"—and a bibliography.

(309)   McKenzie, F. A. The Tragedy of Korea. London: Hodder and Stoughton, 1908. Describes the Japanese penetration of Korea—the steps they took, the reaction of the Koreans, and the excesses of the Japanese as their control increased. There are appendices on the findings of the trial of Viscount Miura, who was implicated in the murder of Queen Min, treaties relating to Korea from 1876 to 1907, and a petition to President Theodore Roosevelt from the Koreans of Hawaii. The author was the sole Western witness to some of the action in the rebellion of 1907. Many photographs.

(310)   Meade, E. Grant. American Military Government in Korea. New York: King's Crown Press, 1951. An analysis of the American Military Government's operations from October, 1945, to October, 1946, in Chŏlla Namdo. The author, who was a member of the American Military Government during this period, provides an introduction to its methods, problems, and pro-

grams, as well as his conclusions on its accomplishments and shortcomings.

(311)   Nelson, M. Frederick. Korea and the Old Orders in Eastern Asia. Baton Rouge: Louisiana State University Press, 1946. Reviews Korea's legal status among nations to 1910 and provides an understanding to Korea's complicated international status. The study is in three parts: (1) "The International Society of Confucian Monarchies" traces the historical development of Korea's position within the Confucian system from early contacts with the Chinese to the coming of the West. (2) "Korea in Conflicting Societies of Nations" presents the clash between Western and Confucian concepts of the status of Korea form the beginning of Western contacts to 1895. (3) "Korea in the Western State System" is a study of Korea's gradual loss of sovereignty from 1894 to 1910. Appended are a list of treaties and agreements concerning Korea, a much abbreviated chronology of Korean rulers, kingdoms and dynasties, and a chronology of Chinese dynasties. The romanization of Korean names is not consistent; many are given in Chinese romanization.

(312)   Republic of Korea Economic Summation [monthly]. Seoul, 1945- . Published by the United States Army Military Government of Korea under the title Summation of the United States Army Military Government Activities in Korea, 1945-1947. Numbers from November, 1945, to March, 1946, were appended to SCAP (Japan) Summaries. Called South Korean Interim Government Activities, 1947-1948. Describes the administrative departments of the American government of occupation and of the Republic of Korea, and gives political and economic data.

(313)   Rossetti, Carlo. Corea e Coreanto. Collezione di monografie illustrate: serie viaggi 3, 4. Bergamo: Instituto italiano d'arti grafiche, 1904-1905. 2 vols. An account, particularly of Seoul, by the Italian representative in Korea at the turn of the century. Many fine photographs.

(314)   Tewksbury, Donald G. Source Materials on Korean Politics and Ideologies. Source Books on Far Eastern Political Ideologies,

II. New York: International Secretariat, Institute of Pacific Relations, 1950. Divided into three parts: "From Isolation to Annexation by Japan," "From Annexation by Japan to World War II," "From World War II to the Korean Crisis of 1950." Composed of treaties, speeches, memorials, petitions, proclamations, and constitutions. Fundamentally, it deals with the Japanese steps toward annexation and the Korean reaction to them, with the Korean independence movement; with the American-Soviet impasse over Korea; and with the statements released in the first few months after hostilities broke out in 1950. Except for its material on the independence movement, the book has little on Korean politics and ideologies.

(315) <u>United Nations Documents Index</u> [monthly]. New York: Document Index Unit of the United Nations Library, 1950- . Lists reports and other documents which are of considerable value for understanding present conditions in Korea, e.g., reports of the United Nations Temporary Commission on Korea.

Korean

(316) Ch'oe Ho-jin 催虎鎭 최호진. <u>Kŭndae Chosŏn Kyŏngje-sa Yŏn-gu</u> 近代朝鮮經濟史研究 근대조선경제사연구 (Researches in Recent Korean Economic History). Seoul: Minjung Sŏgwan, 1947. A well documented study of the Korean production potential at the end of the Yi dynasty by one of Korea's foremost economic historians. Considers the economic characteristics of the people, the social structure, labor conditions, and farming conditions and methods. Contains an extensive bibliography of Korean, Japanese, and Western works on Korean social and economic history.

(317) Chosŏn Kwahakcha Tongmaeng 朝鮮科學者同盟 조선과학자동맹 (Korean Scientists League). <u>Chosŏn Haebang-sa: Sam-il Undong</u> 朝鮮解放史: 三一運動 조선해방사 삼일운동 (History of Korean Liberation: the March First Movement). Seoul: Mun-u Insŏgwan, 1946. Treats at great length the March First Movement of 1919 and later liberation movements. Contains proclamations, petitions, and other papers related to these movements.

Government, Economics, Recent History 115

(318)　Chosŏn Ŭnhaeng Chosa Wŏlbo 朝鮮銀行調査月報 조선은행조사월보 (Monthly Statistical Review of the Bank of Korea). Seoul: Chosŏn Ŭhaeng, 1947- . This journal is an excellent source of banking, currency, and production figures for Korea. Contains articles on national and international economy, research articles on monetary and banking problems, and banking business reports. Written in Korean and English.

(319)　Kim Chong-bŏm 金鐘範 김종범. Chosŏn Singnyang Mundae wa kŭ Taech'aek 朝鮮食糧問題와 그 對策 조선식량문제 와그대책 (Korean Food Supply Problem and Measures to Solve It). Seoul: Ch'anggŏn-sa, 1946. A discussion of the nature, causes, and suggested remedies of the food-supply problem of South Korea immediately after World War II, and the indication of future dangers to the Korean food supply.

(320)　Kim Sŏk-tam 金錫淡 김석담, Yi Ki-su 李基洙 이기수, and Kim Han-ju 金漢周 김한주. Hyŏndae Chosŏn Sahoe Kyŏngje-sa 現代朝鮮社會經濟史 현대조선사회경제사 (Modern Korean Social Economic History). Seoul: Sinhak-sa, 1948. Divided into three parts. (1) General history, by Kim Sŏk-tam, covers conditions at the end of the Yi dynasty, Japanese imperialistic penetration, Korea as a colony and base for Japan, and popular movements. (2) Economic history, by Yi Ki-su, reviews economic developemtns in Korea from 1906 to 1945. (3) Agricultural administrative history, by Kim Han-ju, reviews the agricultural administration and farming conditions during the Japanese occupation.

(321)　Kwanbo 官報 관보 [irregular]. Seoul, 1949- . Published weekly as Chukan Digest, 1948-1949. The official gazette of the Republic of Korea. Contains legislation, presidential decrees, notices of appointments and retirements, and accounts of the activities of government bureaus. Chukan Digest is in English and Korean.

(322)　Kwŏn T'ae-sŏp 權泰燮 권태섭. Chosŏn Kyŏngje ŭi Kibon Kujo 朝鮮經濟의 基本構造 조선경제의 기본구조 (The Basic Structure of Korean Economy). Seoul: Tongsim-sa, 1947.

(323)   Kyŏngje Nyŏn-gam 經濟年鑑 경제년감 (Annual Economic Review). Seoul: Chosŏn Ŭnhaeng, Chosabu, 1948- . Published in 1948 as Chosŏn Kyŏngje Nyŏnbo 朝鮮經濟年報 조선경제 년보 (The Annual Economic Review of Korea). Contains information on all phases of Korean economic life—production, foreign and domestic trade, construction, transportation, currency, banking, population, etc. Reviews laws and ordinances and notes events that affect Korean economy. Many of the statistical tables contain data from the period of Japanese administration as well as from the Republic of Korea. Most of the charts and graphs have English and Korean titles.

(324)   Sudo Kyŏngch'al Paltal-sa 首都警察發達史 수도경찰 발달사 (History of the Metropolitan Police). Seoul: Sudo Kwangu Kyŏngch'al-ch'ŏng, 1947. Largely devoted to the period from 1945 to early 1947—military government ordinances concerned with the police; the organization, training, and reform of the police; and methods of crime detection and prevention. There is a summary of the police systems of the Yi dynasty and Japanese administration. Many charts and graphs.

(325)   Yi Man-gyu 李萬珪 이만규. Yŏ Un-hyŏng Sŏnsaeng T'ujaeng-sa 呂運亨先生鬪爭史 려운형선생투쟁사 (The History of the Fight of Yŏ Un-hyŏng). Seoul: Minju Munhwa-sa, 1946. Recounts the fight for Korean independence by Yŏ Un-hyŏng (Lyuh Woon Hyung), the author's father-in-law. Describes Yŏ's early life, his activities in the twenties, his trip to Moscow, his relations with the Communist Party, his efforts against the Japanese, his imprisonment, and his activities as head of the transient People's Republic formed on September 6, 1945, at Seoul, until his assassination on July 19, 1947. Written with a Communist bias, but nevertheless an important study.

Government, Economics, Recent History   117

Japanese

(326)   Asami Rintarō. Chōsen Hōsei-shi-kō 朝鮮法制史稿(A
Draft History of Korean Legislation). Tōkyō: Ganshō-dō Shoten,
1922. A study of the Korean legal and administrative systems
from the period of the Sam Han to the end of the Yi dynasty.
Well documented. The bibliography contains standard primary
histories and many legal codes.

(327)   Chōsen Ginkō 朝鮮銀行 (Bank of Korea). Sen-Man Keizai
Jū-nen-shi 鮮滿經濟十年史 (A Ten-Year Economic History
of Korea and Manchuria). Keijō: Sawada Shintarō, 1919. Published to commemorate the tenth anniversary of the Bank of Korea. Part one describes banking and currency in Korea before
1910. Part two reviews the financial, agricultural, and industrial conditions in Korea after 1910. Part three discusses industry, railroads, trade, and finance in Manchuria and eastern
Inner Mongolia about 1910. Part four describes the development
of the Bank of Korea. A chronology of the bank's history is separately paged. See also entry 305.

(328)   Chōsen Gyōsei Henshū Sōkyoku 朝鮮行政編輯總局 (Korean Government Editorial Office). Chōsen Tōchi Hiwa 朝鮮
統治秘話 (Secret Story of the Korean Administration). Keijō:
Teikoku Chihō Gyōsei Gakkai, 1937. An account of the unofficial meetings held in Tōkyō by several members of the Diet and
some former members of the Government General to discuss
the independence movement in Korea and the actions of the Government General. The group was not a policy-making body, nor
were its views necessarily the official imperial attitude; but the
account is nevertheless an interesting picture of what Japanese
in comparatively high places thought of the Korean situation.
The group was notably critical of Western missionaries for their
encouragement of Korean independence sentiments.

(329)   Chōsen Jihen no Keii 朝鮮事變の經緯 (Details of the Korean Conflict). Tōkyō: Gaimu-shō, 1951. A pamphlet compiled
by the Research Bureau of the Japanese Foreign office as a supplement to Sengo ni okeru Chōsen no Seiji Jōsei (343). It con-

tains material on: the military and political situation in North and South Korea from 1948 to June, 1950; the North Korean invasion and occupation of most of South Korea; the United Nations drive into North Korea; the entrance of Chinese Communist armies into the Korean conflict; the growing international participation in the war; and the difficulties of finding a solution to the war.

(330)   Chōsen Keizai Nempō 朝鮮經濟年報 (Economic Annual of Korea [1938-1941]). Tōkyō: Kaizō-sha, 1939-1942. The journal of the Korean Branch of the National Federation of Economic Research Organizations. Contains articles on Korean economy and detailed chronologies of economic events of the preceding fiscal year. The report for 1941 contains information on financial, agricultural, and industrial conditions in Korea and reflections upon the importance of Korean economy to the Japanese war effort.

(331)   Chōsen no Keizai Jijō 朝鮮ノ經濟事情 (Korean Economic Condition). Keijō: Chōsen Sōtokufu, 1938. A survey of Korean economy for the year 1936.

(332)   Chōsen Sōtokufu. Chōsen Hōrei Shūran 朝鮮法令輯覽 (Compendium of Laws in Korea). Keijō: Chōsen Gyōsei Gakkai, 1940. 2 vols. A compilation of rescripts, codes, laws, ordinances, statutes, and decrees issued by the Japanese government and the Government General pertaining to or having force in Korea. These are grouped into eighteen sections, e.g., Constitution and Royal Household; Shrines; Religion; Health and Police; Finance; Military Affairs; Law and Courts; Education; Industry. Vol. II contains a chronological index.

(333)   Chōsen Sōtokufu Keimu-kyoku 朝鮮總督府警務局. (Government General Police Bureau). Chōsen Keisatsu no Gaiyō 朝鮮警察ノ概要 (Summary on the Police of Korea [revised]) Keijō: Chōsen Sōtokufu, 1929. Originally published in 1923 and revised at irregular intervals. Contains articles on the history of the police in Korea after 1910; the organization, jurisdiction,

personnel, training of the police; state of law enforcement; condition of Koreans in foreign countries and in Japan; crime in Korea; popular movements, control of newspapers, magazines and motion pictures; control of industry; fire prevention and firemen; public health measures; epidemics and endemic diseases; medicines and control of narcotics; police wages and budget. Appendices contain statistical tables and charts.

(334)　Chōsen Sōtokufu Shisei Nempō 朝鮮總督府施政年報(Annual Report of the Administration of the Government General [1907-1944]). Keijō: Chōsen Sōtokufu, 1908-1945. Called Kankoku Shisei Nempō 韓國施政年報 (Annual Report of the Regency General), 1908-1911. Most of these reports are simply descriptive. Statistical analyses of the Government General's administration were published in the Chōsen Sōtokufu Tōkei Nempō (100). The report for 1939 contains a brief history of the annexation of Korea, material on Korean topography, climate, and population, and a discussion of the organization and functions of the Government General. The report also discusses finance, religions, education, social welfare, agricultural and mineral production, industry, construction, judiciary, police, health, regional government, archaeological and historical research, and Koreans living abroad. See also entry 304.

(335)　Chōsen Tetsudō-shi: Sōshi Jidai 朝鮮鐵道史創始時代 (History of Railways in Korea: Early Period). Keijō: Chōsen Sōtokufu, 1937. The only volume of a planned series of five that were to be prepared by the Government General Railroad Bureau. It deals with international maneuvers for railway concessions, the formation of foreign and Japanese companies, the effect of the Russo-Japanese War, the building of railroads in Korea, and legislation concerning Korean railroads, from 1875 to 1906. Based on documents of the Railroad Bureau and on a shorter work of the same title published by the bureau in 1915 and again in 1929.

(336)　Hosoi Hajime. Sen-Man no Keiei: Chōsen Mondai no Kompon Kaiketsu 鮮滿の經營：朝鮮問題の根本解決

(Administration of Korea and Manchuria: a Basic Solution of the Korean Problems). Tōkyō: Jiyū Tōkyū-sha, 1921. Three parts: (1) a general description of Korea before and after annexation, with emphasis on administration and political activity, including the independence movement; (2) a critical appraisal of Japanese actions and policies in Korea and on the Manchurian border; (3) a collection of documents and notes on factionalism, religious and political movements—e.g., Ch'ŏndo-gyo, Tonghak—and the independence movements after 1910. The book is remarkably candid.

(337)   Im Kwang-ch'ŏl. "Chōsen Minzoku Kaihō Undōshi" 朝鮮民族解放運動史 (The History of the Korean Peoples' Liberation Movement), Rekishi Hyōron 歴史評論, No. 28 (1951) 67-69; no. 29 (1951) 30-40. Describes the Korean independence movement. The first covers the period 1910 to 1919, but gives most attention to the March First (1919) movement. The second gives the history of the Korean Communist Party from 1919 to 1945. Not particularly penetrating, but it has some value for its account of personalities and organizations. The author is a Korean communist.

(338)   Kankoku Kahei Seiri Hōkoku-sho 韓國貨幣整理報告書 (Report on the Regulation of Korean Currency). Keijō: Kankoku Ginkō, 1910. A report compiled in 1909 by the Bank of Korea for the Korean minister of finance on the eve of annexation.[1] The report contains a history of Korean currency from the year 996, which describes the situation before currency regulation, the currency control plan, the regulation and replacing of old coinage in circulation, new Korean currency, the circulation of Japanese currency, the effect of currency regulation and of Japanese troops on Korean economy. There are numerous tables, charts, and graphs.

---

[1]Until November, 1909, the Bank of Korea was called Hanguk Ŭnhaeng in Korean and Kankoku Ginkō in Japanese. In November, 1909, the functions of this bank were transferred to the Japanese bank Daiichi Ginkō. In 1910, the Daiichi Ginkō became the official bank of Korea, thereafter called Chōsen Ginkō in Japanese.

Government, Economics, Recent History   121

(339)   Kida Teikichi 喜田貞吉. <u>Kankoku no Heigō to Kokushi</u>
韓國ノ併合ト國史 (Unification with Korea and its National
History). Tōkyō: Sansei-dō, 1910. Prepared immediately after the annexation to give the Japanese public a brief history of
Korea. It is divided into three parts: the first, a study of ancient Korea, ancient Japanese-Korean relations, and a justification of the annexation partly on the basis of the material presented; the second, a concise general history of Korea; the
third, an account of Japanese-Korean relations in the Meiji era
(1868-1911) which led to the annexation. The principal value of
the book lies in the last section. The book reflects the intense
nationalism of the period, but there are instances of surprising
candor and critical appraisal not to be found in Japanese works
treating the same subjects several decades later.

(340)   Kikuchi Kenjō 菊池謙讓. <u>Kin Gyoku-gin Den</u> 金玉均傳
(Life of Kim Ok-kyun). Edited by Hayashi Kiroku 林毅陸
Tōkyō: Keiō Shuppan-sha, 1944. The first volume of a proposed two-volume life of the Korean reformer written by a Japanese newspaper man, to commemorate the bicentennial of
Kim's death. Most of the book deals with the preparation for
the "Émeuté of 1884," an attempt by Kim and other reformers
to gain control of the government and to effect far reaching
changes toward the Westernization of Korea. The book is an interesting study of the situation that confronted all Korean reformers in this period—their need to rely on a foreign power (with
this group, Japan) in order to carry out a revolution at home,
and the stubborn Korean conservatism that defeated them. The
account is somewhat too partial to Japan. References are sometimes not clear, and the book lacks an index and a bibliography.

(341)   Kikuchi Kenjō. <u>Taiin-gun Den, fu Ōhi no Ishō</u> 大院君傳附
王妃ノ一生 (Biography of the Taewŏn-gun; supplement on the
Life of the Queen [Min]). Keijō: Nikkan Shobō, 1910. The most
available biography of one of the most important figures in nineteenth-century Korea. From the time he became regent in 1864
until his death in 1897, Taewŏn-gun was involved in nearly every
major controversy in Korea and in Korean international relations.

There is a supplementary chapter on the life of Queen Min, Taewŏn-gun's great rival.

The book is based on letters and other records, interviews, and personal observation. Kikuchi, who came to Korea in 1893 as a newspaper man, was involved in court politics during the last years of Taewŏn-gun's regency. However, his account is not always reliable.

(342)   Ri-chō Hōten-kō 李朝法典考 (A Study of Yi Dynasty Legal Codes). Keijō: Chōsen Sōtokufu Chūsū-in, 1936. A study of legal codes of the Yi dynasty—their development, compilation, characteristics, and application. Describes the influence of factionalism in making and interpreting the codes. Critical passages from the codes are cited in the original hanmun. The appendices contain a detailed table of contents, and a chronology of important legal and political events from 1392 to 1910.

(343)   Sengo ni okeru Chōsen no Seiji Jōsei 戦後に於ける朝鮮の政治情勢 (Political Conditions in Korea after the War). Tōkyō: Gaimu-sho, 1948. A pamphlet compiled by the Research Bureau of the Japanese Foreign Office. It deals with the period from August, 1945, to June, 1948: American-Russian exchanges and conferences concerning Korea; political parties, ideological conflict, Communist violence, the interim assembly, and other political problems of South Korea; and conditions in North Korea after liberation, the establishment of a Temporary Peoples' Committee, the expansion of Communist power, the adoption of a constitution of the Korean Democratic Peoples' Republic, and the increasing tension between North and South Korea. There is a twenty-page chronology of events. See also entry 329.

(344)   Shibutani Reiji 澁谷禮治, ed. Chōsen no Kōgyō to Sono Shigen 朝鮮の工業と其の資源 (Korean Industry and Its Resources). Keijō: Chōsen Kōgyō Kyōkai, 1937. A collection of essays by officials in Government General agencies and in industry. Divided into three parts, each separately paged. Part one contains essays of a general nature, such as the place of Korean production within the Japanese Empire, the present state

of industry in Korea, and its future. Part two is divided into six sub-sections with several essays in each on agricultural, forestry, livestock, marine, mineral, and power resources. Part three surveys major industrial fields such as textiles, steel, ceramics, fuels, rubber, paper, fertilizer, brewing and handicraft.

(345)　　Suzuki Takeo 鈴木武雄. Chōsen Keizai no Shin-kōsō 朝鮮 經濟の新構想 (New Concepts of Korean Economy). Tōkyō: Tōyō Keizai Shimpō-sha, 1942. An appraisal of Korean economy in the light of the Great East Asia War (World War II), consideration of Korea as an advance military base for continental expansion, Korea's role in integrating Japanese and Manchurian economies, and the application of city and regional planning to Korea.

(346)　　Suzuki Takeo. Chōsen no Keizai 朝鮮の經濟 (Korean Economy). Tōkyō: Nihon Hyōron-sha, 1942. A compact general handbook of Korean economy. Summarizes Korea's geographical position, geography, population, administrative and economic history. Discusses economic development during the Japanese administration—agriculture (especially rice), stock raising, marine products, forestry, and industry. Concludes with an account of Korea's economic position on the eve of World War II and its role as an advance military base for Japan on the continent of Asia. Contains an extensive bibliography.

(347)　　Tabobashi Kiyoshi. Nis-Shin Seneki Gaikō-shi no Kenkyū 日清戰役外交史の研究 (A Diplomatic History of the Sino-Japanese War). Tōkyō: Tōkō Shoin, 1951. Also published as Memoirs... of the Toyo Bunko (214), Series A, no. 32 (1951). A posthumous work. May be considered to continue his Kindai Nis-Sen Kankei no Kenkyū (300). Contains a documented description of the rivalry between Japan and China over Korea which culminated in the Sino-Japanese War. The part dealing with the political and diplomatic background before the war is primarily concerned with Korean history and is based largely on Korean government documents.

Chinese

(348)　　Ko Ch'ih-feng 葛赤峯. Ch'ao-hsien Ko-ming-chi 朝鮮革命記 (Record of the Korean Revolution). Shanghai: Shang-wu Yin-shu-kuan, 1945. The author, who is a journalist, compiled his material from interviews with cabinet members of the Korean Provisional Government and from this government's publications. The book contains reflections on the Korean revolutionary movement, the problem of recognition of the Provisional Government, the Provisional constitution, Korean political parties, and Korea in Japan's military strategy. Appendices contain material on the underground movement in Korea and the revolutionary activities of Koreans living in America.

(349)　　Pak Ŭn-sik 朴殷植 박은식. Han-kuo T'ung-shih 韓國痛史 (The Tragic History of Korea). By T'ae-baek Kwangno 太白狂奴 태백광노 (The Madman of T'ae-baek) [pseud.] Shanghai: Ta-t'ung Pien-i-chŭ, 1915. The work of a Korean writing in Chinese. Divided into three parts, each separately paged. Part one is a brief outline of Korean geography and history. Part two traces Korean history from 1863 to 1897. Part three covers the period from 1897 to 1911.

(350)　　Pak Ŭn-sik. Han-kuo Tu-li Yŭn-tung chih Hsueh-shih 韓國獨立運動之血史 (Bloody History of the Korean Independence Movement). Shanghai: Wei-hsin-she, 1920. Two parts separately paged. Part one deals with Korean independence movements before 1910, Japanese steps toward annexation, Korean resistance to Japanese control, and oppressive measures introduced by the Japanese after 1910. Part two deals with independence movements after 1910, particularly the March First movement, Japanese atrocities after the March First movement, the establishment of a Provisional republic in 1919, and expressions of sympathy from foreigners. Photographs show demonstrations in 1919, victims of atrocities, and members of the Provisional Republic.

Note: For further information on government, economics, and recent history see 76, 77, 81, 100, 121, 170, 253, 254, 257, 258, 259, 261, 296, 300, 361, 468, 470, 476, 478.

XI

Sociology

Most of the books listed in this chapter describe a social pattern that has existed for centuries among the majority of Korean people. It is a pattern of rural economy, based on the Korean farmer and his family who spend most of their time tilling the fields or working at those cottage industries that make each family nearly self-sufficient. Even recreation is a family affair, the Korean farmer spending his spare hours in such simple pasttimes as conversation, smoking, and listening to the tales of itinerant story-tellers, all within the family circle. These families live in small villages of grass-roofed dwellings. Each group of villages centers around a market town, where on market day the villagers gather to exchange their goods and services, and to engage in holiday festivities. Most Koreans know no larger social or economic activity than the market-day gathering.

In Confucianism, the farmer is more highly regarded than the artisan, the merchant, or the soldier, and the Confucian domestic code is perhaps the strongest force sustaining the existing social pattern. According to this code, women occupy a subordinate position, marriage is arranged by the family, the deceased are given elaborate funerals, and one must honor elders and ancestors.

The Westernization of Korea has been superficial, confined largely to the urban upper classes; most industry lies in the thinly populated North. The Korean War has, of course, disrupted the age-old social pattern in many areas, but just how many permanent changes will come from this one cannot predict.

SOCIOLOGICAL STUDIES OF KOREA
Western

(351)   Osgood, Cornelius. The Koreans and Their Culture. New York: Ronald Press, 1951. A detailed study of Sŏndup'o 船頭浦 선두모, a "typical" Korean village on Kwanghwa-do. Osgood lived on the island in the summer of 1947. His book is the best Western anthropological work on Korea, but his failure to utilize Oriental-language materials resulted in numerous errors, particularly in the second half of the book, which is an analysis of Korean history. The book is reviewed by Evelyn B. McCune in the Journal of the American Oriental Society, LXXI (1951), 284-286.

Korean

(352)   Ch'oe Ik-han 崔益翰 최익한. Chosŏn Sahoe Chŏngch'aeksa 朝鮮社會政策史 조선사회정책사 (History of Korean Social Policy). Seoul: Pangmun Sŏgwan, 1947. A documented study of the measures taken by the government and other organizations to relieve the distress caused by natural calamities, particularly drought, from the early Three Kingdoms period through the Yi dynasty.

(353)   Kim Tu-hŏn 金斗憲 김두헌. Chosŏn Kajok Chedo Yŏn-gu 朝鮮家族制度研究 조선가족제도연구 (Study on the Family System in Korea). Seoul: Ŭryu Munhwa-sa, 1949. An exhaustive, systematic explanation of the Korean family system from the historical as well as from the sociological point of view. Gives special attention to distinguishing between the Chinese and Korean family systems, which are often mistakenly equated. The first half is devoted to the structure and function of the family; the second discusses household mores, marriage, mourning, ancestor worship, and the decay of the patriarchal family system. The study is carefully documented and contains an English table of contents.

(354)   Yi Yŏ-sŏng 李如星 이여성. Chosŏn Poksik-ko 朝鮮服飾考 조선복식고 (Investigation of Korean Costumes and Orn-

aments). Seoul: Paegyang-dang, 1947. An account of dress, and of weaving and dyeing techniques, in ancient Korea, especially during the Three Kingdoms period. Profusely illustrated.

Japanese

(355)   Chōsen Fūzoku Shiryō Shūsetsu: Sen, Hidarinawa, Dakyū, Pakachi 朝鮮風俗資料集説扇縄打毬꽃包 (A Collection of Materials on Korean Customs: Fans, Rope, Polo, Gourds). Keijō: Chōsen Sōtokufu, 1937. A collection of folklore material with kanamajiri annotations. The study is limited and sometimes overemphasizes the similarities between Japan and Korea.

(356)   Chōsen no Shūraku 朝鮮ノ聚落 (Korean Villages). Keijō: Chōsen Sōtokufu, 1933-1935. 3 vols. A detailed study of Korean villages—local history, economic geography, onomatology, and public administration.

(357)   Chōsen Saishi Sōzoku Hōron: Josetsu 朝鮮祭祀相續法論序説 (Treatise on Law with Regard to Inheritance and Religious Observances in Korea: Introduction). Keijō: Chōsen Sōtokufu, 1939. A study of contemporary Korean customs relating to death and religious observances, with an account of their history. Carefully documented, especially with primary sources of the Yi dynasty period.

(358)   Fujita Tōzō 藤田東三 . Chōsen Kon-in-kō 朝鮮婚姻考 (Study on Korean Marriage). Tōkyō: Daidō Shokan, 1941. A valuable treatise on matrimony during the early Yi dynasty. Marriageable age, the wedding ceremony, remarriage, bigamy, and divorce are studied. Based upon the Yijo Sillok (289).

(359)   Imamura Tomo 今村鞆 , ed. Ri-chō Jitsuroku Fūzoku Shiryō Saiyō 李朝實錄風俗資料撮要 (Selection of Materials Related to Customs in the Yi Dynasty Annals). Keijō: Chōsen Sōtokufu, 1939. Intended as an index to sociological material in the Yijo Sillok (289). The editor translated into kanamajiri the entries which deal with the traditions, customs, and beliefs of the Korean people, and arranged them in chronological order.

(360)   Imamura Tomo. Chōsen Fūzoku-shū 朝鮮風俗集 (Compilation of Korean Customs). Keijō: Shidō-kan, 1914. Describes the class system; customs at birth, death, and marriage; festivals; family relationships; legal tradition; superstition; and costume. Based on observation and Korean histories.

(361)   Minji Kanshū Kaitō Ishū 民事慣習回答彙集 (Collection of Customary Replies in Civil Litigation). Keijō: Chōsen Sōtokufu, 1933. Contains the decisions handed down in 324 trials between Korean litigants from 1909 to 1933. These are arranged chronologically. The book contains a detailed table of contents and an index. An outline of family relationships and inheritance customs, prepared by the Government General's Committee on Old Customs and Institutions, is appended.

The book was compiled to supplement the civil code drawn up in 1912 by the Japanese. This code settled most of the civil issues in connection with the annexation, but failed to cover legal problems arising among Koreans, many of which were decided according to customary law unfamiliar to the Japanese tribunals. Therefore, a record of precedents was drawn up to acquaint Japanese jurists with Korean customary law.

Note: For further information on sociology see 80, 83, 84, 95, 98, 101, 102, 173, 185, 187, 195, 199, 200, 206, 385, 386, 387, 388, 389, 390, 393, 446, 452, 454, 457, 458, 462, 488, 491.

XII

Religion and Philosophy

The primordial religion of Korea was animism. Archaeological evidence suggests that the paleo-asiatic inhabitants of the peninsula were animists, and it is known that the Tungusic tribes brought animism into Korea from Manchuria. The Tungusic tribes also brought shamanism, a type of animism. Animism is still a powerful influence among Koreans, especially among the peasantry, who believe that many things and activities are guarded by or governed by spirits. There are many "sacred" places in Korea—especially the tops of high mountains—where gods or demons dwell, and where altars or temples are erected to honor or appease them. The postharvest ceremony of giving tribute to these spirits is perhaps the principal animistic festival. A modern type of Korean shaman is the mudang 무당, a female medium who communicates with spirits by charms, secret rites, and hypnotism.

According to some scholars, Tan-gun was a shaman, according to others, he was a demon, god, or culture-hero of one of the tribes—probably the Puyŏ—who caught the imagination of other tribes and to whom various legends and attributes were gradually assigned. Scholars who argue that he was borrowed from China point out that the earliest known version of the Tan-gun story, in the Samguk Sagi (225), is dated many centuries after the occurrence of the events it relates, when Chinese influence had permeated the peninsula and when Koreans were first becoming conscious of themselves as a nation. Whatever its origins, the Tan-gun story indicates the development of a quite sophisticated form of shamanism and possibly a development toward monotheism. The story is briefly as follows: The son of the Creator promised a tiger and a bear that he would make them into human beings if they would eat only certain foods and remain in darkness for three weeks. Only the bear fulfilled the conditions, and was duly turned into a maiden. The son of the Creator fell in love with his creature, who bore him the semidivine Tan-gun. In manhood, Tan-gun erected an altar on a mountain (several places in Korea claim the honor), ruled the Koreans for 1200 years, and taught them agriculture and other civilized accomplishments. His birthday (The Opening of Heaven Day) is celebrated throughout Korea on the third day of the eleventh month.

The Koreans probably first came into contact with Confucianism in the first century B. C., when the Lo-lang and other Chinese colonies were established. But Confucianism spread slowly in Korea, and was later submerged for several centuries by the Koreans' enthusiastic acceptance of Buddhism, which by the third century had developed a brilliant religious and artistic program in China. In 372, the monk Sundo 順道순도 was sent by the Emperor Fu Chien 符堅 of the Former Ch'in dynasty to preach Buddhism in Koguryŏ. In 384, it entered Paekche, whence in 552 it was transmitted to Japan. Silla received Buddhism comparatively late (in 528), but adopted it with great zeal, made it the state religion, and by its inspiration created a culture of high merit. In the seventh and eighth centuries some of the Silla kings were hostile to the Buddhists and tried to reduce their power and wealth, but when the sympathetic Wang (Koryŏ) dynasty came into power, the Buddhists entered upon a second and longer "golden age." The Koryŏ period marks the height of Korean Buddhism: there were thousands of priests and monks, temple-sponsored arts and education flourished, and Buddhist influence at court was usually strong and sometimes dominant. During the Silla and Koryŏ periods, the Confucianists usually played a subordinate role, although some kings favored them in an effort to stop the abuse of power, the accumulation of wealth, and the growth of superstition among the Buddhists.

The Yi revolution of 1392 was a major reverse in the political power of Buddhism. The early Yi rulers wanted to establish a strong state based on rational ethics and on a political philosophy suitable to the bureaucratic and agrarian character of their kingdom, and they regarded Confucianism, which is primarily a system of social relationships, as much more suitable to their desires than Buddhism. Therefore, like their newly established suzerain, the Ming of China, the Yi became patrons of the Confucianists and organized their monarchy upon the Confucian principles of obedience to and reverence for one's superiors—king, noble, master, teacher, husband, father, elder—and paternal benevolence toward one's inferiors—subject, peasant, servant, disciple, wife, son, younger kinsman. In Confucian schools young men studied the Chinese classics to prepare themselves for positions in the civil service. Scholars were highly respected, and ideally all governors were "sages." Philosophical speculation—which was usually a reinterpretation of Confucian doctrines—thrived; and Korean scholars, especially in the sixteenth century, made important contributions to neo-Confucianism. But just as Buddhism had earlier developed vices when it was in power, so Confucianism developed many deplorable shortcomings: its philosophical speculations (which were often mixed with political issues) created factions at court, its reverence for China often made the Korean mind parochial and subservient, its respect for tradition created a stubborn conservatism that too often tried to rationalize weaknesses into virtues, its contempt for manual labor and technology made Korea in time weak and backward, its respect for scholarship was often merely academic snobbishness. All these shortcomings weakened the Yi government and eventually contributed to its collapse.

The conflict between Buddhism and Confucianism in Korea was generally one of struggle for power confined to the court and the upper class. The triumph of one system did not result in the elimination of the other, only in its loss of prestige and wealth. Just as in "Buddhist" times some Silla and Koryŏ kings had favored the Confucianists, so in "Confucian" times some Yi kings favored Buddhism, or at least were willing to tolerate the Buddhists so long as they caused no trouble. The general attitude of the Confucian toward Buddhism was one of contempt rather than hostility.

Both Buddhism and Confucianism made some attempt to suppress animism. In general, however, Buddhism adapted itself to animism by incorporating some of its spirits or gods into Buddhist temples, and Confucianism generally ignored it as a superstition of the peasants. Perhaps the most notable Confucian influence on the Korean commoner, apart from teaching him to mind his manners and be happy with his place in the great scheme of things, is the encouragement of ancestor worship, a practice which he had already developed as part of animism.

Christianity came into Korea in the seventeenth century, first from Catholic converts at the imperial court in Peking, and later from Catholic missionaries from the West, especially from France. By the late eighteenth century, the Church of Rome was established in Korea and gained many converts during the nineteenth century despite the hostility of the government, which conducted several organized persecutions and executed many priests and other religious. The last persecution, in 1866, resulted in the Western powers' demanding an opening of Korea and a cessation of its anti-Christian activity.

There were only a few Protestant missionaries in Korea before 1850, but in the latter part of the century they came in greater numbers and soon gained considerable influence among the people. Some allied themselves with Koreans who were trying to reform the government and strengthen the nation against Japan; others gained influence at court by their knowledge of Western medicine and technology. Today, the Roman Catholic and several Protestant churches have considerable congregations in Korea.

In 1861, Ch'oe Che-u 崔濟愚 최제우, a scholar of southern Korea, founded a religious reform movement called Ch'ŏndogyo (Teachings of the Heavenly Way), or, especially before 1894, Tonghak, (Eastern learning), as opposed to Sŏhak 西學 서학 (Western learning, or Christianity). Tonghak combined several doctrines of shamanism, Buddhism, and Confucianism in an attempt to furnish the Korean people with a new Oriental faith and ideal. Because it had to combat the corrupt and hostile Yi court, the Tonghak movement soon took on a political role; the "march" of the Tonghak group upon Seoul caused the Manchu to send troops to support the Yi throne and gave the Japanese the excuse they sought to drive the Chinese out of Korea. During the Japanese administration, many Ch'ŏndo-gyo leaders were active in the independence movements.

GENERAL WORKS ON RELIGION IN KOREA
Western

(362)   Clark, Charles Allen. Religions of Old Korea. New York: Revell, 1932. The most comprehensive study of Korean religions. Contains lectures, delivered at the Princeton Theological Seminary in 1921, on Buddhism, Confucianism, Ch'ŏndo-gyo, Shamanism, and other Asiatic sects, and on the early phases of Christianity in Korea; describes their history, doctrines, literature, and arts in Korea. Written by a missionary who, except for some information given him by Korean associates, relied upon Western sources and sometimes accepts accounts of Korean history which have been proved erroneous.

WORKS ON BUDDHISM IN KOREA
Western

(363)   Starr, Frederick. Korean Buddhism. Boston: Marshall Jones Co., 1918. Contains three lectures—"History," "Condition," "Art." Supports the argument that Buddhism is still an influential religion in contemporary Korea. Neither a profound nor detailed work, but it is based on personal observation and contains suggestions for further study. It is also one of the very few Western studies of Korean Buddhism.

(364)   Trollope, Mark Napier. "Introduction to the Study of Buddhism in Corea," TAKBRAS, VIII (1917), 1-41. A brief but informative history of Buddhism in Korea and a summary of its creeds. Contains suggestions to future researchers.

Korean

(365)　　Yi Nŭng-hwa 李能和 이능화. Chosŏn Pulgyo T'ongsa 朝鮮佛教通史 조선불교통사 (A Comprehensive History of Korean Buddhism). Seoul: Sinmung-wan, 1918. 2 vols. Divided into three parts: (1) events related to Buddhism chronologically arranged with extensive quotations from sources; (2) an enumeration of Buddhist sects, with explanations of their creeds and biographies of prominent monks; (3) 200 essays on subjects related to Buddhism, e.g., "The Origin of Korean Phonetic Script," "Korean Music," "Introduction of Mohammedanism, Christianity, Taoism and Confucianism," "Indigenous Religions of Korea." Both volumes contain indices.

(366)　　Yi Nŭng-hwa, "Chosŏn Pulgyo-sa" 朝鮮佛教史 조선불교사 (History of Korean Buddhism), Chōsen-shi Kōza (185), II, [separate paging].　One of the finest introductions to the study of Korean Buddhism, even though the account covers only the Three Kingdoms period. Quotes materials from the Samguk Sagi (225), Samguk Yusa (226), Honchō Kōsō-den 本朝高僧傳 (Biographies of Prominent Priests in Japan), Nihon Bukkyō Ryakushi 日本佛教畧史 (Brief History of Japanese Buddhism), Tongguk T'onggam (244), and other sources.　Contains short accounts of prominent Korean monks, particularly those who transmitted Buddhism to Japan and those who were skilled in military affairs and in literature. Describes temples built during the Three Kingdoms period; and discusses sects and arts of Korean Buddhism. Written in kukhanmun, with a kana paraphrase of the han-gŭl.

Japanese

(367)　　Nukariya Kaiten 忽滑谷快天 Chōsen Zenkyō-shi 朝鮮禪教史 (History of Zen in Korea). Tōkyō: Shunshū-sha, 1930. Consists of lectures originally delivered at Komazawa University. The author is particularly interested in explaining the causes of the decline of Zen Buddhism in Korea. Nukariya, who is a student of Zen throughout the Far East, has a thorough knowledge of Korean history and of Buddhist literature. He supports his argument with many quotations in Chinese from source material, and acknowledges his debt to several Korean abbots and particularly to the Korean authority on Buddhism, Yi Nŭng-hwa.

(368)   Takahashi Tōru 高橋亨. Richō Bukkyō 李朝佛教 (Buddhism During the Yi Dynasty). Tōkyō: Hōbun-kan, 1929. Describes the vicissitudes of Korean Buddhism during the Yi dynasty, and endeavors to show the place of Buddhism in the Yi government by pointing out that Buddhism at first was still an officially recognized religion, that later it retained a strong hold on the people even though not officially recognized, and that finally it showed considerable decay and degeneration. Except for Yi Nŭng-hwa's <u>Chosŏn Pulgyo T'ongsa</u> (365), Takahashi's is perhaps the only systematic Oriental account of Korean Buddhism.

This is the only published volume of a projected outline history of Korean thought, <u>Chōsen Shisō-shi Taikei.</u>

WORKS ON CONFUCIANISM IN KOREA
Western

(369)   Youn, L. Eul Sou (Yun Ŭl-su 尹乙秀윤을수). <u>Le Confucianism en Corée</u>. Paris: Paul Genthner, 1939. The only Western study of Korean Confucianism, but the account stops with the reign of King Sejong. The book is probably at its best in dealing with the conflict between Buddhism and Confucianism in the latter part of the Koryŏ dynasty, and in its account of the philosophical distinctions between Confucianism and neo-Confucianism. References are not always precise and the bibliography is limited.

Korean

(370)   Hong Hŭi 洪熹홍희). "Chosŏn Hakye-sa" 朝鮮學藝史 조선학예사 (History of Korean Literary Accomplishments), <u>Chōsen-shi Kōza</u> (185), II, [separate paging]. Discusses the development of Korean Confucianism from the Three Kingdoms period to the middle of the Yi dynasty, and argues that the year 372, which is recorded as the year of the entry of Confucianism

in Korea, was not really the beginning but the renascence of Confucianism in Korea. The biographical sketches of prominent Confucian scholars are interesting and useful, but the book contains no account of their philosophies.

(371)   Hyŏn Sang-yun 玄相允 현상윤 Chosŏn Yuhak-sa 朝鮮儒學史 조선유학사 (History of Korean Confucianism). Seoul: Minjung Sŏgwan, 1949. Consists of lectures given by the president of Koryŏ University, whose main concern is to trace the influences of Confucianism on the Korean people and on the political and social conditions during the Yi dynasty. Contains biographical sketches of many scholars from the Silla period to 1910, and contains an excellent chapter on the period of Yi Hwang 李滉 이황 (T'oege 退溪 퇴계) and Yi I 李珥 이이 (Yulgok 栗谷 율곡). This book is the best organized study on the history of Korean Confucianism, but gives too much attention to biography and too little to history and philosophy. The detailed table of contents serves as an index.

(372)   Yi Nŭng-hwa. "Chosŏn Yugeji Yangmyŏng Hakp'a" 朝鮮儒界之陽明學派 조선유계지양명학파 (The Yang-ming School of Korean Confucianism), Seikyū Gakusō, 25 (1936), 105-142. An account of the Confucian scholars who were influenced by Wang Shou-jen 王守仁. These were few since the Wang school of Confucian thought was regarded as heretical by its opponent, the Chu Hsi school, which in Korea held political power.

(373)   Yi Sang-baek 李相佰 이상백. "Yupul Yang-gyo Kyodae ŭi Kiyŏn e Taehan Ilyŏn-gu" 儒佛兩敎交代의機緣에對한一硏究 유불양교교대의기연에대한일연구 (On Supplanting of Buddhism by Confucianism). Part I of the Chosŏn Munhwa-sa Yŏn-gu Non-go (488). Originally published in two parts in the Tōyō Shisō Kenkyū 東洋思想研究, Vols. II and III (1938, 1939), an annual of the Research Society of Oriental Thought, Waseda University, Tōkyō. Contends that the Confucian predominance over Buddhism in the later part of the Koryŏ period and early part of the Yi dynasty cannot be explained in terms of their philosophi-

cal and religious systems, but that social and economic reasons enabled Confucianism to supplant Buddhism. The notes and comments at the end of each chapter are particularly valuable.

Japanese

(374)   Oda Shōgo and Ŏ Yun-jŏk. Chōsen Bummyō oyobi Shōbu Jugen; Fu: Chōsen Jugaku Nempyō; Chōsen Jugaku Engenfu 朝鮮文廟及陞廡儒賢附朝鮮儒學年表朝鮮儒學淵源譜(Korean Confucian Temples and Canonized Confucian Sages; Supplement: Chronology of Korean Confucianism; Register of the Origin of Korean Confucianism). Keijō: Chōsen Shigak-kai, 1924. A brief history of Confucian shrines in Korea and biographies of eighteen canonized Confucian sages. Includes poems and essays written by them. A chronology of Korean Confucianism and a chart showing its origin are appended.

(375)   Takada Seiji 高田誠二 and Fujiwara Ichiki 藤原一毅. Nihon no Kyōiku Seishin to Ri Taikei fu Ri Ritsukoku no Gekimō Yōgetsu to Jiji 日本の教育精神と李退溪附李栗谷の擊蒙要訣と時事 (Spirit of Japanese Education and Yi T'oege, with Yi Yulgok's Kyŏngmong Yogyŏl 擊蒙要訣 격몽요결 and Current Events). Keijō: Chōsen Jijō Kyōkai Shuppan-bu, 1934.   Shows the influence of Yi Hwang (T'oege) upon the Japanese Confucianist Ōtsuka Taiya 大塚退野 (1677-1750) and points out that T'oege's philosophy influenced the Meiji educational rescript. Contains a short biography of Yi I (Yulgok) and the original text of his Kyŏngmong Yogyŏl (Essentials of Dispelling Ignorance) with a kanamajiri translation and comments.

(376)   Takahashi Tōru. "Chōsen Jukyō Taikan" 朝鮮儒教大觀 (Survey of Korean Confucianism). Chōsen-shi Kōza (185), III, [separate paging].   Contains a discussion of Korean Confucianism from the end of the Koryŏ period through the Yi dynasty, particularly on neo-Confucianism after its introduction by An Hyang (1243)-1306). Discusses the history of neo-Confucianism and the theories and systems presented by prominent neo-Confucianists.

(377)　　Takahashi Tōru. "Richō Jugaku-shi ni okeru Shuriha Shugiha no Hattatsu" 李朝儒學史に於ける主理派主氣派の發達 (Development of the Schools of Form and Matter in the History of Confucianism in the Yi Dynasty), Chōsen Shina Bunka no Kenkyū 朝鮮支那文化の研究 (Studies of Korean and Chinese Cultures). Edited by the Keijō Teikoku Daigaku Hōbun Gakkai. Tōkyō: Tōkō Shoin, 1929. Pp. 141-281. A detailed study of two of the major schools of thought in neo-Confucianism during the Yi dynasty. The study indicates the fundamental differences between the two schools in their interpretations of human nature, differences which were consequent upon their respective acceptance of the primacy of form or the primacy of matter. The article is based on the writings of Yi I (Yulgok) and Yi Hwang (T'oege), and their followers. The debate between the formalists and the materialists in Korean Confuciansim began with these two philosophers in the sixteenth century, continued for more than 300 years, and often split Confucian scholars into irreconcilable factions but also led to a notable advance and refinement of Confucian thought in Korea.

(378)　　Yun Yong-gyun 尹瑢均윤용균 . Shushi-gaku no Denrai to sono Eikyō ni tsuite 朱子學の傳來とその影響に就いて (Concerning the Introduction of Chu Hsi Philosophy and Its Influence). Edited by Sin Sŏk-ho 申奭鎬신석호 and Suematsu Yasukazu. Keijō, 1933. A posthumous publication. A study of the introduction of Chu Hsi philosophy into Korea, its development and influence, and its political and social implications as revealed by the history of the Yi dynasty. Well documented.

WORKS ON CHRISTIANITY IN KOREA
Western

(379)　　Dallet, Charles. Histoire de l'Église de Corée. Paris: Librairie Victor Palme, 1874. 2 vols. The first systematic account of Catholicism in Korea. The long introduction to Vol. I describes Korean history, institutions, language, morality, and customs; the rest of the work is a detailed account of the Roman Catholic church in Korea from its introduction in 1784 to the persecution of 1866.

(379a)   Yi Nŭng-sik 李能植 이능식 and Yun Chi-sŏn 尹志善 윤지선, trans. Chosŏn Kyohoe-sa: Sŏsŏl 朝鮮教會史序說 조선교회사서설 (History of the Korean Church: Introduction). Seoul: Taesŏng Ch'ulp'an-sa, 1947. A Korean translation of Dallet's introduction, with notes and comments.

(380)   Mutel, Gustave. <u>Documents relatifs aux martyrs de Corée de 1839 et 1846</u>. Hong Kong: Société des Missions Étrangères de Paris, 1924. Contains translations of the sections of the <u>Sŭngjŏng-wŏn Ilgi</u> (265), <u>Hŏnjong Sillok</u> (289), and other Korean official documents which contain accounts of the persecutions of Christians in Korea in 1839 and 1846. Mutel was given permission by the Government General to go through the archives of the old Korean government. He dates every passage by the Chinese and Western calendars, and he gives the Chinese characters as well as the Christian names for the eighty-two martyrs of 1839 and 1846.

(381)   Paik, L. George (Paek Nak-chun 白樂濬 백낙준). <u>The History of Protestant Missions in Korea (1832-1910)</u>. P'yŏngyang: Union Christian College Press, 1929. The most definitive history of Protestant missions in Korea by a Korean scholar trained in Western historical methods. Paik uses few Oriental sources, but his bibliography in Western languages is exhaustive. The introduction furnishes a succinct and useful account of Korea and its religions.

   Korean

(382)   Yi Man-ch'ae 李晚采 이만채 . <u>Pyŏgwi-p'yŏn</u> 闢衛編 벽위편   (Compilations of a Defense Against Heresy). Keijō: Pyŏk Wi-sa, 1931. 7 vols. A compilation of materials about the persecution of Catholics during the reigns of Chŏngjo, Sunjo, and Hŏnjong. The work was begun by Yi Ki-gyŏng 李基慶 이기경 , a Confucian scholar of the reign of King Chŏngjo, and completed by his descendant, Yi Man-ch'ae. Contains an account of the introduction of Catholicism into Korea, its relations with political factions, and the persecutions of its believers; also contains letters of converts and their petitions to the government.

Japanese

(383)   Kusuta Onosaburō 楠田斧三郎 Chōsen Tenshukyō Shoshi 朝鮮天主教小史 (A Short History of Korean Catholicism). Pusan: Privately printed, 1933. Designed for popular use, but it will serve as an introduction to the subject. Fails to use many valuable Korean sources.

(384)   Uragawa Wasaburō 浦川和三郎. Chōsen Junkyō-shi 朝鮮殉教史 (History of Martyrdom in Korea). Ōsaka: Zenkoku Shobō, 1944. A detailed account of persecutions of Christians in 1800-1801 and 1838-1840. Based on the standard works on the subject and on much valuable information the author obtained from Father Leo Pichon, of Seoul. Contains a useful general survey of Catholicism in Korea and gives detailed information on martyrs. Proper names are given only in <u>kana</u>.

WORKS ON OTHER RELIGIONS IN KOREA
Korean

(385)   Son Chin-t'ae 孫晋泰 손진태. Chosŏn Minjok Munwa ŭi Yŏn-gu 朝鮮民族文化의研究 조선민족문화의연구 (Studies on Korean Native Culture). Seoul: Ŭryu Munhwa-sa, 1948. Previously published in several Korean and Japanese journals. A collection of essays on ethnology by one of Korea's outstanding ethnologists. The second part of the book deals with religious beliefs, and contains essays on the traveller's altar, the altar pole, the devil post, the mountain spirit, and other topics. These are studied historically and compared with similar Manchurian and Chinese beliefs and practices.

Japanese

(386)   Murayama Chijun 村山智順. Chōsen no Fuken 朝鮮の巫覡 (Shamans of Korea). Keijō: Chōsen Sōtokufu, 1932. A thorough study of Korean sorcerers and sorceresses. In 1932 there were more than ten thousand shamans in Korea who lived among the people without belonging to any shrine, their effect upon the people is here objectively described.

Religion and Philosophy   141

(387)   Murayama Chijun. <u>Chōsen no Fūsui</u> 朝鮮の風水 (Korean
        Geomancy). Keijō: Chōsen Sōtokufu, 1931. A report on the
        investigation of geomancy, an important aspect of the religious
        beliefs of the Korean populace. The work is a valuable source
        for an understanding of the thought and behavior of the common
        people of Korea.

(388)   Murayama Chijun. <u>Chōsen no Kishin</u> 朝鮮の鬼神 (Korean
        Spirits). Keijō: Chōsen Sōtokufu, 1929. A study of Korean
        demonology. Contains stories about spirits (most of them de-
        mons) popular among the people, conceptions of spirits held by
        Korean scholars and by the populace, and accounts of the meth-
        ods used by Koreans to drive away evil spirits.

(389)   Murayama Chijun. <u>Chōsen no Ruiji Shūkyō</u> 朝鮮の類似
        宗教 (Pseudo-religions of Korea). Keijō: Chōsen Sōtokufu, 1935.
        A study of religions popular among the common people of Korea
        since the founding of Tonghak (Ch'ŏndo-gyo) in 1860. Contains a
        detailed account of the history, organization, creeds, and acti-
        vities of some seventy sects which are offshoots of the major
        religions in Korea. Also contains fine statistical charts which
        show motives for joining and leaving sects, their numbers in
        the various provinces, and their increase or decrease in mem-
        bership. Attributes the rise of these popular religions to the
        religious need of a people who were politically, economically,
        and socially suppressed. It is a valuable book for students both
        of religion and of sociology.

(390)   Murayama Chijun. <u>Shakuten, Kiu; Antaku</u> 釋奠祈雨安宅
        (Sacrifices to Confucius; Prayers for Rain; Sacrifices to Family
        Spirits). Keijō: Chōsen Sōtokufu, 1938. Describes communal
        and private sacrifices practiced among the various classes in
        Korea. Cites passages from the earliest Korean histories to
        show the persistence of the rituals and sacrifices described in
        this book.

<u>Note:</u> For further information on religion and philosophy see
83, 185, 187, 197, 206, 297.

Music

Korean music has always been strongly influenced by that of China, although there have been many independent developments and native adaptations. New instruments were invented in Korea at an early date; for example, the chwago 坐鼓 좌고 (sitting drum), and the hyang p'iri 鄕觱篥 향피리 (tartar pipe), both of which antedate the Christian era. Several instruments were devised during the Three Kingdoms period. The kŏmungo 거문고 (a harp) was developed in Koguryŏ by Wang San-ak 王山岳 왕산악, the chief minister to King Yang-wŏn, and was later made popular in Silla by the composer Ok Po-go 玉寶高 옥보고. King Kasil of Kaya invented a kind of harp called Kaya-gŭm 伽倻琴 가야금, which also became popular in Silla. Silla's musicians produced the hyang pip'a 鄕琵琶 향비파 (Korean lute) and the taegŭm 大 笒 대금, a variety of the T'ang bamboo flute. Paekche produced a harp that seems modeled upon an Assyrian original. Many of these instruments were reproduced without modification for many centuries.

During the Koryŏ and Yi dynasties, Chinese influence became even stronger than it had been during the Three Kingdoms period. The early Yi kings commanded the establishment of musical canons which would conform with Chinese conventions and eliminate native influence. At the command of King Sejong, the musicologist Pak Yŏn 朴堧 박연 brought Korean ceremonial music into conformity with the music of the T'ang and other Chinese courts. Yŏnsan-gun, who preferred the lyrical ballads of the kisaeng, temporarily checked the development toward Chinese orthodoxy, but it was resumed under his successors. Korean music, like most of Korean culture, declined during the Hideyoshi invasions and did not recover until King Chŏngjo and his proteges, Sŏ Myŏng-ŭng and Chŏng Yag-yong, revived an interest at court in classical mu-

Music   143

sic. King Kojong's court included several hundred musicians, whose students preserved Korean classical music after the Japanese annexation.

A rich tradition of folk music was developed among the Korean commoners, although until recent times this music was largely ignored by court composers. Today, Korean musicians are turning increasingly to the folk music of their country, and often use Western musical techniques and instruments.

The best or most available primary and secondary works on Korean music are listed in this chapter. In addition, there is important information on Korean music in the Munhŏn Pigo (83), the Koryŏ-sa (240), the Haedong Yŏksa (241), and in the "Note on Music" of the Sejo Sillok (289).

WORKS ON KOREAN MUSIC
Western

(391)   Eckardt, Andreas. Koreanische Musik. Mitteilungen der Deutschen Gesellschaft für Natur- und Volkerkunde Ostasiens, Vol. XXIV. Tōkyō, 1930. An analysis, description, and history of Korean music. Examples of its melody and harmony are given in Western notation. Contains photographs of instruments. This is the best Western work on the subject.

(392)   Boot, J. L. (Mrs.). "Korean Musical Instruments and An Introduction to Korean Music," TAKBRAS, XXX (1940), 1-31. A compact survey of Korean music with many diagrams, charts, and photographs. Based upon Eckardt's work (391) and other, chiefly Western, sources.

Korean

(393)   Akhak Kwebŏm 樂學軌範 악학 제범 (Examplar for Music). Keijō: Koten Kankō-kai, 1933. 9 books in 3 fascicles. A photo-offset reproduction of the 1610 printing of a work compiled at the command of King Songjong to preserve Pak Yŏn's studies of court music. This is the most complete and best organized work of the Yi dynasty on music. It describes instruments, musical techniques, songs, dances, and ceremonies.

(394)   Chŏng Yag-yong. Aksŏ Kojon 樂書孤存 악서고존 (Gleanings from Music Books). [c. 1800]. 12 books in 4 fascicles. A manuscript of quotations pertinent to musicology from numerous sources, especially classical Chinese literature, arranged by topic. The works are listed in tables of contents for each chapter. Some illustrations.

As an editor and compiler, Chŏng Yag-yong (b. 1762) excelled all other classical scholars of his time. He not only mastered the traditional Oriental learning but undertook pioneer studies in Western learning. Those searching for historical information on specialized musical subjects will find this collection a useful reference. The manuscript is in the East Asiatic Library of the University of California.

(395)   Ham Hwa-jin 咸和鎭 함화진. Chosŏn Ŭmak T'ongnon 朝鮮音樂通論 조선음악통론 (Survey of Korean Music). Seoul: Ŭryu Munhwa-sa, 1948. A comprehensive survey of Korean music from the earliest times to the present, with a chronological chart of major musical events.

(396)   Sŏng Kyŏng-nin 成慶麟 성경린. Chosŏn ŭi Aak 朝鮮의雅樂 조선의아악 (Korean Court Music). Seoul: Pangmun Sŏgwan, 1947. A short history of the development of court ceremonial music, with descriptions of instruments, songs, and dances.

(397)   Sŏng Kyŏng-nin. Chosŏn Ŭmak Tokpon 朝鮮音樂讀本 조선음악독본 (Korean Music Reader). Seoul: Ŭryu Munhwa-sa, 1947. A handbook of Korean music written in han-gŭl. Contains a concise account of Korean music from its origins to the present. Apparently intended as a textbook.

Japanese

(398)   Tanabe Hisao 田邊尚雄. Tōyō Ongaku-shi 東洋音樂史 (History of Oriental Music). Tōyō-shi Kōza 東洋史講座 (Lectures on Oriental History), Vol. XIII. Tōkyō: Yūsan-kaku, 1930. Contains a partly annotated bibliography of Western and Oriental materials on Korean music.

Note: For further information on music see 83, 84, 187, 297, 365, 441, 442.

XIV

Language

Korean is a polysyllabic, agglutinative language of the Altaic family, similar to Japanese in morphology and syntax: i.e., (1) particles are placed after substantives to indicate their function; (2) the sentence order is always subject, object, and verb; (3) modifying words, phrases, and clauses precede the words they modify; (4) verbs have neither person nor number, and are conjugated by adding auxiliary suffixes to the stem; (5) there are no articles nor relative pronouns; and (6) nouns usually have neither person nor number. The Korean vocabulary contains numerous Chinese words, and some words from Jürchen, Manchu, and Mongolian. Modern Korean retains vestiges of vowel harmony, which is a prominent characteristic of other Altaic languages. Spoken Korean expresses degrees of politeness by different verbal suffixes.

Little is known about early Korean. Chinese accounts indicate only that the Sam Han spoke similar dialects and that the northern tribes—the Ye, Okcho, and Koguryŏ—spoke languages related to that of the Puyŏ. Silla and the lower classes of Paekche spoke a Han dialect; Koguryŏ and the upper classes of Paekche spoke a Puyŏ dialect. The language spoken at the Koryŏ period resembled modern Korean.

The Koreans have two scripts: the older—hanmun—was borrowed from China in the Three Kingdoms period; the other—han-gŭl—was invented by King Sejong in 1443. Hanmun consists of Chinese characters written according to the laws of Chinese grammar and syntax, but usually read with Korean pronunciation. Until the twentieth century, hanmun remained the script of most scholars and educated Koreans, many of whom regarded Sejong's script with contempt. Late in the Three Kingdoms period the Koreans devised a supplementary charactery—idu—which used certain Chinese characters only for their phonetic value in order to indicate particles and verbal suffixes. The invention of idu is usually attributed to Sŏl Ch'ong 薛聰 설총 (b. 655), but some authorities believe it was devised earlier. In the Koryŏ period kugyŏl and t'o, which some authorities regard as identical with idu, were used for this purpose.

In 1446, King Sejong issued a proclamation, the preface to which read in part as follows:

Our national language differs from Chinese and has no affinity with written Chinese. Therefore, what our people wish to say cannot be said in the Chinese manner. And so, having compassion upon our people in this deplorable situation, we have devised a new writing of twenty-eight characters, so that our people may readily learn it and use it in their daily affairs.

The "new writing" consisted of seventeen consonants and eleven vowels—twenty-eight symbols that could be conveniently combined to represent the sounds of Korean speech. Each Korean syllable cluster consisted of two or sometimes three symbols— the initial (a consonant), the medial (a vowel), and sometimes the final (a consonant). King Sejong called this script hunmin chŏngŭm, i.e., "correct sound for teaching the people" (see 407). About a century later, it was called ŏnmun, or "vernacular script," and was also referred to as panjŏl, from the Chinese term for phonetic representation. During the so-called ŏnmun period, which lasted until 1893, the script was considerably revised, particularly by the scholar Ch'oe Se-jin, who discarded the symbol ㆁ . For a short time (1894-1910) the script was called kungmun, or national script. Early in the twentieth century it was given the name han-gŭl, or Korean script, by the great Korean linguist, Chu Si-gyŏng. The Chosŏn Ŏ Hakhoe (Korean Language Association) has, since its formation in 1933, encouraged the use of han-gŭl. It has reduced the script to twenty-four symbols—fourteen consonants and ten vowels—and has formulated rules to standardize the spelling of Korean. Modern Korean is usually written in kukhanmun, which comprises both hanmun and han-gŭl.

WORKS ON THE KOREAN LANGUAGE
Western

(399)   Gale, James S. Korean Grammatical Forms. Seoul: Trilingual Press, 1894. A handbook of 164 verbal endings and connectives. Contains more than a thousand sentences, with English translations, to illustrate the use of these grammatical forms.

(400)   Rahder, Johannes. "Comparative Treatment of the Japanese Language," Monumenta Nipponica, VII (1951), 198-208; VIII (1952), 239-288. A comparative study intended principally "to link old Japanese word families to related word families in Korean, Ainu, Tungus, Mongolian, Turkic, Sinitic, Tibeto-Burmese, Thai, Austrio-Asiatic and Austronesian languages." The second part discusses Korean-Japanese phoneme correspondence.

(401)   Ramstedt, G. J. A Korean Grammar. Helsinki: Suomalais-Ugrilaninen Seura, 1939. Divided into six chapters: phonetics, morphology, postpositions and adverbs, uninflected words, word formation, and sentence structure. Presents many original interpretations of Korean grammar, e.g., regards the adjective as a verb. This is one of the most thorough and systematic grammars of Korean, but it is suitable only for the advanced student. It uses a difficult system of romanization instead of han-gŭl. Had the author used han-gŭl, and had he followed the unified system of spelling, he could have avoided many involved and laborious explanations.

(402)   Ramstedt, G. J. Studies in Korean Etymology. Helsinki: Suomalais-Ugrilaninen Seura, 1949. An etymological dictionary of Korean words arranged according to the alphabetic order of romanized Korean. Contains illustrations of phoneme correspondence between Korean and Mongolian, Turkish, Tungus, Manchurian, Japanese, and other languages, but the relationship between the Korean word and its equivalent in another language is not always clearly shown. Also illustrates the difference between North and South Korean dialects.

(403)   Rogers, Michael C. <u>Outline of Korean Grammar</u>. Berkeley: Department of Oriental Languages of the University of California, 1953. A brief study of Korean grammar designed for advanced students. The material could have been presented more clearly by using <u>han-gŭl</u>, as well as romanization, throughout the book; instead, <u>han-gŭl</u> is used only in the first chapter.

Korean

(404)   Ch'oe Hyŏn-bae 崔鉉培 최현배. <u>Chosŏn Malbon</u> 조선 말본 (Korean Grammar). Seoul: Chŏng-ŭm-sa, 1948. A high school grammar condensed from the author's voluminous <u>Uri Malbon</u> 우리 말 본 (Our Grammar), which was unavailable to the compilers of the <u>Guide</u>. It is divided into phonetics, parts of speech, and syntax; and emphasizes Korean grammatical terms. This is perhaps the most thorough and systematic Korean grammar.

(405)   Ch'oe Hyŏn-bae. <u>Han-gŭl Kal</u> 한글 갈 (A Study of <u>Han-gŭl</u>). Keijō: Chŏng-ŭm-sa, 1942. A detailed account of the history and theory of <u>han-gŭl</u>. Discusses all historical and theoretical problems connected with the study of <u>han-gŭl</u>, traces its development and use, and examines critically the many theories of its origins and grammar. Discusses the romanization of <u>han-gŭl</u> and <u>han-gŭl</u> transcription of other languages, and presents systems for doing both. A title and author index is appended.

(406)   Ch'oe Hyŏn-bae. <u>Kŭlja ŭi Hyŏngmyŏng</u> 글자의 혁명 (Revolution of Written Script). Seoul: Kunjŏngch'ŏng Mungyo-bu, 1947. Argues for the elimination of Chinese characters from Korean writing, and for the horizontal writing of <u>han-gŭl</u>. Ch'oe's plan for writing <u>han-gŭl</u> horizontally calls for the deforming of the traditional syllable cluster and changes in some letters so that <u>han-gŭl</u> may be adapted to the typewriter and linotype.

(407)   Chosŏn Ŏ Hakhoe. <u>Hunmin Chŏng-ŭm</u> 訓民正音 훈민정음 (Correct Sound in Teaching the People). Seoul: Chosŏn Ŏ Hakhoe, 1946. A facsimile of King Sejong's <u>Hunmin Chŏng-ŭm</u>, which was discovered in 1940 in Kyŏngsang Pukto.

(408)   Chu Si-gyŏng 周時經주시경. Chosŏn Ŏ Munbŏp 朝鮮語
文法조선어문법 (Korean Grammar). 2nd ed. Seoul: Chŏng-
ŭm-sa, 1946. A posthumous publication. Contains three essays
on Korean language by Chu Si-gyŏng (1876-1914), who was perhaps the first to study Korean by modern linguistic techniques.
Also contains a short biography of Chu Si-gyŏng by Kwŏn Tŏk-kyu
權悳奎권덕규.

(409)   Hong Ki-mun 洪起文홍기문. Chŏng-ŭm Paldal-sa 正音
發達史정음발달사 (History of the Development of Han-gŭl).
Seoul: Sŏul Sinmun-sa Ch'ulp'an-guk, 1946. 2 vols. An examination of materials relative to the Hunmin Chŏng-ŭm. Vol. I contains portions of the Hunmin Chŏng-ŭm in modern Korean and
critical notes. Vol. II discusses Sejong's reasons for inventing
han-gŭl, the process of its proclamation, later revisions, King
Sejong's policies on its use, persons who contributed to devising
the script, and scholars who opposed the use of han-gŭl.

(410)   Hong Ki-mun. Chosŏn Munbŏp Yŏn-gu 朝鮮文法研究조
선문법연구 (Studies in Korean Grammar). Seoul: Sŏul Sinmun-
sa, 1947. A thorough study of Korean grammar divided into:
"Letters and Phonetics," "Some Basic Studies," "Parts of Speech,"
and "Syntax." The foreword is by the author's father, Hong Pyŏk-
ch'o 洪碧初홍벽초, a novelist.

(411)   Kim Pyŏng-je 金炳濟김병제. Han-gŭl Match'umbŏp Haesŏl 한글맞춤법解說한글맞춤법해설 (An Exposition on the
Han-gŭl Spelling System). Seoul: Chŏng-ŭm-sa, 1946. A pamphlet which shows the correct spelling of han-gŭl. Selects words
and phrases that are often misspelled, shows how they should be
spelled and explains why.

(412)   Kim Yun-gyŏng 金允經김윤경. Chosŏn Munja kŭp Ŏhak-sa
朝鮮文字及語學史조선문자급어학사 (History of Korean
Letters and Language). Seoul: Chinhak Ch'ulp'an Hyŏphoe, 1946.
First printed in 1938. A detailed history of Korean by the dean of
the Chosun (Chosŏn) Christian University. Discusses the linguistic
classification and the scope of Korean, and surveys the origin and

history of han-gŭl. Includes the original text of the Hunmin Chŏng-ŭm. The bibliography of Oriental and Western works is exhaustive.

(413)　　Pang Chong-hyŏn 方鐘鉉 방종현, ed.　Chosŏn Munhwa Ch'ongsŏl 朝鮮文化叢說 조선문화총설 (Essays on Korean Culture). Seoul: Tongsŏng-sa, 1947. A pamphlet containing sixteen articles on language, literature, and ethnology by Korean scholars. About half are on language, e.g., "Hunmin Chŏng-ŭm and Vowels," by Yi Sung-nyŏng 李崇寧 이숭녕; "Study of Consonant Assimilations" and "The Past and Future of Korean Language," by Kim Hyŏng-gyu 金亨奎 김형규; "What is the National Language?" by Yi Hi-sŭng 李熙昇 이희승.

(414)　　Pang Chong-hyŏn. Hunmin Chŏng-ŭm T'ongsa 訓民正音通史 훈민정음통사 (Survey History of Korean Script). Seoul: Ilsŏngdang Sŏjŏm, 1948. A concise but not very systematic survey of han-gŭl. Discusses written Korean before the invention of han-gŭl, and the invention and development of han-gŭl.

(415)　　Sŏk Chu-myŏng 石宙明 석주명. Cheju-do Pang-ŏn-jip 濟州島方言集 제주도방언집 (Collection on the Cheju-do Dialect). Seoul: Sŏul Sinmun-sa Ch'ulp'an-bu, 1947. Divided into three parts: (1) a list of about 10,000 dialect words and phrases of Cheju-do, and their standard Korean equivalents; (2) essays on the Cheju-do and other Korean dialects, e.g., differences between the speech of northern and southern Cheju-do, dialect words of Cheju-do derived from old Korean and foreign languages; (3) essays on miscellaneous subjects related to the Cheju-do dialects.

(416)　　Yi Hi-sŭng. Chosŏn Ŏhak Non-go 朝鮮語學論攷 조선어학론고 (Essays on Korean Language). Seoul: Ŭryu Munhwa-sa, 1947. Contains sixteen essays, originally published in journals and newspapers before 1945, on Korean linguistics, e.g., "On the Problem of the Final Use of ㅎ," "Concerning Korean Standard Language," "Concerning Foreign Derivative Words," "On Temporal Auxiliary Verbs," and "An Introduction to the Methodology of Korean Language Studies."

(417)　　Yi Kŭng-no 李克魯 이극노. <u>Silhŏm Tohae Chosŏn Ŏ Ŭm-sŏng-hak</u> 實驗圖解朝鮮語音聲學 실험도해조선어음성학 (Illustrated Korean Phonetics). Seoul: Amun-gak, 1947. A pamphlet which describes Korean phonetics on the basis of experiments the author made with an artificial mouth and kymograph in 1928 at the University of Paris.

(418)　　Yi Sung-nyŏng. "Moŭm Chohwa Yŏn-gu" 母音調和研究 오음조화연구 (A Study of Vowel Harmony), <u>Chindan Hakpo</u>, 16 (1949), 1-110. A critical examination of Ogura Shimpei's theory of vowel harmony, a review of the study of vowel harmony during the past 500 years, and the author's theories on the subject.

(419)　　Yi Sung-nyŏng. <u>Chosŏn Ŏ Ŭmunnon Yŏn-gu</u> 朝鮮語音韻論研究 조선어음운론연구 (Studies on Korean Phonology). Seoul: Ŭryu Munhwa-sa, 1949. An exhaustive study of the extinct vowel symbol ㆍ.

Japanese

(420)　　Maema Kyōsaku 前間恭作. <u>Keirin Ruiji Raigen Kō</u> 鷄林類事麗言攷 (Study of Koryŏ Words in Chi-lin-lei Shih). Memoirs... of the Toyo Bunko (214), Series A, no. 3 (1925). A commentary on Koryŏ words in the <u>Chi-lin-lei Shih</u> (A Korean Miscellany) by Sun Mu 孫穆 (twelfth century).

(421)　　Maema Kyōsaku. <u>Ryūka Kogo Sen</u> 龍歌故語箋 (Comments on Old Words in <u>Yongbi Ŏ Ch'ŏn-ga</u>), Memoirs... of the Toyo Bunko (214), Series A, no. 3 (1924). A commentary on old words in the <u>Yongbi Ŏ Ch'ŏn-ga</u> (1445). See entry 451.

(422)　　Ogura Shimpei. <u>Chōsen Gogaku-shi</u> 朝鮮語學史 (History of the Korean Language). Keijō: Ōsaka-yago Shoten, 1920. A detailed survey of the characteristics of the Korean language and an account of the origin of written Korean. A large part of the book is a discussion of Korean studies of Japanese, Chinese, Manchurian, Mongolian, Jürchen, Khitan, and other languages. Contains photographs of old Korean texts. The index is in <u>kana</u> order.

(423)   Ogura Shimpei. Chōsen ni okeru Kenjō-hō Sonkei-hō no Jo-dōshi 朝鮮に於ける謙讓法尊敬法の助動詞 (The Humble and Honorific Auxiliary Verb in Korea). Memoirs... of the Toyo Bunko (214), Series A, no. 26 (1938). An excellent historical and descriptive account of humble and honorific Korean auxiliary verbs. Contains an English resume and a han-gŭl index of the auxiliary verbs.

(424)   Ogura Shimpei. Chōsen-go Hōgen no Kenkyū 朝鮮方言の研究 (Studies in Korean Dialects). Tōkyō: Iwanami Shoten, 1944. 2 vols. Vol. I contains dialectical words arranged by subjects—e.g., astronomy, climate, rivers, food, animals—in the international phonetic symbols. Vol. II contains essays previously published in journals and pamphlets, and an account of regional dialects, with maps.

(425)   Ogura Shimpei. Kyōka oyobi Ritō no Kenkyū 鄕歌及び吏讀の研究(Study of Hyangga and Idu). Keijō: Keijō Imperial University, 1929. A handbook of hyangga 鄕歌 향가 and idu divided into three parts: (1) a thorough study of hyangga, with comprehensive commentary on the hyangga in the Samguk Yusa (226); (2) a study of idu used in official documents; (3) essays on vowel harmony, the development of double consonants, and the development of honorific auxiliary verbs.

Note: For further information on language see 73, 74, 185, 206, 365, 487.

XV

Literature

Before the twentieth century, Korean literature had two separate although partly overlapping traditions—a native or "folk" literature, most of it unwritten, which was composed largely for the lower classes; a formal or "Chinese" literature, most of it in hanmun, which was composed by and for the upper classes. Korea's native literature first developed in prehistoric times from religious ceremonies, mythology, and folklore, Korea's "Chinese" literature first developed in the Three Kingdoms period from the influence of Buddhism and Confucianism. The distinction between these two literatures increased in the Koryŏ and Yi periods, as Confucian scholars became ever more disdainful of native Korean culture and ever more devoted to being "Chinese." Korean folk literature consists principally of songs (all folk poetry was intended to be sung), "prose" fiction, mask plays (or mask dances), and puppet shows; formal literature consists principally of poetry in Chinese verse-forms, prose fiction, and literary essays. "Operatic" performances, that is, the formal singing of poems by either groups or soloists, were popular with all classes, but except for these and the mask plays, Korea had no important drama. The Confucianists held the theatre in contempt, although they performed annually an intellectual play, the Kwŏlhŭi  (The Drama of the Palace Gate) to commemorate the removal of the capital to Seoul at the inception of the Yi dynasty.

Probably the oldest Korean verse-form is called tosolga 兜率歌 도솔가, a term which is believed to be a transliteration of tŏtsori 덧소리 , or "sounds for appeasing spirits or gods." Early Chinese accounts of Korea relate that the people sang and danced at religious ceremonies, and it is probable that the first Korean poetry was "hymns" of praise or prayer composed for these festivities. The most important poems of the Three Kingdoms period are the hyangga of Silla—idu poems of four, eight, or ten phrases (each phrase has five or sometimes six syllables), many of them Buddhist songs. There are fourteen hyangga in the Samguk Yusa (226), which were probably copied from a lost ninth-century anthology, the Samdaemok 三代目 삼대목. Hanmun poems of the Three Kingdoms and later periods are in the Samguk Sagi (225), the Chŭngbo Munhŏn Pigo (83), and the "Akji" 樂志 악지 (Music Section) of the Koryŏ-sa (240), which also contains thirty-one sok-ak 俗樂 속악, or popular songs, of Koryŏ. Two important han-gŭl anthologies were compiled in the reign of Sejong: the Yongbi Ŏ Ch'ŏn-ga (451); and the Wŏrin Ch'ŏn-gang Chigok 月印千江之曲 월인천강지곡 (Songs of the Moon's Reflection on a Thousand Rivers), which contains Buddhist hymns translated by command of King Sejong.

Sijo 時調 시조, kasa 歌辭 가사, and chapka 雜歌 잡가 were popular verse-forms of the Yi period. Most sijo were composed in three lines, each of four phrases, and each phrase of a fixed number of syllables: 3, 4, 3(4), 4; 3, 4, 3(4), 4; 3, 5, 4, 3. Kasa usually contained eight phrases, each of eight syllables. Chŏng Ch'ŏl 鄭澈 정철 (1536-1593), style Songgang 松江 송강, was the most outstanding poet of the kasa form. Chapka were long narrative poems sung by male professional entertainers called soritkun 소릿군 or kwangdae 광대.

Prose fiction was first written in the Three Kingdoms period, e.g., Hwawang-yu 花王喩 화왕유 (Parable of the Flower Kingdom), by Sŏl Ch'ŏng, and Chap-jŏn 雜傳 잡전 (Miscellaneous Stories), by Kim Tae-mun 金大問 김대문, are from Silla. Hanmun remained the principal vehicle of prose fiction in the Yi period, although there were also many tales written in han-gŭl for ladies, who could not read hanmun, and translations into han-gŭl of Buddhist and Confucian tales. One of the best of these, the Kuunmong 九雲夢 구운몽, by Kim Man-jung 金萬重 김만중 (1617-1682), was translated by James S. Gale: The Cloud Dream of the Nine (London: O'Connor, 1922). Much han-gŭl prose fiction is anonymous, some because Confucian scholars regarded anything not written in hanmun as trivial, some because it contains satirical attacks upon the injustices and inequalities of the Yi period.

Korean literature since 1900 reveals both a profound Western influence and the Korean desire to create a new, distinct national culture. Han-gŭl and kukhanmun have displaced hanmun as the principal script; "folk" literature has been compiled in anthologies and studied as a serious cultural heritage; Western ideas and literary forms have been used by Korean writers. Prose fiction of the first two decades urged new ideas of education and morality, political liberalism, and national independence, e.g., Ŭn Sege 銀世界 은세계 (The Silvery World), first modern Korean novel (1908), by Yi In-jik 李仁植 이인직 ; Hwa ŭi Hyŏl 花의血 화의혈 (Blood of Flowers), by Yi Hae-jo 李海朝 이해조 ; Mujŏng 無情 무정 (The Heartless), by Yi Kwang-su 李光洙 이광수. The principal type of prose fiction in the twenties was the naturalistic novel, e.g., T'angnyu 濁流 탁류 (The Muddy Stream), by Ch'ae Man-sik 蔡萬植 채만식 ; Pulgŭn Chwi 붉은 쥐 (Red Mouse), by Kim Ki-jin 金基鎮 김기진 ; Sanyang Kae 사냥개 (The Hunting Dog), by Pak Yŏng-hi 朴英熙 박영희 ; and Kananhan Saram-dŭl 가난한 사람들 (The Poor), by Yi Ki-yŏng 李箕永 이기영. Historical novels and novels-of-the-soil were prominent in Korean prose fiction of the thirties, e.g., Yi Sun-sin 李舜臣 이순신, by Yi Kwang-su, and Unhyŏn-gung ŭi Pom 雲峴宮의봄 운현궁의봄 (Spring of the Unhyŏn Palace), by Kim Tong-in 金東仁 김동인 ; Hŭrk 흙 (The Soil), by Yi Kwang-su, and Sangnoksu 常綠樹 상록수 (The Evergreen Tree), by Sim Hun 沈薰 심훈. Hong Myŏng-hi's 洪命憙 홍명희 long novel, Im Kŏ-jŏng 林巨正 림거정, published in 1928, combines several of these types; it is a realistic account of life among the lower classes in the Yi period.

Many modern Korean poets abandoned the traditional Oriental verse forms to experiment with the free-verse styles of recent Western poetry. Outstanding among these free-verse poets are: Kim Yŏng-nang 金永郎 김영랑, a lyric poet whose dominant mood is aestheticism; Kim Ki-rim 金起林 김기림, noted for his subtle, intellectual verse; and the Catholic poet, Chŏng Chi-yong 鄭芝溶 정지용. Other modern poets—Chŏng In-bo, Yi Ŭn-sang 李殷相 이은상, and Yi Pyŏng-gi 李秉岐 이병기, for example—use sijo and other traditional verse forms.

The modern Korean literary essay also reveals both Western and traditional influences: Yi Tae-jun's 李泰俊 이태준 Musŏrok 無序錄 무서록 (Random Notes) combine modern Western and traditional Oriental perceptions; Yi Ŭn-sang's essays often show a strong Buddhist influence; Yi Yang-ha 李敭河 이양하, on the other hand, reveals in his writings the strong influence of English culture upon his thinking.

GENERAL WORKS ON KOREAN LITERATURE
Korean

(426)   Kim Sa-yŏp 金思燁 김사엽. <u>Chosŏn Munhak-sa</u> 朝鮮文學史 조선문학사 (History of Korean Literature). Seoul: Chŏngŭm-sa, 1948. From ancient times to 1910. Emphasizes the "native" literature, that is, works written in <u>kukhanmun</u> and <u>han-gŭl</u>, and works handed down orally, rather than Korea's "Chinese" literature.

(427)   Min Pyŏng-do 閔丙燾 민병도, ed. <u>Chosŏn Yŏktae Yŏryu Mun-jip</u> 朝鮮歷代女流文集 조선역대여류문집 (Selections from Korean Women Writers of the Classical Period). Seoul: Ŭryu Munhwa-sa, 1950. Contains poems, novels, essays, diaries, and other writings by fifteen women of the Yi period. All of the works but three are in <u>hanmun</u>, and two of the <u>han-gŭl</u> works are facsimiles of the manuscripts. Contains explanatory notes by Yi Pyŏng-gi and Yi Pyŏng-do.

(428)   Mun Il-p'yŏng 文一平 문일평. <u>Chosŏn Munhwa Yesul</u> 朝鮮文化藝術 조선문화예술 (Korean Culture and Arts). Seoul: Chogwang-sa, 1946. A survey of Korean culture and art which includes a historical account of Korean authors.

(429)   Paek Ch'ŏl 白鐵 백철. <u>Chosŏn Sinmunhak Sajo-sa</u> 朝鮮新文學思潮史 조선신문학사조사 (History of Modern Literary Thought in Korea). Seoul: Susŏn-sa, 1948. A survey of Korean literary trends from about 1880 to 1925, divided into such categories as nationalism, aestheticism, romanticism, and naturalism. Contains long passages from some of the works discussed. See also 430.

(430)   Paek Ch'ŏl. Chosŏn Sinmunhak Sajo-sa: Hyŏndae-p'yŏn 朝鮮新文學思潮史現代篇 조선 신 문 학 사 조 사 현 대 편 (History of Modern Literary Thought in Korea: Contemporary Period). 2d ed. Seoul: Paeg-yang-dang, 1950. Continues the survey of modern Korean literature begun in the Chosŏn Sinmunhak Sajo-sa (429). Emphasizes the literature of social consciousness written between 1924 and 1934, and brings the account down to the time of publication. Contains long passages from the works discussed. The content and organization of this book are superior to the earlier work.

(431)   Sŏ Kŏ-jŏng. Tongmun-sŏn 東文選 동 문 선 (Anthology of Korean Literature). Keijō: Chōsen Kosho Kankō-kai, 1914. 7 vols. A modern edition of a collection of poems and other Korean writings in hanmun from the Silla to the early Yi period. Compiled by Sŏ in 1478 in 154 books in 45 fascicles, and supplemented by Sin Yong-gae 申用溉 신 용 개 during the reign of Chungjong (1506-1545).

(432)   Yang Chu-dong 梁柱東 양 주 동, ed. Sangju Kungmunhak Kojŏn Tokpon 詳註國文學古典讀本 상 주 국 문 학 고 전 독 본 (Annotated Reader of Classical Korean Literature). Seoul: Pangmun Ch'ulp'an-sa, 1947. An anthology of Korean literature designed as a college text. Arranged in reverse chronological order.

(433)   Yi Hi-sŭng (Lee Hi-seung). Chosŏn Munhak Yŏn-gu-ch'o 朝鮮文學硏究鈔 조 선 문 학 연 구 초 (Some Studies in Korean Literature). Seoul: Ŭryu Munhwa-sa, 1946. Contains a valuable exposition of six well-known kasa, views on the origin of sijo, and other essays.

(434)   Yi Hi-sŭng. Chŏngjŏng Yŏktae Chosŏn Munhak Chŏnghwa: Kwŏnsang 訂正歷代朝鮮文學精華卷上 정 정 력 대 조 선 문 학 정 화 권 상 (Revised Essentials of Korean Literature Throughout History: Volume One). Seoul: Pangmun Ch'ulp'an-sa, 1948. A high-school and college text. Contains prose fiction, sijo, songs, essays, and other writings in reverse chronological order. Uses the spelling prescribed by the Korean Language Association. The manuscript of the second volume was destroyed in the Korean War.

(435)   Yi Yun-jae. Munye Tokpon 文藝讀本 문예독본 (Literary Reader). Seoul: Hansŏng Tosŏ Chusik Hoesa, 1945. A high-school and college text in two parts. Contains prose fiction, poetry, plays, and essays by contemporary Korean writers, with brief data about the authors and the persons named in the selections. Part one contains comparatively simple readings; part two, more advanced readings.

WORKS ON KOREAN POETRY
Western

(436)   Grigsby, Joan S., trans. The Orchid Door: Ancient Korean Poems. Kobe: Thompson and Co., 1935. Contains free-verse translations of poems by Korean scholars and of a few love songs by kisaeng. The introduction contains a sketchy account of Korean history and a discussion of the method of translation used in the book.

(437)   Zong In-sob (Chŏng In-sŏp 鄭寅燮 정인섭), trans. An Anthology of Modern Poems in Korea. Seoul: Munhwa-dang, 1948. Contains 125 poems by 100 modern Korean poets. Part one contains poems selected by their authors at the translator's request. Part two contains poems selected for translation by Chŏng. These two parts contain the original poem as well as the English translation. Part three contains only the English translations. The introduction contains a survey by Chŏng of modern Korean poetry.

Korean

(438)   Chi Hŏn-yŏng 池憲英 지헌영. Hyangga Ryŏyo Sinsŏk 鄉歌麗謠新釋 향가려요신석 (New Expositions of Silla and Koryŏ Songs). Seoul: Chŏng-ŭm-sa, 1947. A short exposition of Silla and Koryŏ songs. Contains the original poems, brief notes on historical background, interpretations of difficult words and phrases, and free translations into kukhanmun. Part one contains songs of the upper classes; part two, songs of the lower classes.

(439)   Cho Yun-je 趙潤濟 조윤제. Chosŏn Siga ŭi Yŏn-gu 朝鮮詩歌의研究 조선시가의연구 (A Study of Korean Poetry). Seoul: Ŭryu Munhwa-sa, 1948. Contains essays on hyangga,

sijo, kasa, and many other subjects of Korean poetry. Many of
the essays had been published in journals during the preceding
twenty years.

(440)   Cho Yun-je. Chosŏn Siga Sagang 朝鮮詩歌史綱 조선
시가사강 (Outline History of Korean Poetry and Song). Rev. ed.
Keijō: Pangmun Ch'ulp'an-sa, 1937. An account of Korean poetry from ancient times to 1910, divided into eight periods according to dominant verse forms. Shows how social conditions affected Korean poetry. This is one of the most comprehensive and best organized studies of Korean poetry by a Korean scholar.

(441)   Ham Hwa-jin. Chŭngbo Kagok Wŏllyu 增補歌曲源流 증
보가곡원류 (Revised Source Book of Korean Songs). Seoul: Chosŏn Munhwa-gwan, n.d. A revision from the manuscript of the Kagok Wŏllyu, an anthology of Korean songs compiled by Pak Hyo-gwan in 1876. The Kagok Wŏllyu, also known as Haedong Akchang 海東樂章 해동악장 (Korean Songs) and Ch'ŏnggu Akchang 青丘樂章 청구악장 (Songs of the Green Hills [Korea]) is regarded by many scholars as better organized, better documented, and more precise than the earlier and more famous Ch'ŏnggu Yŏng-ŏn (442) and Haedong Kayo (443). This edition contains an essay on the musical setting and organization of the songs.

(442)   Kim Ch'ŏn-t'aek 金天澤 김천택. Ch'ŏnggu Yŏng-ŏn 青丘
永信 청구영신 (Eternal Words of the Green Hills). Keijō: Keijō Teikoku Daigaku, 1930. A modern edition of the oldest and largest extant anthology of Korean poetry. Compiled by the singer, Kim, in 1727. It contains more than a thousand sijo and kasa from the late Koryŏ period to the early eighteenth century classified by their tunes, and also brief biographies of the known authors (about 140), who range from kings to kisaeng. See also 441 and 443.

(443)   Kim Su-jang 金壽長 김수장. Haedong Kayo 海東歌謠
해동가요 (Anthology of Songs of the Eastern Sea [Korea]). Keijō: Keijō Teikoku Daigaku, 1930. A modern edition of a work compiled by Kim Su-jang in 1763. Contains 883 songs, including 149

by the compiler, of Koryŏ and Yi poets. The poets' names, styles, and titles are listed in the preface. See also 441 and 442.

(444) Kim T'ae-jun 金台俊 김태준, trans. Koryŏ Kasa 高麗歌詞 고려가사 (Songs of Koryŏ). Keijō: Hagye-sa, 1939. Contains free renderings into modern Korean of sixteen songs of Koryŏ and one song of Paekche, and an introduction, notes, and comments.

(445) Ko Chŏng-ok 高晶玉 고정옥. Chosŏn Minyo Yŏn-gu 朝鮮民謠研究 조선민요연구 (A Study of Korean Folk Songs). Seoul: Susŏn-sa, 1949. Examines the origin and development of Korean folk songs, and defines their form and content. Classifies the songs into twenty-three types. The book is well documented and contains a topical index of first lines.

(446) Lim Hwa 林和 림화, ed. Chosŏn Minyo-sŏn 朝鮮民謠選 조선민요선 (Selected Folk Songs of Korea). Keijō: Hakye-sa, 1939. Contains songs which were never before written down. These are arranged by subject and their places of origin are given. Includes Cheju-do folk songs collected by Kim T'ae-jun and an interpretation of Korean folk songs by Yi Chae-uk.

(447) Pak Yun-ch'ŏl 朴允哲 박윤철, ed. Sijo-jip 時調集 시조집 (Collected Sijo). Seoul: Minjung Sŏ-gwan, 1946. Contains 555 sijo of the Koryŏ and Yi periods in chronological order.

(448) Pang Chong-hyŏn. Ko-sijo Chŏnghae 古時調精解 고시조정해 (Detailed Commentary on Old Sijo). Seoul: Ilsongdang Sŏjŏm, 1949. Contains old sijo arranged by the han-gŭl order of the first word of each poem, gives the correct spelling and explains the meaning of difficult or doubtful words; and gives data about authors and source materials of old sijo. Contains indices of first lines, of authors, and of important words in old sijo.

(449) Pang Ŭng-mo 方應謨 방응모. Hyŏndae Chosŏn Munhak Chŏnjip: Siga-jip 現代朝鮮文學全集詩歌集 현대조선문학전집시가집 (Collected Works of Contemporary Korean Literature: Poetry Section). Keijō: Chosŏn Ilbo-sa, 1938. Contains poems by thirty-three contemporary Korean writers and biographical sketches of the authors.

(450) Yang Chu-dong. Ryŏyo Chŏnju 麗謠箋注 려묘전주 (A Commentary on Koryŏ Songs). Seoul: Ŭryu Munhwa-sa, 1947. Contains a detailed study of sixteen Koryŏ songs—historical, linguistic, textual. Lists some 130 sources.

(451) Yi Sang-ch'un 李常春 이상춘. Chuhae Yongbi Ŏ Ch'ŏn-ga 註解龍飛御天歌 주해용비어천가 (A Commentary to Dragons Flying to Heaven). Seoul: Tonghwa Ch'ulp'an-sa, 1946. A modern edition of an anthology of songs written in 1445 to praise six kings of the Yi dynasty. Contains the original text and brief notes.

Japanese

(452) Kim Kyo-hwan 金教煥 김교환, trans. Chōsen Minyō-shū 朝鮮民謠集 (Anthology of Korean Folk Songs). By Kim So-un 金素雲 김소운 [pseud.]. Tōkyō: Shinchō-sha, 1941. Contains kanamajiri translations of Korean folk songs, children's songs, and women's songs. The preface is by the Japanese poet, Kitahara Hakushu 北原白秋.

WORKS ON KOREAN PROSE FICTION
Korean

(453) An Hoe-nam 安懷南 안회남. Chosŏn Tanp'yŏn Munhak Sŏnjip: Cheiljip 朝鮮短篇文學選集第一輯 조선단편문학선집제일집 (Anthology of Korean Short Stories: Volume One). Seoul: Pŏmjang-gak, 1946. Contains short stories and a play by seventeen contemporary Korean writers. The text is in han-gŭl.

(454) Ch'oe Sang-su 崔常壽 최상수. Chosŏn Mingan Chŏnsŏl-jip 朝鮮民間傳說集 조선민간전설집 (Collected Folk Tales of Korea). Seoul: Ŭryu Munhwa-sa, 1947. Contains 114 Korean folk tales arranged by subject.

(455) Lim Hwa. Wŏnbon Ch'unhyang-jŏn 原本春香傳 원본춘향전 (The Original Story of Spring Fragrance). Keijō: Hagye-sa, 1939. A modern edition of a long narrative poem written anonymously in han-gŭl in the eighteenth century. The text is a reprint of the Chŏnju 全州 전주 version—the Yolyŏ Ch'unhyang Sujŏlgara

열여춘향수절가라 (Song of the Faithfulness of the Virtuous Wife, Spring Fragrance) printed in the eighteenth century (?) and believed by many scholars to be the oldest printing. The 1939 edition also contains an essay by Kim T'ae-jun which gives a modern interpretation of the story, and discusses its authorship and its first printing. An adaptation by Yun Tal-sŏn 尹達善윤달선 in Chinese for opera is appended.

(456) Pak Chi-wŏn 朴趾源 박지원. Yangban-jŏn 兩班傳 양반전 (Stories of Aristocrats). Seoul: Chosŏn Kŭmyung Chohap Yŏnhaphoe, 1947. Contains seven satirical tales by Pak Chi-wŏn (1737-1805) translated into modern han-gŭl by Yi Sŏk-ku 李奭求 이석구. The well known Hŏ Saeng-jŏn 許生傳 허생전 (Tale of Hŏ Saeng) is included.

(457) Son Chin-t'ae 孫晉泰 손진태 Chosŏn Minjok Sŏlhwa ŭi Yŏn-gu 朝鮮民族說話의研究 조선민족설화의연구 (Studies in Korean Legends and Folk Tales). Seoul: Ŭryu Munhwa-sa, 1947. A comparative, ethnological study of Korean, Chinese, and Japanese legehds which argues that Korean culture was strongly influenced by China and Mongolia, and that it influenced Japanese culture.

(458) Yi Kwang-su. Ilsŏl Ch'unhyang-jŏn 一說春香傳 일설춘향전 (A Modern Story of Spring Fragrance). Keijō: Hansŏng Tosŏ Chusik Hoesa, 1929. A modern-dress version of the Ch'unhyang-jŏn in simple han-gŭl. See 455.

(459) Yi Ŭn-sang. Chosŏn Sahwa-jip: Samguk Sidae-p'yŏn 朝鮮史話集三國時代篇 조선사화집삼국시대편 (Korean Historical Romance: Three Kingdoms Period). Keijō: Tonggwang-sa, 1931. Contains narratives from the Samguk Sagi (225), Samguk Yusa (226), Koryŏ-sa (240), and other ancient works rendered into modern fictional forms. Written in han-gŭl with some Chinese characters in parentheses.

WORKS ON THE KOREAN LITERARY ESSAY
Korean

(460)　Yi Ŭn-sang. Nosan Munsŏn 鷺山文選 로산문선 (Anthology of Nosan). Seoul: Yŏngch'ang Sŏgwan, 1947. Contains travelogues and essays, several of them literary studies, e.g., the writings of the monk Sŏsan 西山 서산, the poetry of Noge 蘆溪 로계, Korean children's songs, the effects of the Manchu invasions on sijo. Also contains Korean translations of all Chinese poems cited in the essays.

WORKS ON KOREAN DRAMA
Japanese

(461)　Innami Takaichi 印南高一. Chōsen no Engeki 朝鮮の演劇 (Korean Theatricals). Tōkyō: Hokkō Shobō, 1944. An account of traditional folk plays, mask dances, puppet shows, and "operas," and also of the new Korean drama to 1944. Contains the text of the puppet show Kkoktukkaksi 꼭두각시 and of the mask dance Pongsan T'al 봉산탈, and photographs of Korean dances and musical instruments. Based largely upon Kim Chae-ch'ŏl's 金在喆 김재철 Chosŏn Yŏn-gŭk-sa 朝鮮演劇史 조선연극사 (History of Korean Drama) and Chŏng No-sik's 鄭魯湜 정로식 Chosŏn Ch'ang-gŭk-sa 朝鮮唱劇史 조선창극사 (History of Korean Opera), neither of which was available to the compilers of the Guide.

Note: For further information on literature see 99, 185, 187, 197, 264, 297, 370, 425.

Education

Formal education in Korea was largely in the hands of the Confucianists from the Three Kingdoms period until the twentieth century. The Buddhists played a secondary role in Korean education even when they dominated the government. The first school was established by royal command in Koguryŏ in 372 to instruct sons of noblemen, and similar schools were founded later in Paekche and Silla. During the Silla and Koryŏ periods many Buddhist neophytes and Confucian students went to China to study. The kwagŏ 科擧 과거, or Confucian civil-service examination system, was known in the Silla period, but the dominance of Buddhism and the hostility of the hereditary nobles prevented its full development until the Yi period.

Until the twentieth century, little education was given to the lower classes. In theory, the Confucian civil-service examinations were open to all males, but social and economic conditions prevented the lower class from preparing for them. Buddhist education was more readily available to the lower classes, and the Buddhists increasingly recruited neophytes from among the common people. After King Sejong's time, some commoners were taught to read and write han-gŭl.

The sŏdang 書堂 서당 were small, private "elementary" schools which were first established by the Confucianists during the Koryŏ period and became numerous during the Yi period. Boys entered the sŏdang at seven or eight years, were taught Chinese characters, and memorized selected passages from the works of Confucius. The secondary level of Confucian education consisted of the hyanggyo 鄕校 향교, or local phrontistery, and sŏwŏn 書院 서원, or academy. The hyanggyo, which flourished from the fourteenth to the eighteenth century, were provincial colleges modeled after the Four Institutes in Seoul and intended to prepare students for final degrees. The first sŏwŏn—the Sosu Sŏwŏn 紹修書院 소 수 서 원 —was founded in 1541 by Chu Se-bung 周世鵬 주 세 붕 to honor the shade of the thirteenth-century Confucian, An Yu 安裕 안 유 , and in 1551 was enriched by the government's generous gift of land, serfs, books, and other awards. Soon other sŏwŏn were established, like the first ostensibly to honor the memory of a famous local scholar, but also to form literary and political clubs independent of the capital. The sŏwŏn, which gradually displaced the hyanggyo, became locally narrow and adamant, and in the later Yi period were often the meeting-places of factional groups.

The highest school in Korea during the Yi period was the Sŏnggyun-gwan 成均館 성 균 관 , or Confucian College, in Seoul, which was a sort of scholastic honorary society and a gathering-place of Korean intellectuals. The Four Institutes were associated with this college, each of them staffed by two instructors and two professors, supervised by a director appointed by the crown, and limited to one hundred students.

Examinations were on three levels—district, provincial, and national. Every hundred days the prefect of each district held a general examination, and successful candidates were entitled to take the provincial examinations. These, held at three-year intervals by the provincial governor in his palace, were specialized —military science, literature, language, law, medicine, cosmography, and the "degree" course—and a candidate prepared to be examined in one of these subjects. The national examinations, held in Seoul the following spring, were also specialized. Successful candidates in all fields except literature and military science were awarded the chinsa 進士 진 사 (doctor), saeng-wŏn 生員 생 원 (licentiate), or a similar degree, and usually given a position in the government. Students of literature and military science were granted the privilege of a yet higher examination —one held in the royal palace with the king as one of the arbitrators. They were graded "A," "B," or "C," but all received very special honors and usually a high political appointment.

The Confucianists equated knowledge with the philosophy of Confucius; therefore, their schools stressed thorough instruction in the Chinese classics and a reverence for all that the Master had said. Original inquiry and a critical attitude were discouraged; thoroughness and conformity were the qualities expected of a student—qualities which readily degenerated into pedantry and rote memorization. Moreover, because Confucian schooling was given only to males of the upper classes, and because it was so closely connected with politics, it developed many corruptions and abuses, especially in the late Yi period.

The first Western school in Korea was an English-language school for interpreters opened by the crown in 1883. In 1886, the crown appointed three Americans to teach some thirty sons of noblemen, and in the same year Methodist missionaries founded Ihwa Haktang 梨花學堂 이화학당 (now Ewha [Ihwa] Women's University), the first Korean college for women. P'yŏng-yang Union Christian College was founded early in the twentieth century, and Chosun (Chosŏn) Christian College (now a university) in 1915. Westernized education in Korea was encouraged by the Japanese and many schools, including Keijō Imperial University, were built by them. However, the Japanese refused Koreans equal educational opportunities, prohibited the use of Korean in schools, and tried to use education as a device for making Koreans loyal subjects of the Japanese emperor. These restrictions and abuses are said to have angered the Koreans more than any of the other oppressive measures of the Japanese. After 1945, the Republic of Korea launched a "democracy and nationalism" program of education, and school attendance, both in North and South Korea, increased greatly in the brief period between liberation and the Korean War.

WORKS ON KOREAN EDUCATION
Western

(462)   Hulbert, Homer B. "National Examination in Korea," TAK-BRAS XIV (1923), 9-32. Consists mainly of passages from chronicles and other records chronologically arranged which show how the civil-service examinations affected Korean culture.

(463)   Kim, Helen K. Rural Education for the Regeneration of Korea. New York: Teachers College, Columbia University, 1931. Surveys the Japanese school system in Korea, argues that the factor which kept the system from rendering a greater service to the people was discrimination against Koreans, and advocates cultural autonomy and vocational training for Koreans.

(464)   Roe, Chungil Y. The True Function of Education in Social Adjustment: A Comparative Estimate and Criticism of the Educational Teachings of Confucius and the Philosophy of John Dewey with a View to Evolving a Project for a System of National Education Which Will Meet the Needs of Korea. Lincoln [University of Nebraska], 1927. Argues "that neither Confucius nor Dewey has succeeded in finding a basic aim for education which is entirely adequate to the needs of Korea," and presents the "doctrine of survival-efficiency... which facilitates the synthesis of the best elements of both oriental and occidental philosophies of education."

(465)   Underwood, Horace H. Modern Education in Korea. New York: International Press, 1926. A history of Korean education from 1883. Most of the account deals with the schools of the Protestant missionaries. Contains many charts and tables.

Korean

(466)   Sosu Sŏwŏn Tŭngnok 紹修書院謄錄 소수서원등록 (Records of Sosu Sŏwŏn). Item 17 of the Chōsen Shiryō Sōkan (183). Keijō, 1937. A photolith reproduction of the records of the Sosu Sŏwŏn from 1547 to 1669, and a printing of the text with modern punctuation and the idu rendered in reduced type.

(467)   Yi Man-gyu. Chosŏn Kyoyuk-sa 朝鮮教育史 조선교육사 (History of Korean Education). Seoul: Ŭryu Munhwa-sa, 1947. 2 vols. A detailed survey of Korean education interpreted in terms of social and economic patterns. Vol. I is particularly valuable because it contains information hard to find elsewhere. A chronology of Korean education from 285 to 1943 is appended. An informative work, but written with a leftist bias.

Japanese

(468)   Meiji ikō Kyōiku Seido Hattatsu-shi 明治以降教育制度
発達史 (History of the Development of the Educational System
since Meiji). Tōkyō: Kyōiku-shi Henshū-kai, 1939. 12 vols.
A detailed account of the government-supported schools of the
Japanese Empire from kindergarten to college since 1911. Volume X, which has more than a thousand pages, deals with Korea.

Note: For further information on education see 83, 84, 185, 187, 370.

XVII

Special Reference Materials and Addenda

Here are listed the most important available works on Korean ranks and titles, Korean chronologies, and also a few works which came to the attention of the compilers of the Guide too late to be listed in their proper chapters.

Korean Ranks and Titles

The understanding of Korean court and military ranks and titles is one of the most difficult problems for the student of Korean history, and unfortunately there is no adequate Western work on the subject. In general, Korean military and administrative designations are largely patterned upon China's from the Silla period until 1910, Japan's from 1910 to 1945, and the Western republics' after 1945; but there were, of course, many differences.

WORKS ON KOREAN RANKS AND TITLES
Western

(469)   Des Rotours, Robert. Traité des fonctionnaires et Traité de l'armée, traduit de la Nouvelle Histoire des T'ang. Bibliothèque de l'Institut des Hautes Études Chinoises, Vol. VI. Leyden: Brill, 1947-1948. 2 vols.   An account of the T'ang government of China, which gives some indirect knowledge of Silla and Koryŏ ranks and titles because these were largely patterned after the T'ang system.

(470)   Korea (Republic). Bureau of Public Information. Reference Handbook, Government of the Republic of Korea. Seoul, 1949. Standardizes the names of Korean government agencies and organizations, describes them in detail, lists the officials, and gives Chinese characters, romanization, and English translations of the names of all government groups.

(471)   Mayers, William F. The Chinese Government: A Manual of Chinese Titles Categorically Arranged and Explained, with an Appendix. 2d ed. Shanghai: Kelly and Walsh, 1886. Offers some indirect knowledge of ranks and titles of the Yi period, although the book is chiefly about late Ch'ing times rather than the Ming and T'ang dynasties, upon which the Yi government was patterned.

(472)   Wilkinson, William H. The Corean Government: Constitutional Changes, July 1894 to October 1895, with an Appendix on Subsequent Enactments to 30th June 1896. Shanghai: Statistical Department of the Inspectorate General of Customs, 1897. The only Western work which is anything near an adequate account of the Korean legal and administrative systems before 1910. Divided into three parts: (1) the legal and administrative systems before 1894, which is based chiefly on the Taejŏn Hoet'ong (473); (2) the reorganized government after the reforms of 1894-1895; (3) a chronological summary of the resolutions and acts which changed the government. The book has a subject index, an index of romanized Korean names, ranks, etc., and an index of Chinese characters arranged according to radicals.

Korean

(473)   Chugyo Taejŏn Hoet'ong 註校大典會通 주교대전회통 (Annotated Collection of Fundamental Statutes). Keijō: Chōsen Sōtokufu Chūsū-in, 1939. A reprint with annotations of the Taejŏn Hoet'ong (1865), which is a compendium of the major law codes of the Yi period. Contains laws on administration, land, rites and ceremonies, military organization, public works, etc., and names the responsible officials. The text is punctuated and includes kunten, and there is a kana index of the annotations. Also contains a 75-page kanamajiri account of the background of the Taejŏn Hoet'ong and the organization of the Korean government.

(473a)   Yakubun Taiten Kaitsū 譯文大典會通 . Keijō: Chōsen Sōtokufu Chūsū-in, 1921. A Japanese translation of the Taejŏn Hoet'ong.

Special Reference Materials   171

Japanese

(474)   Kuroi Jodō 黒井怒堂. "Shiragi Shoki Kankai Meigi ni tsuite no Shin-kenkyū" 新羅初期官階名義 に就いての新研究 (New Researches on the Names of Official Ranks in the First Age of Silla), Kōkogaku Zasshi 考古學雜誌, XIV (1924), 470-483. Based on the Samguk Sagi (225). Studies Buddhist and Sanskrit influence on titles of the early Silla period.

(475)   Imanishi Ryū. "Shiragi Kan-igō-kō" 新羅官位號考 (Study of Official Ranks and Titles in Silla). Shiragi-shi Kenkyū (231), pp. 267-281. Based on ancient source materials of Korea, China, and Japan.

(476)   Kurumada Atsushi 車田篤. Chōsen Gyōseihō-ron 朝鮮行政法論 (Treatise on Korean Administrative Law). Rev. ed. Keijō: Chōsen Hōsei Kenkyū-kai, 1935. 2 vols. A description of the administrative system of the Government General.

(477)   Shiratori Kurakichi. "Chōsen Kodai Kammei-kō" 朝鮮古代官名考 (Study of the Official Names in Ancient Times in Korea), Shigaku Zasshi, VII (1896), 271-295. A study of titles in the Three Kingdoms period.

(478)   Shisei Nijūgo-nen-shi 施政二十五年史 (History of Twenty-five Years of Administration). Keijō: Chōsen Sōtokufu, 1935. An official account of the Government General's administration valuable for information about official titles after 1910.

See also entries 83, 177, 191, 192, 217, 304, 312, 334.

Korean Chronology

Korean chronology becomes increasingly inaccurate and unreliable as one traces it back toward the time of Christ, but it is more accurate than Japanese chronology, probably because the Koreans learned astronomy from the Chinese several centuries before the Japanese. Ironically, most of the information in Western languages about Korean chronology is in works on Japanese chronology, and there is no adequate Western work on the subject.

WORKS ON KOREAN CHRONOLOGY
Western

(479)   Allen, Horace N. A Chronological Index: Some of the Chief Events in the Foreign Intercourse of Korea from the Beginning of the Christian Era to the Twentieth Century. Seoul: Methodist Publishing House, 1901. Divided into seven parts: (1) a chronology of important events in Korea from the time of the birth of Christ to 1876, based mainly on Griffis' Corea (168) and therefore often unreliable; (2) a chronology of events from 1876 to 1901, based on first-hand knowledge, which is detailed and accurate; (3) Korean treaties and agreements from 1876 to 1901; (4) the names of all diplomatic officials in Korea from the time of the establishment of legations and consulates; (5) the names of the chiefs of the Korean Foreign Office since 1882; (6) the names of the commissioners of the Korean Customs Service; (7) a selected reading list on Korea.

(480)   Aston, W. G. "Early Japanese History," Transactions of the Asiatic Society of Japan, XVI (1889), 39-75. Refers to Korean chronologies to correct errors in dates of early Japanese history.

(481)   Clement, Ernest W. "Comparative Chronological Tables of the Christian Era, Japanese Eras and Emperors, Chinese Emperors and Eras, and Korean Kings, with Years of the Sexagenary Cycles, from 660 B. C. to 1910 A. D.," Transactions of the Asiatic Society of Japan, XXXVII, pt. 2 (1910), 133-303. A useful work, but it does not contain many of the tables found in Korean and Japanese chronologies, e. g., 186, 485, 486, nor does it emphasize Korea. See also entry 484.

(482)   Gaspardone, Émile. "La Chronologie ancienne du Japon," Journal Asiatique, CCXXX (1938), 235-277. Probably the best-known Western study on Japanese chronology. Contains numerous references to Korean chronology.

(483)   Hoang, P. "Concordances des chronologies néoméniques chinoise et européene," Variétés Sinologiques, XXIX (1910), 1-569. Provides one with the means of dating Asiatic events by the Julian and Gregorian calendars, and of Western events by the Chinese

calendar. Based on the Chinese work, Li-tai Ch'ang-shu Chi-yao 歷代長術輯要 (Compendium of Historical Chronology).

(484) Tchang, Mathias. "Synchronismes Chinois," Variétés sinologiques, XXIV (1905), 1-530. Similar in material to Clement (481), but gives a broader coverage, and includes all Far Eastern calendars based on lunar reckonings and on the notations of cyclical characters.

Korean

(485) Ŏ Yun-jŏk. Tongsa Nyŏnp'yo 東史年表 동사년표 (Chronologies of Korean History). Keijō: Pomun-sa, 1915; Chōsen Shigak-kai, 1934. Contains detailed tables on the Korean kings from Tan-gun to 1910, a comparative yearly chronology of Korean, Japanese, and Chinese rulers, and a list of important events in Korean history. Unlike the Chōsen Nempyō (486), which stresses Japanese-Korean relations, this book deals chiefly with internal affairs and Sino-Korean relations.

Japanese

(486) Mori Junzaburō 森潤三郎. Chōsen Nempyō 朝鮮年表 (Chronological Tables of Korea). Tōkyō: Shunyō-dō, 1904. Contains comparative chronologies of Korea, China, and Japan from ancient times to 1903, a large map of Korea, an account of Korean historical geography, genealogies of Korean rulers, a list of capitals, a yearly summary of important events in Japanese-Korean relations, and a summary of Korean and Japanese relations with Tsushima. See also 485.

See also entries 171, 186, and 374..

ADDENDA
Western

(487) Horne, E. C., and S. S. Yun. Introduction to Spoken Korean. New Haven: Institute of Far Eastern Languages, Yale University, 1951. 2 vols. The most complete practical Korean grammar available. It is accompanied by soundscriber records. Grammatical constructions are introduced progressively, and there are

many illustrative sentences for each. The authors use their own system of romanization, which is simple and well suited to their purpose. The book contains an index of grammatical constructions and glossaries.

Korean

(488) Chosŏn Munhwa-sa Yŏn-gu Non-go 朝鮮文化史研究論攷 조선문화사연구론고 (Essays on the Study of Korean Cultural History). Seoul: Ŭryu Munhwa-sa, 1947. Divided into four parts: (1) [see entry 373]; (2) the origin of discrimination against the offspring of concubines; (3) the origin of the prohibition of the remarriage of widows; and (4) the life of Chŏng To-jŏn (Sambong), an important figure at the time of the Yi revolution.

Japanese

(489) Fujita Ryōsaku. Chōsen no Rekishi 朝鮮の歴史. (History of Korea). Tōkyō: Fukumura Shoten, 1953. From prehistoric times to 1945. It contains much general information and gives some attention to Korean cultural history. The chapters on early Korea are particularly rewarding. A small and compact volume which is easy to read.

(490) Imai Kichinosuke 今井吉之助. Chōsen Kankei Zasshi-rui 朝鮮關係雜誌類 (Magazine Articles about Korea). Tōkyō, 1953. [Manuscript.] A bibliography of articles about Korea published in Japanese periodicals between 1882 and 1926. The list complements the periodical bibliography found in the special issue (July, 1953) of the Rekishigaku Kenkyū (58), which lists articles for 1927 to 1953. The manuscript is in the East Asiatic Library of the University of California.

(491) Shōtoku Chōsen Shinshi Tōjō Gyōretsu-zu 正德朝鮮信使登城行列圖 (A Picture of the Korean Envoy's Procession to Edo in 1711). Item 20 of the Chōsen Shiryō Sōkan (183). 1938. A collotype of a scroll painting made about 1711. Some parts are in color. Captions identify the persons depicted. A 27-page kanamajiri commentary is boxed with the scroll.

APPENDICES

Chronological List of Rulers and Dynasties

ANCIENT KOREA (2333 B.C.-108 B.C.)

Largely legendary until c. 200 B.C. Tan-gun is a semidivine mythical figure; Kija (Ch'i-tzu) was supposedly a scholar from China who founded a dynasty that reigned until 194 B.C.; Wiman (Weiman) was a usurper from China. He and two successors ruled Korea until 108 B.C.

A. Period of Tan-gun 檀君 단 군 (2333 B.C.-1122 B.C.)
B. Period of Kija 箕子 기 자 (1122 B.C.-194 B.C.)
C. Period of Wiman 衛滿 위 만 (194 B.C.-108 B.C.)

CHINESE COLONIES (108 B.C.-313 A.D.)

Introduction of Chinese culture into Korea and gradual cultural and political development of the Sam Han and other Korean tribes.

A. Period of Four Prefectures (108 B.C.-82 B.C.)
   Lo-lang (Nangnang) 樂浪 낙 랑; Lin-t'un (Nimdun) 臨屯 림 둔; Hsüan-t'u (Hyŏndo) 玄菟 현 도; Chen-fan (Chinbŏn) 眞番 진 번.

B. Period of Two Prefectures (82 B.C.-204 A.D.)
   Lo-lang; Hsüan-t'u.

C. Period of Three Prefectures (204-313)
   Lo-lang; Hsüan-t'u; Tai-fang (Taebang) 帶方 대 방.

THREE KINGDOMS AND UNIFIED SILLA
(313-935; traditional dates: 57 B.C.-935 A.D.)

A. Karak 駕洛 가락 (?42-562)
A small state in the basin of the Naktong River ruled by the Kim 金 김 dynasty. It had several divisions and was called by several names. It was absorbed by Silla in 562.

1. T'aejo 太祖 태조 (42-199)
2. To Wang 道王 도왕 (199-253)
3. Sŏng Wang 成王 성왕 (253-291)
4. Tŏk Wang 德王 덕왕 (291-346)
5. Myŏng Wang 明王 명왕 (346-407)
6. Sin Wang 神王 신왕 (407-421)
7. Hye Wang 惠王 혜왕 (421-451)
8. Chang Wang 莊王 장왕 (451-492)
9. Suk Wang 肅王 숙왕 (492-521)
10. Yang Wang 讓王 양왕 (521-532)
11. Mal Wang 末王 말왕 (532)

B. Paekche 百濟 백제 (?18 B.C.-660 A.D.)

Ruled by the Puyŏ 扶餘 부여 dynasty. Generally in close alliance with Japan. Occupied by T'ang China and Silla in 660; and finally defeated by Silla in 663.

1. Onjo Wang 溫祚王 온조왕 (18 B.C.-28 A.D.)
2. Taru Wang 多婁王 다루왕 (28-77)
3. Kiru Wang 己婁王 기루왕 (77-128)
4. Kaeru Wang 盖婁王 개루왕 (128-166)
5. Ch'ogo Wang 肖古王 초고왕 (166-214)
6. Kusu Wang 仇首王 구수왕 (214-234)
7. Saban Wang 沙伴王 사반왕 (234)
8. Koi Wang 古爾王 고이왕 (234-286)
9. Chaekkye Wang 責稽王 책계왕 (286-298)
10. Punsŏ Wang 汾西王 분서왕 (298-304)
11. Piryu Wang 比流王 비류왕 (304-344)
12. Ke Wang 契王 계왕 (344-346)
13. Kŭnch'ogo Wang 近肖古王 근초고왕 (346-375)
14. Kŭn-gusu Wang 近仇首王 근구수왕 (375-384)
15. Ch'imnyu Wang 枕流王 침류왕 (384-385)
16. Chinsa Wang 辰斯王 진사왕 (385-392)
17. Asin Wang 阿莘王 아신왕 (392-405)
18. Chŏnji Wang 腆支王 전지왕 (405-420)
19. Kuisin Wang 久爾辛王 구이신왕 (420-427)
20. Piyu Wang 毗有王 비유왕 (427-455)
21. Kaero Wang 盖鹵王 개로왕 (455-475)
22. Munju Wang 文周王 문주왕 (475-477)

23. Samgǔn Wang 三斤王 삼근왕 (477-479)
24. Tongsŏng Wang 東城王 동성왕 (479-501)
25. Munyŏng Wang 武寧王 무녕왕 (501-523)
26. Sŏng Wang 聖王 성왕 (523-554)
27. Widŏk Wang 威德王 위덕왕 (554-598)
28. Hye Wang 惠王 혜왕 (598-599)
29. Pŏp Wang 法王 법왕 (599-600)
30. Mu Wang 武王 무왕 (600-645)
31. Ŭija Wang 義慈王 의자왕 (645-660)
32. P'ungjang Wang 豊璋王 풍장왕 (660-663)

C. Koguryŏ 高句麗 고구려 (?37 B.C.-668 A.D.)

Ruled by the Ko 高 dynasty. The years 313 to 552 were the period of Koguryŏ dominance in the peninsula; thereafter, the kingdom gradually declined and was finally overthrown by T'ang China and Silla.

1. Tongmyŏngsŏng Wang 東明聖王 동명성왕 (37 B.C.-19 B.C.)
2. Yurimyŏng Wang 琉璃明王 유리명왕 (19 B.C.-18 A.D.)
3. Taemusin Wang 大武神王 대무신왕 (18-44)
4. Minjung Wang 閔中王 민중왕 (44-48)
5. Mobon Wang 慕本王 모본왕 (48-53)
6. T'aejo Wang 太祖王 대조왕 (53-146)
7. Ch'adae Wang 次大王 차대왕 (146-165)
8. Sindae Wang 新大王 신대왕 (165-179)
9. Kogukch'ŏn Wang 故國川王 고국천왕 (179-197)
10. Sansang Wang 山上王 산상왕 (197-227)
11. Tongch'ŏn Wang 東川王 동천왕 (227-248)
12. Chungch'ŏn Wang 中川王 중천왕 (248-270)
13. Sŏch'ŏn Wang 西川王 서천왕 (270-292)
14. Pongsang Wang 烽山王 봉상왕 (292-300)
15. Mich'ŏn Wang 美川王 미천왕 (300-331)
16. Kogugwŏn Wang 故國原王 고국원왕 (331-371)
17. Sosurim Wang 小獸林王 소수림왕 (371-384)
18. Kogugyang Wang 故國壤王 고국양왕 (384-391)
19. Kwanggaet'o Wang 廣開土王 광개토왕 (391-412)
20. Changsu Wang 長壽王 장수왕 (413-491)

21. Munja Wang 文咨王 문자왕 (492-519)
22. Anjang Wang 安藏王 안장왕 (519-531)
23. Anwŏn Wang 安原王 안원왕 (531-545)
24. Yang-wŏn Wnag 陽原王 양원왕 (545-559)
25. P'yŏng-wŏn Wang 平原王 평원왕 (559-590)
26. Yŏng-yang Wang 嬰陽王 영양왕 (590-618)
27. Yŏngnyu Wang 榮留王 영류왕 (618-642)
28. Pojang Wang 寶藏王 보장왕 (642-668)

D. Silla 新羅 신라 (?57 B.C.-935 A.D.)

Ruled variously by the Pak 朴박, Sŏk 昔석, and Kim 金김 families, although principally by the last. The years 552 to 660 were the period of Silla dominance among the Three Kingdoms, and after 660 the peninsula was united under Silla's rule. The period of united Silla is generally divided into three phases—greatness (660-780), decline (780-887), and disintegration (887-935).

1. Hyŏkkŏse Wang 赫居世王 혁거세왕 (57 B.C.-3 A.D.) Pak
2. Namhae Wang 南解王 남해왕 (4-24) Pak
3. Yuri Wang 儒理王 유리왕 (24-57) Pak
4. T'alhae Wang 脫解王 탈해왕 (57-80) Sŏk
5. P'asa Wang 婆娑王 파사왕 (80-112) Pak
6. Chima Wang 祇摩王 지마왕 (112-134) Pak
7. Ilsŏng Wang 逸聖王 일성왕 (134-154) Pak
8. Adalla Wang 阿達羅王 아달라왕 (154-184) Pak
9. Pŏrhyu Wang 伐休王 벌휴왕 (184-196) Sŏk
10. Naehae Wang 奈解王 내해왕 (196-230) Sŏk
11. Chobun Wang 助賁王 조분왕 (230-247) Sŏk
12. Ch'ŏmhae Wang 沾解王 첨해왕 (247-261) Sŏk
13. Mich'u Wang 味鄒王 미추왕 (262-284) Kim
14. Yurye Wang 儒禮王 유례왕 (284-298) Sŏk
15. Kirim Wang 基臨王 기림왕 (298-310) Sŏk
16. Hŭlhae Wang 訖解王 흘해왕 (310-356) Sŏk
17. Naemul Wang 奈勿王 내물왕 (356-402) Kim
18. Silsŏng Wang 實聖王 실성왕 (402-417) Kim
19. Nulchi Wang 訥祇王 눌지왕 (417-458) Kim
20. Chabi Wang 慈悲王 자비왕 (458-479) Kim
21. Soji Wang 炤知王 소지왕 (479-500) Kim
22. Chijŭng Wang 智證王 지증왕 (500-514) Kim

Rulers and Dynasties 181

23. Pŏphŭng Wang 法興王 법흥왕 (514-540) Kim
24. Chinhŭng Wang 眞興王 진흥왕 (540-576) Kim
25. Chinji Wang 眞智王 진지왕 (576-579) Kim
26. Chinp'yŏng Wang 眞平王 진평왕 (579-632) Kim
27. Sŏndŏk Yŏwang* 善德女王 선덕여왕 (632-647) Kim
28. Chindŏk Yŏwang* 眞德女王 진덕여왕 (647-654) Kim
29. Muryŏl Wang 武烈王 무열왕 (654-661) Kim
30. Munmu Wang 文武王 문무왕 (661-681) Kim
31. Sinmun Wang 神文王 신문왕 (681-692) Kim
32. Hyoso Wang 孝昭王 효소왕 (692-702) Kim
33. Sŏngdŏk Wang 聖德王 성덕왕 (702-737) Kim
34. Hyosŏng Wang 孝成王 효성왕 (737-742) Kim
35. Kyŏngdŏk Wang 景德王 경덕왕 (742-765) Kim
36. Hyegong Wang 惠恭王 혜공왕 (765-780) Kim
37. Sŏndŏk Wang 宣德王 선덕왕 (780-785) Kim
38. Wŏnsŏng Wang 元聖王 원성왕 (785-798) Kim
39. Sosŏng Wang 昭聖王 소성왕 (799-800) Kim
40. Aejang Wang 哀莊王 애장왕 (800-809) Kim
41. Hŏndŏk Wang 憲德王 헌덕왕 (809-826) Kim
42. Hŭngdŏk Wang 興德王 흥덕왕 (826-836) Kim
43. Hŭigang Wang 僖康王 희강왕 (836-838) Kim
44. Minae Wang 閔哀王 민애왕 (838-839) Kim
45. Sinmu Wang 神武王 신무왕 (839) Kim
46. Munsŏng Wang 文聖王 문성왕 (839-857) Kim
47. Hŏnan Wang 憲安王 헌안왕 (857-861) Kim
48. Kyŏngmun Wang 景文王 경문왕 (861-875) Kim
49. Hŏn-gang Wang 憲康王 헌강왕 (875-886) Kim
50. Chŏnggang Wang 定康王 정강왕 (886-887) Kim
51. Chinsŏng Yŏwang* 眞聖女王 진성여왕 (887-897) Kim
52. Hyogong Wang 孝恭王 효공왕 (897-912) Kim
53. Sindŏk Wang 神德王 신덕왕 (912-917) Pak
54. Kyŏngmyŏng Wang 景明王 경명왕 (917-924) Pak
55. Kyŏng-ae Wang 景哀王 경애왕 (924-927) Pak
56. Kyŏngsun Wang 敬順王 경순왕 (927-935) Kim

*Queen

E. Later Paekche (892-936)

Proclaimed officially in 900; destroyed by Koryŏ.
   1. Chinhwŏn Wang 甄萱王 진훤왕 (892-935)
   2. Sin-gŏm Wang 神劒王 신검왕 (936)

F. Later Koguryŏ (901-918)

Called Majin 摩震 마진 (904-910) and T'aebong 泰封 태봉 (910-917); destroyed by Koryŏ.
   1. Kung-ye 弓裔 궁예 (901-918)

KORYŎ KINGDOM (918-1392)

Established by Wang Kŏn 王建 왕건 and ruled by the Wang 王 왕 dynasty (except from 1375 to 1389). After 950, the rulers of Koryŏ were vassals of one of the Chinese dynasties or sometimes another foreign prince; in this list the dynasty to whom a Koryŏ king was vassal is named after his dates of reign.

   A. Period of Establishment (918-997)
      1. T'aejo 太祖 태조 (918-943)
      2. Hyejong 惠宗 혜종 (944-945)
      3. Chŏngjong 定宗 정종 (946-949)
      4. Kwangjong 光宗 광종 (950-975) Sung 宋
      5. Kyŏngjong 景宗 경종 (976-981) Sung
      6. Sŏngjong 成宗 성종 (982-997) Sung and Khitan 契丹

   B. Period of Prosperity (998-1122)
      7. Mokchong 穆宗 목종 (998-1009) Sung and Khitan
      8. Hyŏnjong 顯宗 현종 (1010-1031) Sung and Khitan
      9. Tŏkjong 德宗 덕종 (1032-1034) Sung and Khitan
      10. Chŏngjong 靖宗 정종 (1035-1046) Sung and Khitan
      11. Munjong 文宗 문종 (1047-1083) Sung and Khitan
      12. Sunjong 順宗 순종 (1083) Sung and Khitan
      13. Sŏnjong 宣宗 선종 (1084-1094) Sung and Khitan
      14. Hŏnjong 獻宗 헌종 (1095) Sung and Khitan
      15. Sukjong 肅宗 숙종 (1096-1105) Sung and Khitan
      16. Yejong 睿宗 예종 (1106-1122) Sung and Khitan

Rulers and Dynasties   183

C. **Period of Decline (1123-1374)**
  I. Control by Influential Nobles
     17. Injong 仁宗 인 종 (1123-1146) Chin 金
     18. Ŭijong 毅宗 의 종 (1147-1170) Chin
  II. Presumptuous Control by Generals (1171-1259)
     19. Myŏngjong 明宗 명 종 (1171-1197) Chin
     20. Sinjong 神宗 신 종 (1198-1204) Chin
     21. Hŭijong 熙宗 희 종 (1205-1211) Chin
     22. Kangjong 康宗 강 종 (1212-1213) Chin
     23. Kojong 高宗 고 종 (1214-1259) Chin
  III. Relations with the Yüan 元 Imperial House (1260-1374)
     24. Wŏnjong 元宗 원 종 (1260-1274) Yüan
     25. Ch'ungnyŏl Wang 忠烈王 충 렬 왕 (1275-1308) Yüan
     26. Ch'ungsŏn Wang 忠宣王 충 선 왕 (1309-1313) Yüan
     27. Ch'ungsuk Wang 忠肅王 충 숙 왕 (1314-1330) Yüan
     28. Ch'unghye Wang 忠惠王 충 혜 왕 (1331-1332) Yüan
     [27] Ch'ungsuk Wang* (1332-1339) Yüan
     [28] Ch'unghye Wang* (1340-1344) Yüan
     29. Ch'ungmok Wang 忠穆王 충 목 왕 (1345-1348) Yüan
     30. Ch'ungjŏng Wang 忠定王 충 정 왕 (1349-1351) Yüan
     31. Kongmin Wang 恭愍王 공 민 왕 (1352-1374) Ming 明

D. **Period of Disintegration (1375-1392)**
     32. Sin-u** 辛禑 신 우 (1375-1388) Northern Yüan
     33. Sinch'ang** 辛昌 신 창 (1389)
     34. Kongyang Wang 恭讓王 공 양 왕 (1389-1392)
         Pro-Ming

CHOSŎN KINGDOM (1392-1910)

Ruled by the Yi dynasty, which was established by the revolt of General Yi Sŏng-ge 李成桂 이 성 게 (T'aejo) against the last of the Wang monarchs. The Yi monarchs were vassals of Ming China until 1623, and of Ch'ing 清 China from 1623 to 1895.

*Restored to the throne
**Considered a usurper

A. Period of Establishment (1392-1400)
   1. T'aejo 太祖 태조 (1392-1398)
   2. Chŏngjong 定宗 정종 (1399-1400)

B. Period of Greatness (1401-1494)
   3. T'aejong 太宗 태종 (1401-1418)
   4. Sejong 世宗 세종 (1419-1450)
   5. Munjong 文宗 문종 (1451-1452)
   6. Tanjong 端宗 단종 (1453-1455)
   7. Sejo 世祖 세조 (1456-1468)
   8. Yejong 睿宗 예종 (1469)
   9. Sŏngjong 成宗 성종 (1470-1494)

C. Period of Internal Disorganization (1495-1567)
   10. Yŏnsan-gun 燕山君 연산군 (1495-1506)
   11. Chungjong 中宗 중종 (1506-1544)
   12. Injong 仁宗 인종 (1545)
   13. Myŏngjong 明宗 명종 (1546-1567)

D. Period of Exhaustion (1568-1724)
   14. Sŏnjo 宣祖 선조 (1568-1608)
   15. Kwanghae-gun 光海君 광해군 (1609-1623)
   16. Injo 仁祖 인조 (1623-1649)
   17. Hyojong 孝宗 효종 (1650-1659)
   18. Hyŏnjong 顯宗 현종 (1660-1674)
   19. Sukchong 肅宗 숙종 (1675-1720)
   20. Kyŏngjong 景宗 경종 (1721-1724)

E. Period of Revival (1725-1800)
   21. Yŏngjo 英祖 영조 (1725-1776)
   22. Chŏngjo 正祖 정조 (1777-1800)

F. Period of Decline (1801-1910)
   23. Sunjo 純祖 순조 (1801-1834)
   24. Hŏnjong 憲宗 헌종 (1835-1849)
   25. Ch'oljong 哲宗 철종 (1850-1863)
   26. Kojong 高宗 고종 (Yi T'ae Wang 李太王 이태왕)
       (1864-1907) Assumed title of emperor in 1897;
       Japanese protectorate established in 1906.
   27. Sunjong 純宗 순종 (Yi Wang 李王 이왕) (1907-1910)

GOVERNMENT GENERAL (1910–1945)

Korea subject to Japanese rule and administered by a governor general who was appointed by, and responsible only to, the Japanese crown. All governors, except Admiral Viscount Saitō, were generals of the Imperial Japanese Army.

1. Terauchi Masakata 寺内正毅 (1910–1916)
2. Hasegawa Yoshimichi 長谷川好道 (1916–1919)
3. Saitō Makoto 齊藤實 (1919–1927)
4. Ugaki Issei* 宇垣一成 (1927)
5. Yamanashi Hanzō 山梨半造 (1927–1929)

[3] Saitō Makoto (1929–1931)
[4] Ugaki Issei (1931–1936)

6. Minami Jirō 南次郎 (1936–1942)
7. Koiso Kuniteru 小磯國昭 (1942–1944)
8. Abe Nobuyuki 阿部信行 (1944–1945)

*Acting governor general

Publishing Houses and Societies

Korean

Amun-gak 稚文閣 아문 각
Anak Myŏnhak-hoe 安岳勉學會 안 악 면 학 회
Ch'anggŏn-sa 創建社 창 건 사
Chindan Hakhoe 震檀學會 진 단 학 회
Chinhak Ch'ulp'an Hyŏphoe 震學出版協會 진 학 출 판 협 회
Chogwang-sa 朝光社 조 광 사
Chŏng-ŭm-sa 正音社 정 음 사
Chosŏn Ch'ulp'an Munhwa Hyŏphoe 朝鮮出版文化協會 조 선 출 판 문 화 협 회
Chosŏn Ch'ulp'an Hyŏphoe 朝鮮出版協會 조 선 출 판 협 회
Chosŏn Ilbo-sa 朝鮮日報社 조 선 일 보 사
Chosŏn Kŭmyung Chohap Yŏnhap-hoe 朝鮮金融組合聯合會 조 선 금 융 조 합 연 합 회
Chosŏn Mungo 朝鮮文庫 조 선 문 고
Chosŏn Munhwa-gwan 朝鮮文化館 조 선 문 화 관
Chosŏn Ŏ Hakhoe 朝鮮語學會 조 선 어 학 회 (Korean Language Research Association)
Chosŏn Ŏ Sajŏn Kanhaeng-hoe 朝鮮語辭典刊行會 조 선 어 사 전 간 행 회
Chosŏn Tongsin-sa 朝鮮通信社 조 선 통 신 사
Chosŏn Ŭnhaeng 朝鮮銀行 조 선 은 행 (Bank of Korea)
Haedong Munhwa-sa 海東文化社 해 동 문 화 사
Hagye-sa 學藝社 학 예 사
Hansŏng Tosŏ Chusik Hoesa 漢城圖書株式會社 한 성 도 서 주 식 회 사
Hanyang Sŏwŏn 漢陽書院 한 양 서 원
Hongmun Sŏgwan 弘文書館 홍 문 서 관
Ilsŏng-dang Sŏjŏm 一誠堂書店 일 성 당 서 점

Kong-ŏp Munhwa-sa 工業文化社 공업문화사
Kŭmnyong Tosŏ Chusik Hoesa 金龍圖書株式會社 금룡도서주식회사
Kyemong Kurakpu 啓蒙俱樂部 계몽구락부
Minju Munhwa-sa 民主文化社 민주문화사
Minjung Sŏgwan 民衆書館 민중서관
Minu-sa 民友社 민우사
Munhwa-dang 文化堂 문화당
Munu Insŏgwan 文友印書館 문우인서관
Myŏngmun-dang 明文堂 명문당
Paegyang-dang 白揚堂 백양당
Pangmun Ch'ulp'an-sa 博文出版社 박문출판사
Pangmun Sŏgwan 博文書館 박문서관
Pŏmjang-gak 凡章閣 범장각
Pyŏgwi-sa 闢衛社 벽위사
Sinhak-sa 新學社 신학사
Sinmun-gwan 新文館 신문관
Sinsaeng-sa 新生社 신생사
Sŏul Sinmun-sa 서울新聞社 서울신문사
Sŏul Sinmun-sa Ch'ulp'an-bu 서울신문社出版部 서울신문사출판부
Sŏul Sinmun-sa Ch'ulp'an-guk 서울신문社出版局 서울신문사출판국
Sudo Kwan-gu Kyŏngch'al-ch'ŏng 首都管區警察廳 수도관구경찰청 (Metropolitan District Police Bureau)
Susŏn-sa 首善社 수선사
Taehan Yŏn-gam-sa 大韓年鑑社 대한연감사
Taesŏng Ch'ulp'an-sa 大成出版社 대성출판사
Tŏkhŭng Sŏrim 德興書林 덕흥서림
Tongbang Munhwa-sa 東邦文化社 동방문화사
Tonggwang-sa 東光社 동광사
Tonghwa Ch'ulp'an-sa 同和出版社 동화출판사
Tongji-sa 同志社 동지사
Tongmyŏng-sa 東明社 동명사
Tongsim-sa 同心社 동심사
Tongsŏng-sa 東省社 동성사
Ŭryu Munhwa-sa 乙酉文化社 을유문화사

Yi Ch'ungmugong Kinyŏm-hoe 李忠武公記念會 이충무공기념회
    (Society to Commemorate Yi Ch'ungmugong [Yi Sun-sin])
Yŏngch'ang Sŏgwan 永昌書館 영창서관
Yŏnhak-sa 研學社 연학사

Japanese

Chijin Shokan 地人書館
Chikazawa Shoten 近澤書店
Chōsen Gakkai 朝鮮學會 (Korean Studies Society)
Chōsen Gyōsei Gakkai 朝鮮行政學會 (Korean Administration Studies Society)
Chōsen Jijō Kyōkai Shuppan-bu 朝鮮事情協會出版部
Chōsen Kenkyū-kai 朝鮮研究會 (Korean Research Society)
Chōsen Kōgyō-kai 朝鮮鑛業會 (Korean Mining Association)
Chōsen Kōkogak-kai 朝鮮考古學會 (Korean Archaeology Society)
Chōsen Koseki Kenkyū-kai 朝鮮古蹟研究會 (Society for the Study of Korean Antiquities)
Chōsen Kosho Kankō-kai 朝鮮古書刊行會 (Society for the Publication of Old Korean books)
Chōsen Shigak-kai 朝鮮史學會 (Historical Society of Korea)
Chōsen-shi Henshū-kai 朝鮮史編修會 (History of Korea Compilation Society)
Chōsen Sōtokufu 朝鮮總督府 (Government General of Korea)
Chōsen Sōtokufu Chūsū-in 朝鮮總督府中樞院 ([Korean Advisory] Central Council to the Government General of Korea)
Daiichi Shobō 第一書房
Dōbun-kan 同文館
Fukumura Shoten 福村書店
Fuzam-bō 富山房
Ganshō-dō Shoten 巖松堂書店
Hakubun-kan 博文館
Hakuyō-sha 白揚社
Heibon-sha 平凡社
Hōbun-kan 寶文館
Hokkō Shobō 北光書房
Hoshino Tokuji 星野德治

Hōun-sha 寶雲社
Isobe Kōyō-dō 磯部甲陽堂
Iwanami Shoten 岩波書店
Jiyū Tōkyū-sha 自由討究社
Kaikō-sha 偕行社 (The Military Club)
Kaizō-sha 改造社
Kankoku Ginkō 韓國銀行 (Bank of Korea)
Keijō Nippō-sha 京城日報社
Keijō Teikoku Daigaku 京城帝國大學 (Keijō Imperial University)
Keijō Teikoku Daigaku Fuzoku Toshokan 京城帝國大學附屬圖書館 (Keijō Imperial University Library)
Keijō Teikoku Daigaku Hōbungaku-bu 京城帝國大學法文學部 (Keijō Imperial University Faculty of Law and Letters)
Kōbun-dō 弘文堂
Koji Ruien Kankō-kai 古事類苑刊行會
Kokusai Bunka Shinkō-kai 國際文化進興會 (International Culture Advancement Society)
Kokusho Kankō-kai 國書刊行會
Koten Kankō-kai 古典刊行會
Kōtetsu Shoin 鋼鐵書院
Kyōiku-shi Henshū-kai 教育史編輯會
Kyōto Teikoku Daigaku 京都帝國大學 (Kyōto Imperial University)
Maruzen 丸善
Minami Manshū Tetsudō Kabushiki Kaisha 南滿洲鐵道株式會社 (South Manchuria Railroad Company)
Musashino Shoin 武藏野書院
Nichi-Man Bunka Kyōkai 日滿文化協會
Nihon Gaimu-shō 日本外務省 (Japanese Foreign Office)
Nihon Hyōron-sha 日本評論社
Nihon Rekishi Chiri Gakkai 日本歷史地理學會 (Japanese Historical Geography Society)
Nihon Shuppan Kyōdō Kabushiki Gaisha 日本出版協同株式會社
Ogiwara Sei Bunkan 荻原星文館
Ōsaka-yago Shoten 大阪屋號書店
Ōyashima Shuppan-sha 大八洲出版社
Ri-ō-shoku 李王職 (Yi Royal Household)

Rōan Kinen Zaidan 魯庵記念財團 (Foundation to Commemo-
    rate Rōan [Marshal Terauchi Masakata])
Sansei-dō 三省堂
Sawada Shintarō 澤田信太郎
Seiken-sha 清閑舍
Seiko Hakkō-sho 青壺發行所
Seikyū Gakkai 青丘學會
Shidō-kan 斯道館
Shigaku Kenkyū-kai 史學研究會 (Historical Science Society)
Shinchō-sha 新潮社
Shinkō-sha 進光社
Shomotsu Dōkō-kai 書物同好會
Shunshū-sha 春秋社
Shunyō-dō 春陽堂
Shuppan Nyūsu-sha 出版ニュース社
Sōbun-kaku 叢文閣
Sōkoku-sha 祖國社
Taidō Shokan 大同書館
Taiyō-sha 大洋社
Takagiri Shoin 高桐書院
Teikoku Chihō Gyōsei Gakkai 帝國地方行政學會 (Imperial
    Regional Administration Study Society)
Tōhō Kenkyū-kai 東方研究會
Tōkō Shoin 刀江書院
Tōkyō-dō 東京堂
Tōkyō Shoseki-shō Kumai Jimusho 東京書籍商組合事務所
Tōkyō Teikoku Daigaku 東京帝國大學 (Tōkyō Imperial Univer-
    sity)
Tōyō Bunko 東洋文庫
Tōyō Kaizai Shimpō-sha 東洋經濟新報社
Tōyō Kyōkai 東洋協會
Tōyō Kyōkyai Gakujutsu Chōsa-bu 東洋協會學術調查部
Wakabayashi Shunwa-dō 若松春和堂
Waseda Daigaku Shuppan-bu 早稲田大學出版部 (Waseda Uni-
    versity Press)
Yamagawa Shuppan-sha 山川出版社
Yonkai Shobō 四海書房

Yoshikawa Hanshichi 吉川半七
Yōtoku-sha 養德社
Yūsan-kaku 雄山閣
Zauhō Kankō-kai 座右寶刊行會
Zenkoku Shobō 全國書房

Chinese

Ching-hua In-shu-kuan 京華印書館
Shang-wu Yin-shu-kuan 商務印書館 (Commercial Press)
Ta-t'ung Pien-i-chū 大同編譯局
Wei-hsin-she 維新社

Mongolian

Mongɤul Udx-a Jin Xorij-a

PLACES OF PUBLICATION IN THE FAR EAST

Korea

Korean	Japanese
Pusan 釜山 부산	Fusan
P'yŏng-yang 平壤 평양	Heijō
Seoul (Sŏul) 서울	
Kyŏngsŏng 京城 경성	Keijō
Hanyang 漢陽 한양	Kanyō
Hansŏng 漢城 한성	Kanjō

Japan

Kyōto 京都
Okazaki 岡崎
Tambaichi 丹波市
Tōkyō 東京
Yokohama 横濱

China

Chung-king 重慶
Shanghai 上海
K'ai-lu 開魯

Glossary

Note: (K), (J), and (C) indicate that the word is Korean, Japanese, or Chinese.

hanmun 漢文 한문 (K): a script written in Chinese characters. Hanmun appears to be indistinguishable from Chinese, but most Koreans read it by their pronunciation and syntax. For the purposes of the Guide, works by Koreans written in Chinese characters have been classified as "Korean" and regarded as being in hanmun.

han-gŭl 한글 (K): the present name of the script invented by King Sejong. It contained 17 consonants and 11 vowels when it was proclaimed in 1446; various modifications reduced these to 14 consonants and 10 vowels. Words are written in syllable clusters. Han-gŭl was also called hunmin chŏng-ŭm, ŏnmun, panjŏl (q.v.), and kungmun.

hwarang 花郞 화랑 (K): an institution of Silla organized to train young nobles in the arts of war and government. By extension, the word came to mean a spirit of warrior valor.

idu 吏讀 이두 (K): Chinese characters used phonetically to represent Korean auxiliary verbs and connectives. Invented early in the period of unified Silla. It is similar to kugyŏl (q.v.) and t'o in method and purpose, and also resembles the Japanese manyōgana 萬葉假名.

kana 假名 (J): a Japanese syllabary of forty-seven symbols. There are two types of kana: (1) hiragana 平假名, which gives a cursive or abbreviated form of a character which has the sound of the kana syllable; (2) katakana 片假名, which gives the essential or characteristic portion of a character which has the sound of the kana syllable. Kana is a simple way of writing Japanese words usually used in conjunction with Chinese characters (see kanamajiri).

kanamajiri 假名交 (J): Japanese script composed of Chinese characters and kana (q.v.). Most nouns and verbs are in characters; particles, verbal suffixes, adjectival, and adverbial inflections are in kana.

kambun 漢文 (J): Japanese script written in Chinese characters. Kambun seems indistinguishable from Chinese, but the Japanese usually read it by their pronunciation and syntax, and often insert kunten (q.v.) to indicate the latter. It is essentially the Japanese equivalent of the Korean hanmun (q.v.).

kisaeng 妓生 기생 (K): Korean female entertainers skilled in singing, dancing, playing musical instruments, and in the art of polite conversation. Similar to the Japanese geisha 藝者.

Korea: the present English name for the country and peninsula, derived from Koryŏ (K). The country, or portions of it, has been called by many names throughout its history, and several of these names are still used for patriotic, poetic, or other reasons. The most important are given below with some explanation of when or where they are chiefly used.

    Chosŏn (K): the Koreans' name for their country during the Yi period and still the most frequent Korean designation. Chōsen (J) is the Japanese form used during most of the Japanese occupation period. Ch'ao-hsien (C) is the Chinese equivalent, used chiefly to refer to Korea of Kija and Wiman.

    Sam Han (K), San Kan (J), San-han (C): properly the three tribes of early Korean history, but by extension has been used to indicate Korea as a whole. Similarly, Samguk (K), Sankoku (J) and San-kuo (C) mean properly the Three Kingdoms, but by extension have been used to indicate Korea in later ages.

    Silla (K), Shiragi, Shinra (J), Hsin-lo (C): used to designate Korea after the tenth century, although the name is usually confined to the historical kingdom. Only very rarely has this extension been given to Paekche (K)—Kudara, Hakusai (J), Pai-chi (C)—and to Koguryŏ (K)—Kōkurai, Koma (J), Kao-chü-li (C).

Koryŏ 高麗 고려 (K), Koma, Korai (J), Kao-li (C): usually confined to the historical kingdom.

Taehan Cheguk 大韓帝國 대한제국 (K), Taikan Teikoku (J), Ta-han Ti-kuo (C): used especially during the so-called Korean Empire (1897-1910). Han-guk 韓國 한국 (K), Kankoku (J), and Han-kuo (C) are shorter forms of these names, and also variants of Sam Han, etc.

Taehan Min-guk 大韓民國 대한민국 (K), Taikan Minkoku (J), Ta-han Min-kuo (C): the official name of the Republic of Korea; and Chosŏn Inmin-guk 朝鮮人民國 조선인민국 (K), Chōsen Jinminkoku (J), Ch'ao-hsien Jen-min-kuo (C)—the official name of the Democratic People's Republic of Korea.

In addition, these names are also frequently used for Korea:

    Chindan 震檀 진단 (K), Shindan (J), Chen-t'an (C)
    Ch'ŏnggu 青邱 청구 (K), Seikyū (J), Ch'ing-ch'iu (C)
    Haedong 海東 해동 (K), Kaitō (J), Hai-tung (C)
    Kyerim 鷄林 계림 (K), Keirin (J), Chi-lin (C)
    Kŭnyŏk 槿域 근역 (K), Kan-iki (J), Chin-yüeh (C)
    Sohwa 小華 소화 (K), Shōka (J), Hsiao-hua (C)
    Taedong 大東 대동 (K), Taidō (J), Ta-tung (C)
    Tongguk 東國 동국 (K), Tōkoku (J), Tung-kuo (C)

kugyŏl 口訣 구결 (K): Chinese characters or parts of Chinese characters first used during the Koryŏ period to represent Korean auxiliary verbs and connectives in hanmun (q.v.) in order to facilitate the reading of the text according to Korean syntax. T'o is a script similar to kugyŏl in method and purpose, and both are similar to idu (q.v.).

kukhanmun 國漢文 국한문 (K): Korean script composed of Chinese characters and han-gŭl (q.v.) used in Korea since the invention of han-gŭl but especially by recent Korean writers and publishers. Most nouns are written in characters; most of the other parts of speech in han-gŭl.

kungmun 國文 구 문 (K): see han-gŭl.

kunten 訓點 (J): marks used in kambun (q.v.) texts to indicate how to read the text according to Japanese syntax.

okp'yŏn 玉篇 옥 편 (K): Korean dictionaries of Chinese characters which give the Korean pronunciation of the characters, usually in han-gŭl in the recent okp'yŏn. Early okp'yŏn used the Chinese method called fan-ch'ieh 反切, in which the initial sound of one character was combined with the final sound of another to indicate the pronunciation of the character in question.

ŏnmun 諺文 언 문 (K): see han-gŭl.

panjŏl 反切 반 절 (K): Originally, a Korean word for fan-ch'ieh (see okp'yŏn). By extension, it became one of the names for Sejong's script (see han-gŭl).

Po-hai 渤海 (C): a Manchurian state which existed from the eighth to the early tenth century and which contained much of present northeastern Korea. Called also Palhae 발해 (K) and Bokkai (J).

Tamna-guk 耽羅國 담 라 국 (K): The Korean name for Cheju-do before the Yi period. Called also Tanra-koku (J) and Tan-lo-kuo (C).

t'o 吐 토 (K): see kugyŏl.

MAPS

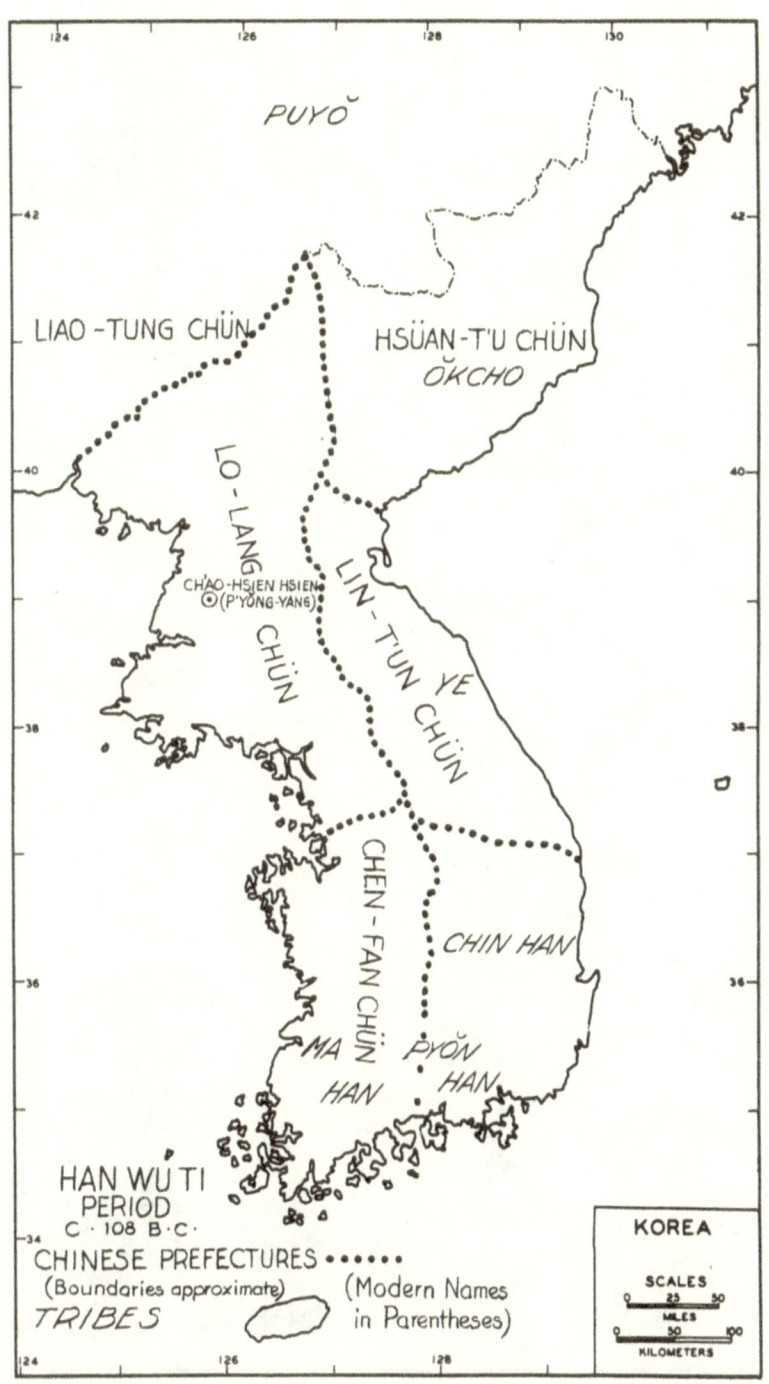

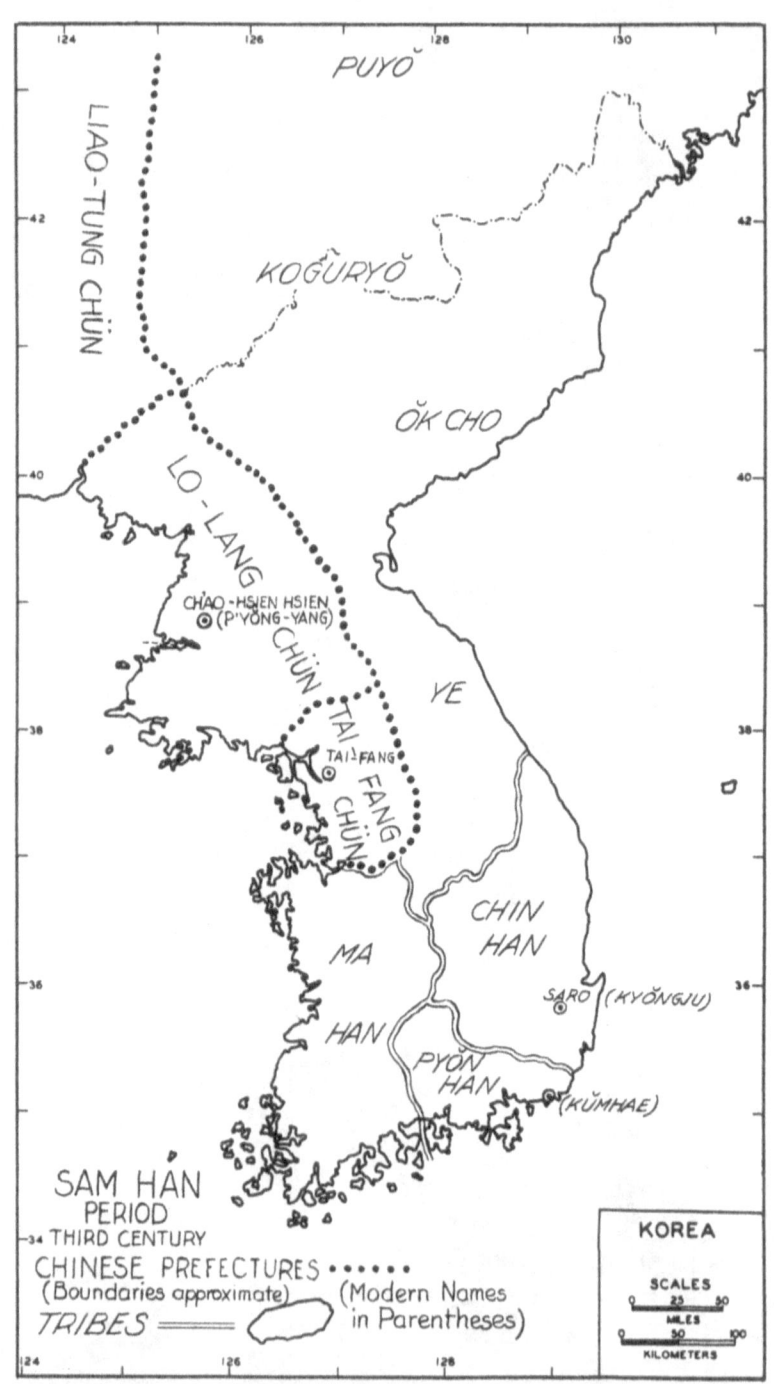

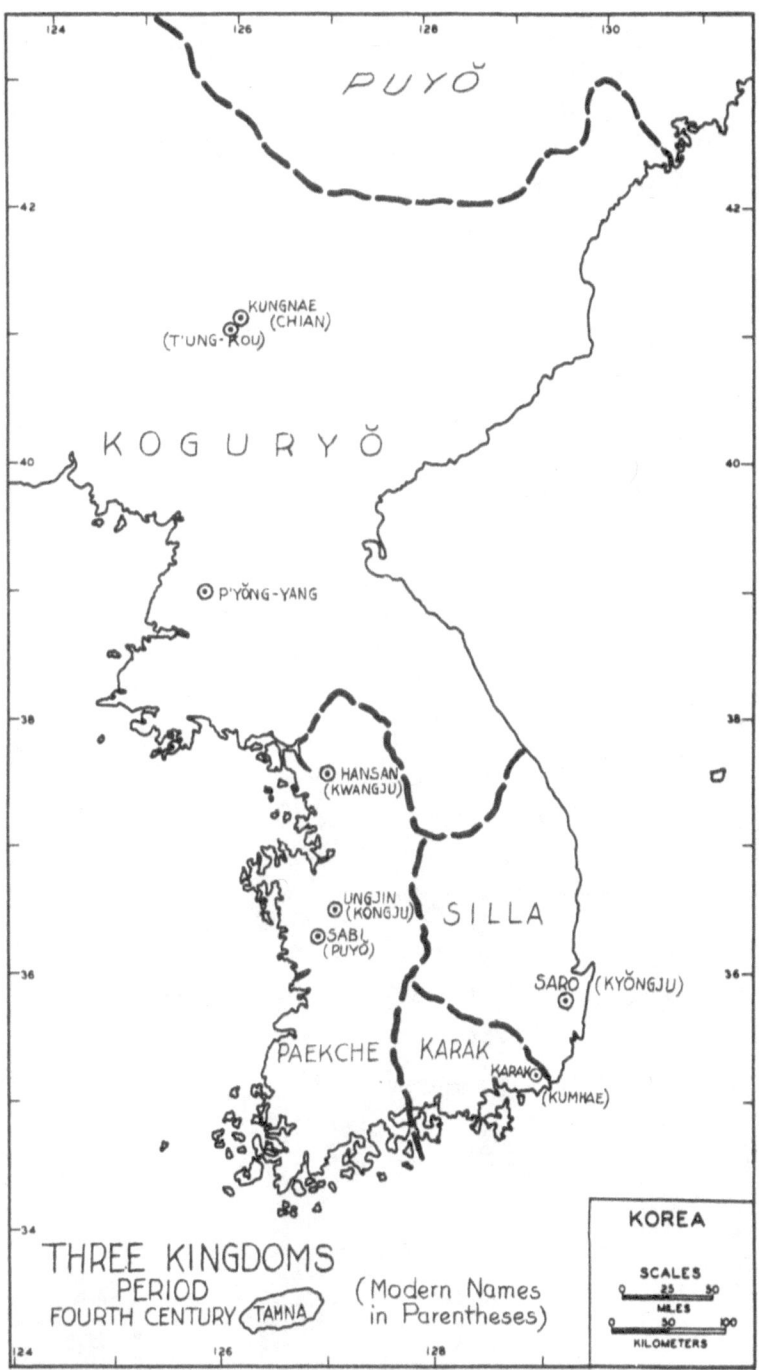

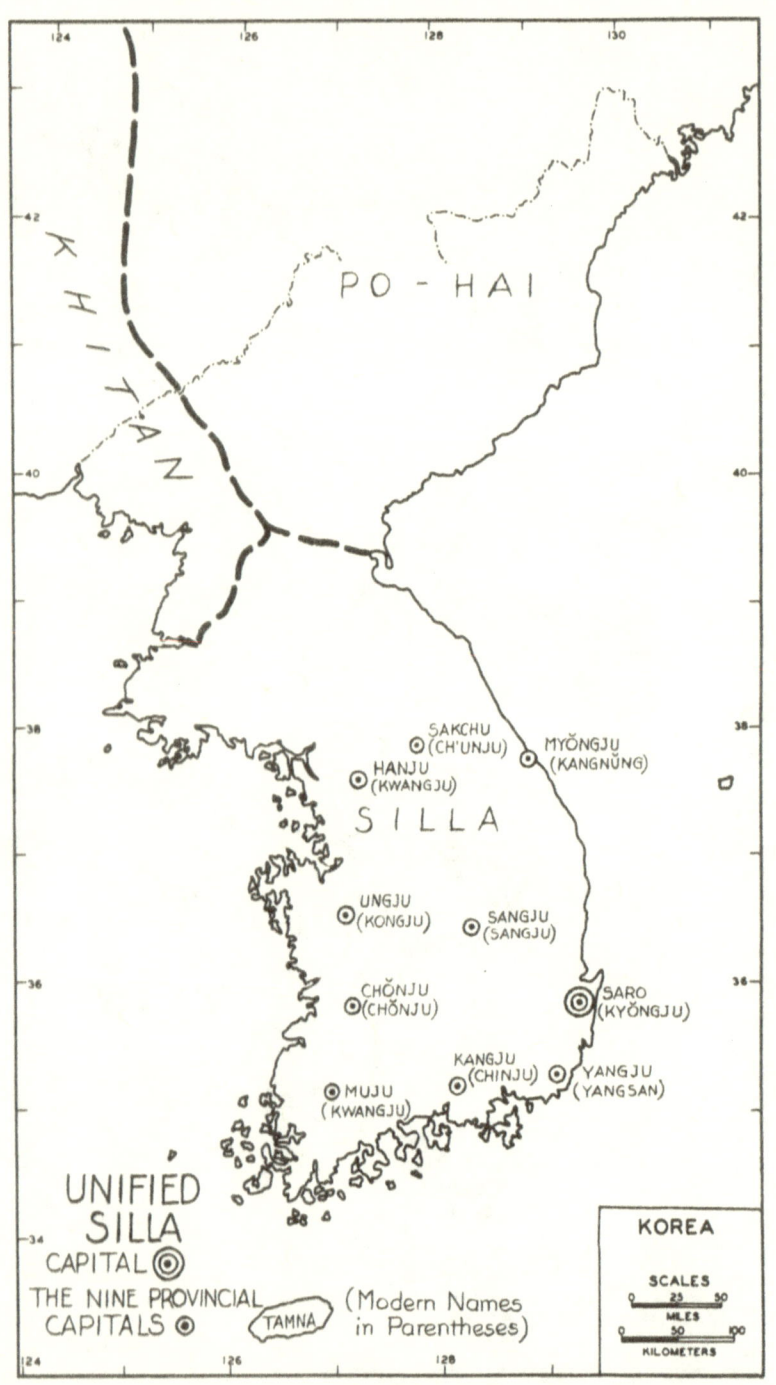

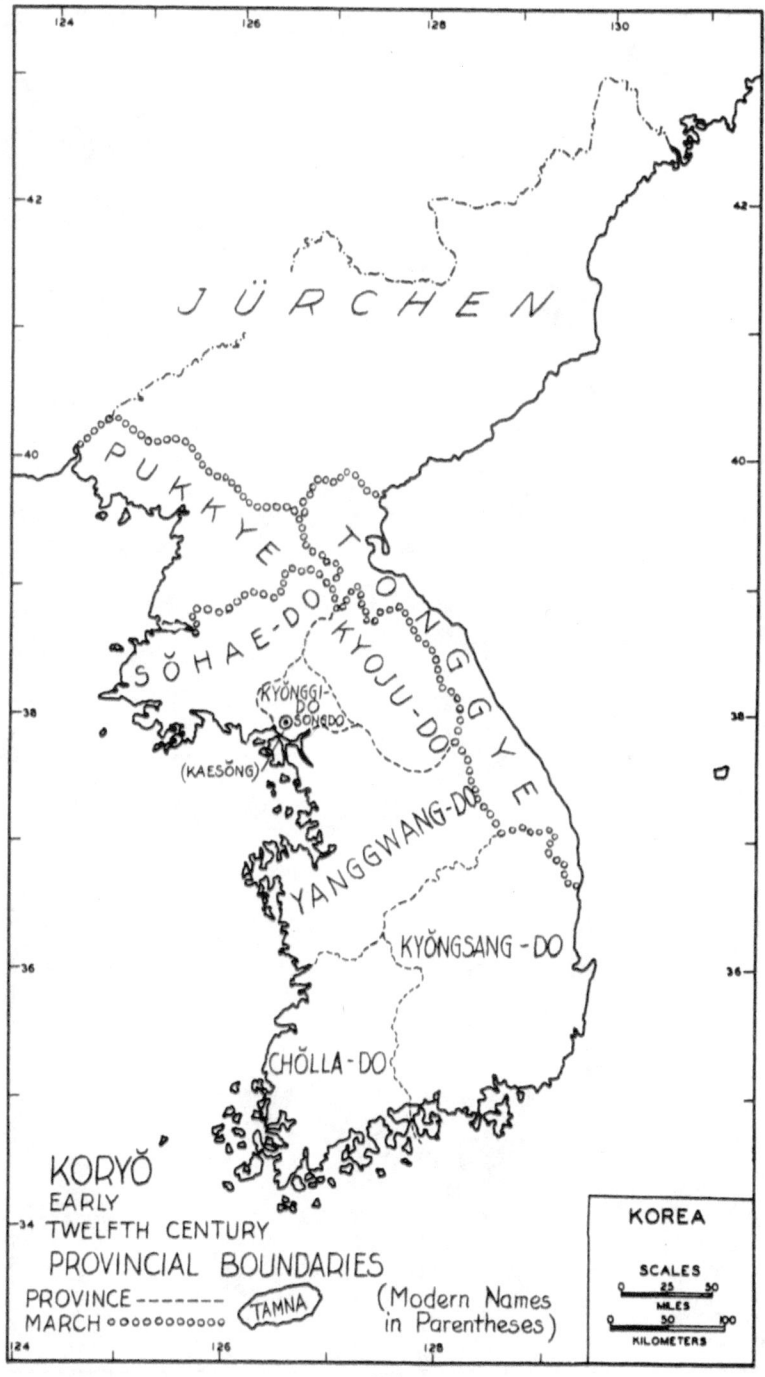

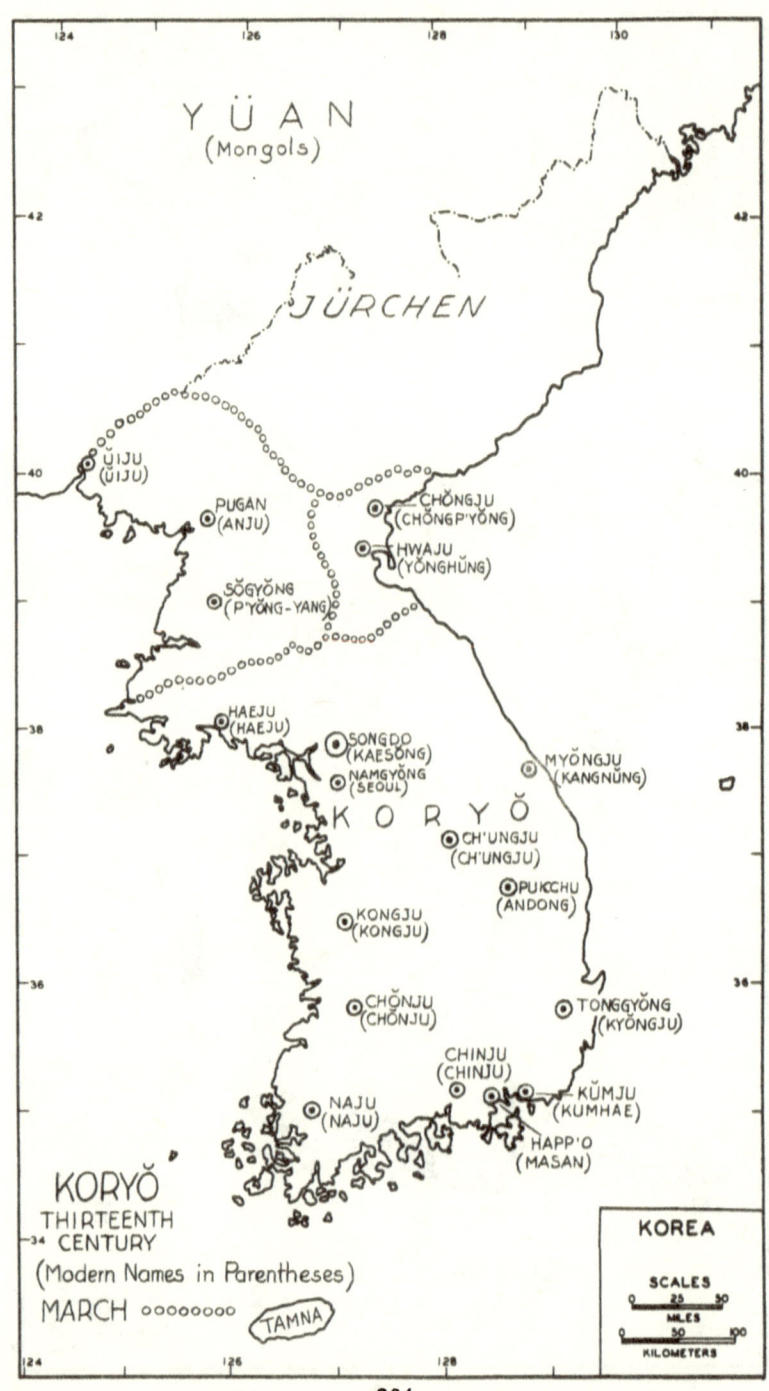

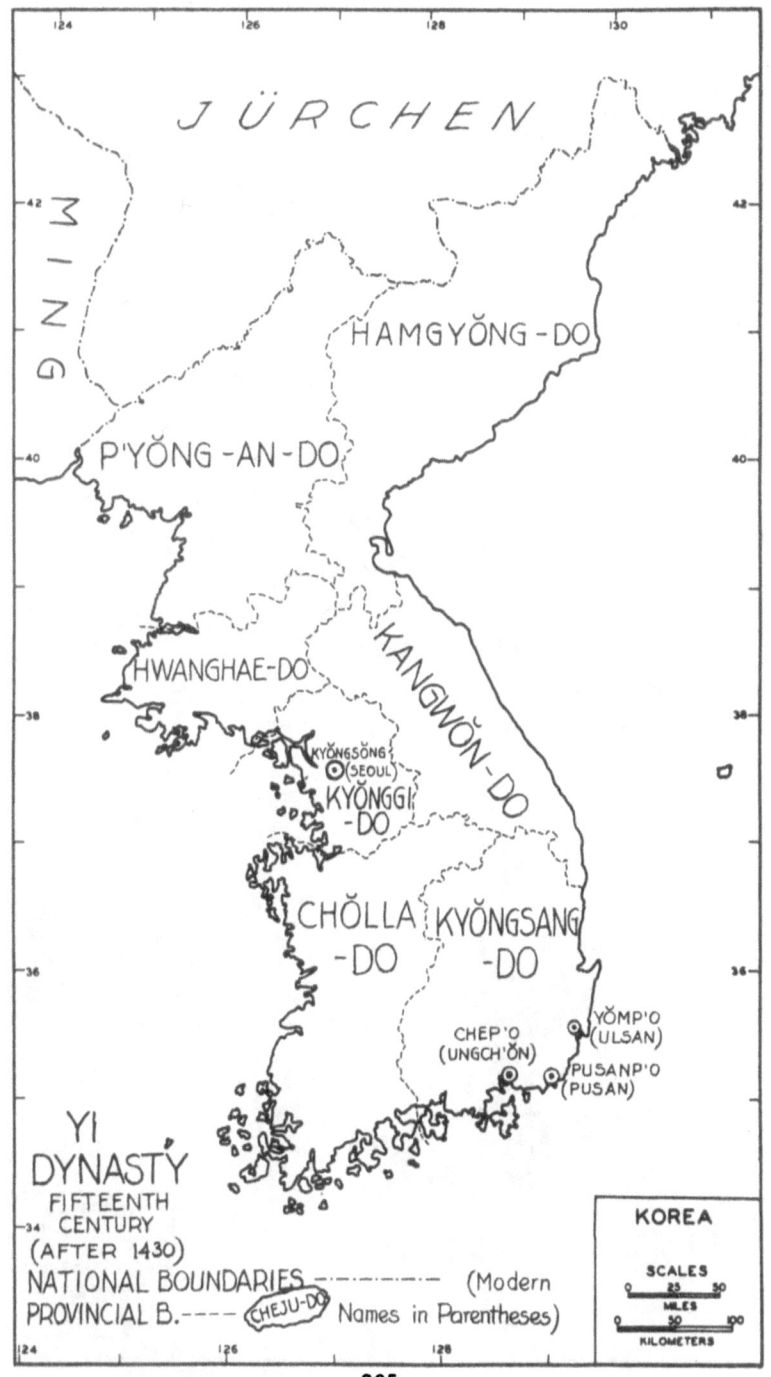

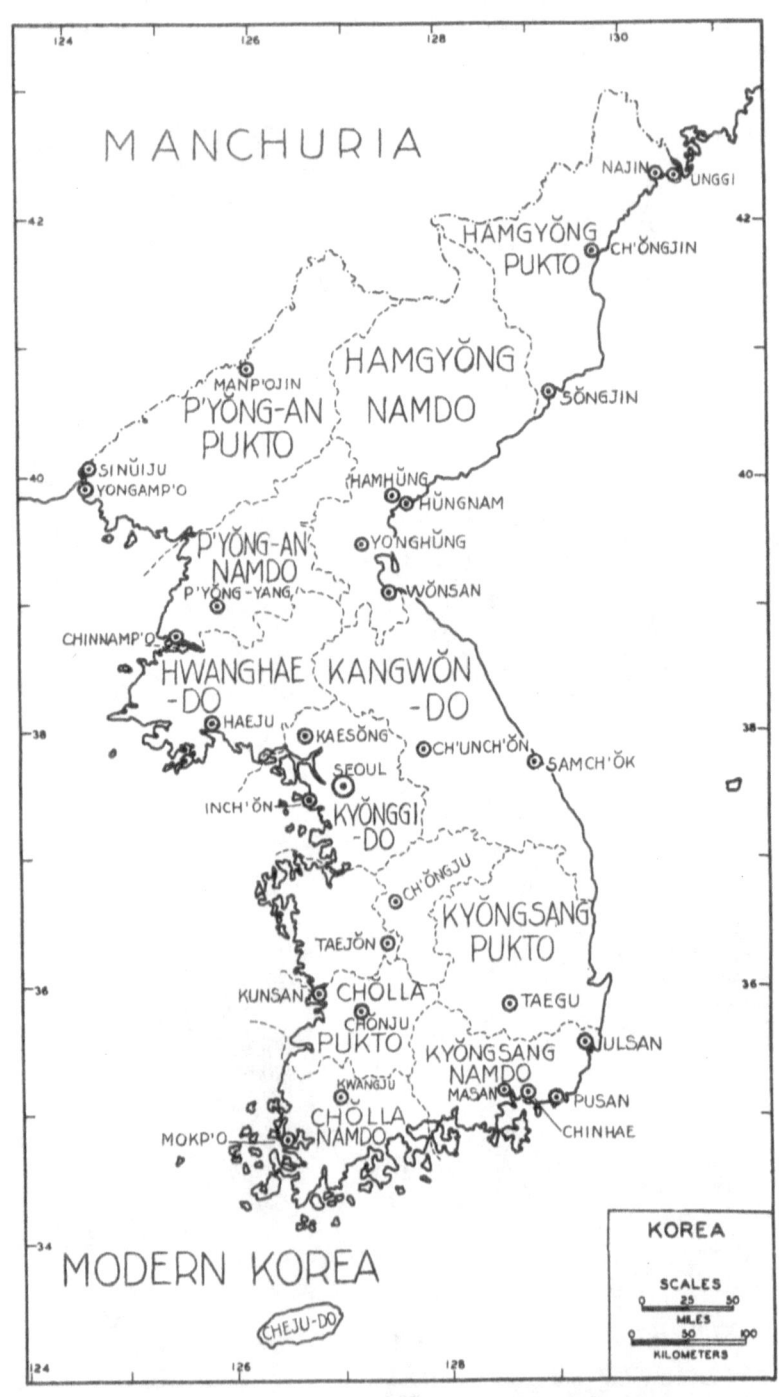

INDICES

Index of Titles

Note: Reference is to entry number

An Account of the Shipwreck of a Dutch Vessel on the Coast of the Isle of Quelpart 255
Akhak Kwebŏm 393
Aksŏ Kojon 394
American Military Government in Korea 310
Annual Report on the Administration of Tyosen [1907-1937] 304
An Anthology of Modern Poems in Korea 437
Archaeology of Korea: A Selected Bibliography 123
Bibliographie Coréene 7
Bibliographie von Japan, 1933-1935 13
Bibliography of the Japanese Empire, 1906-26 12
Bibliography of Western Language Material on Korea 11
Biblioteca Sinica 6
Bulletin of Far Eastern Bibliography 5
Bunken Hōkoku 27
Bunroku Keichō no Eki 298
Bunrui-shi 185: II
Catalogue of the Le Blond Collection of Corean Pottery 130
A Catalogue of the Romanized Geographical Names of Korea 89
Ch'ao-hsien Fu 303
Ch'ao-hsien Ko-ming-chi 348
Ch'ao-hsien Ti-li 121
Ch'ao-hsien Tung-shih 193a
Chayu Sege 48
Cheju-do Pang-ŏn-jip 415
Chesŭng Pangnyak 284
Chindan Hakpo 49

The Chinese Expedition to Manchuria Under the Wei Dynasty 224
The Chinese Government: A Manual of Chinese Titles 471
The Chinese Reader's Manual 97
Chinese Social and Political Science Review 32
Chinese Traditional Historiography 94
Chingbirok 291
Chin-gwan Kwanbyŏng P'yŏn-o Ch'aek Chan-gwŏn 263
Ch'obon Chingbirok 292
Ch'onggu Yŏng-ŏn 442
Chŏngjŏng Yŏktae Chosŏn Munhak Chŏnghwa Kwŏnsang 434
Chŏng-ŭm Paldal-sa 409
Chŏng-wŏn Chŏn-gyo 265
Chōsen 53
Chōsen Bijutsu Taikan 138
Chōsen Bijutsu-shi 158
Chōsen Bummyō oyobi Shōbu Jugen 374
Chōsen Bunka Shiron 196
Chōsen Bunka-shi 187
Chōsen Bunka-shi Kenkyū 199
Chōsen Fūzoku Shiryō Shūsetsu: Sen, Hidarinawa, Dakyū, Pakachi 355
Chōsen Fūzoku-shū 360
Chōsen Gakuhō 54
Chōsen Gogaku-shi 422
Chōsen Gyoseihō-ron 476
Chōsen Hōbutsu Koseki Zuroku 139
Chōsen Hōrei Shūran 332

Chōsen Hōsei-shi-kō 326
Chōsen Ippan-shi 185: I
Chōsen Jihen no Keii 329
Chōsen Jimmei Jisho 78
Chōsen Jimmei-roku 79
Chōsen Jukyō Taikan 376
Chōsen Junkyō-shi 384
Chōsen Kagaku-shi 195
Chōsen Kaika-shi 207
Chōsen Kankei Zasshi-rui 490
Chōsen Keisatsu no Gaiyō 333
Chōsen Keizai Nempō 330
Chōsen Keizai no Shin-kōsō 345
Chōsen Kinsei-shi 192
Chōsen Kinseki Sōran 140
Chōsen Kinseki-kō 149
Chōsen Kobunka Sōkan 164
Chōsen Kodai Bunka no Kenkyū 157
Chōsen Kodai Kammei-kō 477
Chōsen Kodai Kenkyū Dai-ichi-bu: Shiragi Karō no Kenkyū 233
Chōsen Kodai no Bosei 162
Chōsen Kodai no Bunka 163
Chōsen Kofun Hekiga-shū 141
Chōsen Kōkogaku Kenkyū 143
Chōsen Kokuhō Taikan 160
Chōsen Kon-in-kō 358
Chōsen Koseki Zufu 142
Chōsen Koseki Zufu Kaisetsu 142a
Chōsen Koshi no Kenkyū 220
Chōsen Koyūshoku Jiten 101
Chōsen-Manshū-shi 200
Chōsen Minyō-shū 452
Chōsen Minzoku Kaihō Undōshi 337
Chōsen Nempyō 486
Chōsen ni okeru Chishitsu oyobi Kōbutsu no Chōsa Enkaku narabi ni Bunken 106
Chōsen ni okeru Kenjō-hō Sonkei-hō no Jodōshi 423
Chōsen no Engeki 461
Chōsen no Fuken 386
Chōsen no Fūsui 387
Chōsen no Keizai 346
Chōsen no Keizai Jijō 331

210   Index of Titles

Chōsen no Kenchiku to Geijutsu 159
Chōsen no Kishin 388
Chōsen no Kōgyō to Sono Shigen 344
Chōsen no Nenjū Gyōji 102
Chōsen no Rekishi 489
Chōsen no Ruiji Shūkyō 389
Chōsen no Seimei Shizoku ni Kansuru Kenkyū Chōsa 80
Chōsen no Shūraku 356
Chōsen oyobi Manshū 55
Chōsen Rekidai Jitsuroku Ichiran 289a
Chōsen Rekishi Chiri 120
Chōsen Rekishi Tokuhon 197
Chōsen Saishi Sōzoku Hōron: Josetsu 357
Chōsen Shakai Keizai-shi 234
Chōsen Shiryō Shūshin 184
Chōsen Shiryō Sōkan 183
Chōsen Shiseki Kaidai Kōgi 20
Chōsen Shiwa 206
Chōsen Shogaka Retsuden 166
Chōsen Shoshi 204
Chōsen Sōtokufu Keimu-kyoku 333
Chōsen Sōtokufu Kotosho Mokuroku 17
Chōsen Sōtokufu Shisei Nempō 334
Chōsen Sōtokufu Tōkei Nempō 100
Chōsen Sōtokufu Tosho Mokuroku 22
Chōsen Tenshukyō Shoshi 383
Chōsen Tetsudō-shi: Sōshi Jidai 335
Chōsen to Sono Geijutsu 165
Chōsen Tōchi Hiwa 328
Chōsen Tosho Kaidai 18
Chōsen Tsūshi 193
Chōsen Yonsen-nen-shi 188
Chōsen Zenkyō-shi 367
Chōsen-eki 301
Chōsen-gō Hōgen no Kenkyū 424
Chōsengo Jiten 70
Chōsen-shi [1901] 191

Index of Titles 211

Chōsen-shi [1909] 201
Chōsen-shi [1932-1940] 182
Chōsen-shi [1951] 190
Chōsen-shi Gaisetsu 202
Chōsen-shi Henshū-kai Jigyō Gaiyō 182a
Chōsen-shi Kōza 185
Chōsen-shi no Shiori 198
Chōsen-shi no Shirube 189
Chōsen-shi Taikei 186
Chosŏn Haebang-sa: Sam-il Undong 317
Chosŏn Hakye-sa 370
Chosŏn Kajok Chedo Yŏn-gu 353
Chosŏn Kwahak-sa 195a
Chosŏn Kyohoe-sa: Sŏsŏl 379a
Chosŏn Kyŏngje Nyŏnbo. See: Kyŏngje Nyŏn-gam.
Chosŏn Kyŏngje ŭi Kibon Kujo 322
Chosŏn Kyoyuk-sa 467
Chosŏn Malbon 404
Chosŏn Mingan Chŏnsŏl-jip 454
Chosŏn Minjok Munwa ŭi Yŏn-gu 385
Chosŏn Minjok Sŏlhwa ŭi Yŏn-gu 457
Chosŏn Minyo Yŏn-gu 445
Chosŏn Minyo-sŏn 446
Chosŏn Misul-sa 134
Chosŏn Misul-sa Yŏn-gu 137
Chosŏn Munbŏp Yŏn-gu 410
Chosŏn Munhak Yŏn-gu-ch'o 433
Chosŏn Munhak-sa 426
Chosŏn Munhwa Ch'ongsŏl 413
Chosŏn Munhwa Yesul 428
Chosŏn Munhwa-sa Yŏn-gu Non-go 488
Chosŏn Munja kŭp Ŏhak-sa 412
Chosŏn Ŏ Munbŏp 408
Chosŏn Ŏ Ŭmunnon Yŏn-gu 419
Chosŏn Oegu-sa 239
Chosŏn Ŏhak Non-go 416
Chosŏn Poksik-ko 354
Chosŏn Pulgyo T'ongsa 365
Chosŏn Pulgyo-sa 366
Chosŏn Sahoe Chŏngch'aek-sa 352

Chosŏn Sahwa-jip: Samguk Si-dae-p'yŏn 459
Chosŏn Sanggosagam 217
Chosŏn Siga Sagang 440
Chosŏn Siga ŭi Yŏn-gu 439
Chosŏn Singnyang Mundae wa kŭ Taech'aek 319
Chosŏn Sinmunhak Sajo-sa 429
Chosŏn Sinmunhak Sajo-sa: Hyŏndae-p'yŏn 430
Chosŏn Sinsa Pogam 76
Chosŏn Tanp'yŏn Munhak Sŏnjip: Cheiljip 453
Chosŏn T'app'a ŭi Yŏn-gu 135
Chosŏn ŭi Aak 396
Chosŏn ŭi Kŏsŏk Munhwa Yŏn-gu 132
Chosŏn Ŭmak Tokpon 397
Chosŏn Ŭmak T'ongnon 395
Chosŏn Ŭnhaeng Chosa Wŏlbo 318
Chosŏn Yŏksa 174
Chosŏn Yŏktae Yŏryu Mun-jip 427
Chosŏn Yŏngam 77
Chosŏn Yugeji Yangmyŏng Hak-p'a 372
Chosŏn Yuhak-sa 371
Chosŏnŏ K'ŭn Sajŏn 72
Chosŏnŏ Sajŏn 71
Chosŏn-sa Kaesŏl 177
Chosŏn-sa Taegwan. See: Kuk-sa Taegwan
Chosŏn-sa Yŏn-gu 227
Chosŏn-sa Yŏn-gu-ch'o 228
A Chronological Index: Some of the Chief Events in the Foreign Intercourse of Korea 479
La Chronologie ancienne du Japon 482
Chugyo Taejŏn Hoet'ong 473
Chuhae Yongbi Ŏ Ch'ŏn-ga 451
Chukan Digest. See: Kwanbo
Ch'ulp'an Taegam 16
Chŭngbo Kagok Wŏllyu 441
Chŭngbo Munhŏn Pigo 83
Chŭngjŏng Kyorinji 266
Chungjŏng Namhan-ji 112

Ch'ungmukong Chŏnsŏ. See entry 272
Climate of Korea 109
Climatic Regions 109
La code pénal de la Corée 306
Comparative Chronological Tables . . . from 660 B.C. to 1910 A.D. 481
Comparative Treatment of the Japanese Language 400
Concordances des chronologies néoméniques chinoise et européene 483
Le Confucianism en Corée 369
Corea e Coreanio 313
Corea, the Hermit Nation 168
Corean Books and Their Authors 14
The Corean Government 472
Corean Pottery 128
La Corée jusqu'au IXe Siécle 223
Décoration Coréene 126
Documents relatifs aux martyrs de Corée de 1839 et 1846 380
Early Japanese History 480
Economic History of Chosen 305
The Exchange of Envoys between Korea and Japan during the Tokugawa Period 262a
Far Eastern Quarterly 8
Far Eastern Survey 33
Gaikan Chōsen-shi 203
Gaikō-bu 246
Gazetteer to Maps of Korea 90
Gendai Tōa Jimmei Kan 81
Genkō no Shin-Kenkyū 247
Geographic Publications of Hermann Lautensach on Korea 104
God, Mammon, and the Japanese 261
Haedong Chŏgukki 276
Haedong Kayo 443
Haedong Yŏksa 241
Hakp'ung 50
Hamel P'yoryugi 287
Han Dynasty Mythology and the Korean Legend of Tangun 211

Han-gŭl Kal 405
Han-gŭl Match'umbŏp Haesŏl 411
Han-kuo Tu-li Yŭn-tung chih Hsueh-shih 350
Han-kuo T'ung-shih 349
Harvard Journal of Asiatic Studies 34
Hideyoshi's Invasions of Korea 260
Histoire de l'Église de Corée 379
History of Corea, Ancient and Modern 173
The History of Korea 169
A History of Korean Art 127
History of Lo-lang 212
The History of Protestant Missions in Korea (1832-1910) 381
A History of the Korean People 167
Hoku-Manshū oyobi Tōbu Shiberiya Chōsa Hōkoku 153:II
The Horace Allen Manuscript Collection at the New York Public Library 259
Ho-u Ch'ong kwa Ŭnnyong Ch'ong 133
Hsüan Ho Feng Shih Kao Li T'u Ching 251
Hunmin Chŏng-ŭm 407
Hunmin Chŏng-ŭm T'ongsa 414
Hwarang-do Yŏn-gu 229
Hyangga Ryŏyo Sinsŏk 438
Hyangt'o 51
Hyŏndae Chosŏn Munhak Chŏnjip: Siga-jip 449
Hyŏndae Chosŏn Sahoe Kyŏngje-sa 320
Ilbon Wanghwan Ilgi 268
Ilsŏl Ch'unhyang-jŏn 458
Introduction to Spoken Korean 487
Introduction to the Study of Buddhism in Corea 364
The Invention of Printing in China and Its Spread Westward 124

Japan Weekly Mail 35
Japanese Expansion on the Asiatic Continent 171
The Japanese Trading Post at Pusan 262b
Jeke Juvan Ulus Un Mandǔsan Tǫry Jin Kǫke Sudar 252
K. B. S. Bibliographical Register of Important Works written in Japanese on Japan and the Far East. 9
Kagok Wŏllyu. See: Chŭngbo Kagok Wŏllyu
Kankoku no Heigō to Kokushi 339
Kankoku Kahei Seiri Hōkōku-sho 338
Kankoku Shisei Nempō. See: Chōsen Sōtokufu Shisei Nempō
Keijō Teikoku Daigaku Fuzoku Toshokan, Wakan Shomei Mokuroku 23
Keirin Ruiji Raigen Kō 420
Keishū Kinkan-tsuka to Sono Ihō 153: III
Kenkenroku 296
Kich'o Kuksa Sajǒn 85
Kin Gyoku-gin Den 340
Kindai Chōsen Seiji-shi 302
Kindai Nis-Sen Kankei no Kenkyū 300
Kinsei Chōsen-shi 192a
Koji Ruien. See entry 246
Kōkai-kun Jidai no Man-Sen Kankei 299
Kōkuri Jidai no Iseki 153: V(2)
Kokushi Jiten 86
Kōrai Tōji no Kenkyū 154
Kōrai-shi Kenkyū 249
Kōrai-shi Retsu-den Jimmei Sakuin 240a
Korea: An Annotated Bibliography of Publications in Far Eastern Languages 3
Korea: An Annotated Bibliography of Publications in the Russian Language 2
Korea: An Annotated Bibliography of Publications in Western Languages 1

Korea and the Old Orders in Eastern Asia 311
Korea, eine Landeskunde auf Grund eigener Reisen und der Literatur 107
Korea: Land, Volk, Schicksal 108
Korea Magazine 36
Korea Mission Field 37
Korea (1926-36) mit Nachtragen aus alterer Zeit 103
Korea Review 38
Korea Today 308
Korea: Treaties and Agreements 253
Korean-American Relations 257
Korean Buddhism 363
A Korean Grammar 401
Korean Grammatical Forms 399
Korean Musical Instruments and An Introduction to Korean Music 392
Korean Relations with China and Japan, 1800-1864 262
Korean Relations with Japan 256
Korean Repository 39
Korean Review 40
Korean Survey 41
Korean Treaties 254
Koreanische Musik 391
The Koreans and Their Culture 351
Koreia 110
Koryǒ Kasa 444
Koryǒ-sa 240
Koryǒ-sa Chǒryo 242
Koryǒ-sa Chǒryo Pogan 243
Kosa Ch'waryo 269
Koseki Chōsa Gaihō 151
Koseki Chōsa Hōkoku [1916-1938] 152
Koseki Chōsa Tokubetsu Hōkoku 153
Ko-sijo Chǒnghae 448
The Kōtaiō Monument 131
Kudara Bijutsu 148
Kudara-shi Kenkyū 232

Kukcho Pogam 270
Kukhan Myŏngmun Sinokp'yŏn 69
Kuksa Kaesŏl 178
Kuksa Taegwan 181
Kuksa Yoron 180
Kŭlja ŭi Hyŏngmyŏng 406
Kŭmsu Kangsan 4
Kŭndae Chosŏn Kyŏngje-sa Yŏn-gu 316
Kungmin Chosŏn Yŏksa 175
Kunmun Tŭngnok 293
Die Kunst Chinas, Japans, und Koreas 129
Kwanbo 321
Kyōka oyobi Ritō no Kenkyū 425
Kyŏngje Nyŏn-gam 323
The Legend of the King Tunming, the Founder of Fu-yu-kuo 216
Man-Sen Chiri Rekishi Kenkyū 56
Man-Sen-shi Kenkyū Chūsei 248
Man-Sen-shi Kenkyū Jōsei-hen 219
Manshū Rekishi-chiri 222
A Manual of Korean Geographical and Other Proper Names Romanized 91
Map of Korea 92
Maps of Korea 104
Meiji ikō Kyōiku Seido Hattatsu-shi 468
Meiji Nenkan Chōsen Kenkyū Bunken-shi 24
Memoirs of the Research Department of the Toyo Bunko 214
Miam Ilgi-ch'o 290
Mimana Kōbō-shi 236
Minji Kanshū Kaitō Ishū 361
Minjok ŭi T'aeyang 295
Modern Education in Korea 465
Modern Korea 307
Monumentica Nipponica 42
Moŭm Chohwa Yŏn-gu 418
Munye Tokpon 435
Muromachi Jidai no Nis-Sen Kankei 250

Nanhu Chamnok 294
Nanjung Ilgi-ch'o; Imjinjang-ch'o 288
National Examination in Korea 462
New Life Korean-English Dictionary 67
Nihon Chiri Taikei 119
Nihon no Kyōiku Seishin to Ri Taikei fu Ri Ritsukoku no Gekimō Yōgetsu to Jiji 375
Nik-kan Jōko-shi no Rimen 235
Nik-Kan Koshi Dan 237
Nik-Kan Kodai-shi Shiryō 221
Nippon Chōsen Hikaku Kenchiku-shi 161
Nippon Shuppan Nenkan 28
Nippon Sōsho Sakuin 19
Nis-Sen Kankei no Shiteki Kōsatsu to Sono Kenkyū 194
Nis-Shin Seneki Gaikō-shi no Kenkyū 347
Northeast Asia, a Selected Bibliography 10
Nosan Munsŏn 460
Nosongdang Ilbon Haengnok 279
Notes on the History of Korea 213
Numerical Categories of Korea 95
Oda Sensei Shōju Kinen Chōsen Ronshū 205
Old Korean Geographical Works 105
On Race Struggles in Korea 215
The Orchid Door 436
Outline of Korean Grammar 403
Ōyano-hon. See entry 247.
Pacific Affairs 43
A Partial Bibliography of Occidental Literature on Korea 15
The Passing of Korea 170
Place Name Index for Korea (Chōsen) 93
Pohanjae-jip 277

Publications in Japanese on
  Korean Anthropology   122
Pugyŏ Yosŏn   114
Pukhan-ji   117
Pyŏgwi-p'yŏn   382
Rakurō   146
Rakurō Iseki   151:1935
Rakurō Kofun   151:1933, 1934
Rakurō Ōkō-bo   155
Rakurō Saikyō-zuka   150
Rakurō-gun Jidai no Iseki   153:IV
Recent Geographical Works on
  Korea   104
Reference Handbook, Government of the Republic of Korea   470
Rekishi Chiri   57
Rekishigaku Kenkyū   58
Religions of Old Korea   362
Republic of Korea Economic
  Summation   312
Research Monographs on Korea
  44
Ri Shun-shin Zenshū   272
Richō Bukkyō   368
Ri-chō Hōten-kō   342
Ri-chō Jitsuroku Fūzoku Shiryō
  Saiyō   359
Richō Jugaku-shi ni okeru Shuriha Shugiha no Hattatsu   377
Richō Senso Shūsei Jitsuroku to
  Kensō Kaishū Jitsuroku ni
  tsuite   289b
Richō-shi Taizen   297
Ridoku Shūsei   73
Ri-ō-ke Hakubutsukan Shozō Shashin-chō   156
Romanization of the Korean Language Based Upon Its Phonetic
  Structure   74
Rural Education for the Regeneration of Korea   463
Ryōsan Fufu-tsuka to Sono Ibutsu
  153: V(1)
Ryŏyo Chŏnju   450
Ryūka Kogo Sen   421
Sach'ŏnnyŏn Munhŏn T'onggo   84
Sadae Mun-gwe   273
Saishin Chōsen Rekishi Chiri Jiten
  87

Samban Resik   274
Sambong-jip   264
Samguk Sagi   225
Samguk Yusa   226
Sangsik Kuksa   179
Sangju Kungmunhak Kojŏn Tokpon   432
Seikyū Gakusō   59
Sengo ni okeru Chōsen no Seiji
  Jōsei   343
Sen-Man Keizai Jū-nen-shi
  327
Sen-Man no Keiei: Chōsen Mondai no Kompon Kaiketsu   336
Shakuten, Kiu; Antaku   390
Shien   60
Shigaku Bunken Mokuroku   25
Shigaku Zasshi   61
Shinkō Ō no Boshi Junkyō-hi to
  Shiragi no Tōhokukyō   153:VI
Shinsen Jimmei Daijiten   82
Shinshobu Bunrui Mokuroku   26
Shinzō Tōkoku Yochi Shōran Sakuin   118a
Shiragi Kan-igō-kō   475
Shiragi Koga no Kenkyū   145
Shiragi Shoki Kankai Meigi ni
  tsuite no Shin-kenkyū   474
Shiragi-shi   230
Shiragi-shi Kenkyū   231
Shirin   62
Shisei Nijūgo-nen-shi   478
Shōtoku Chōsen Shinshi Tōjō
  Gyōretsu-zu   491
Shuppan Nenkan [1930-1941]   29
Shuppan Nenkan [1948]   30
Shushi-gaku no Denrai to sono
  Eikyō ni tsuite   378
Sijo-jip   447
Silhŏm Tohae Chosŏn Ŏ Ŭmsŏnghak   417
Simyang Changgye   275
Sin Chosŏn Chiri   116
Sinjajŏn   68
Sinjŭng Tongguk Yŏji Sŭngnam
  118
Sok Mujŏng Pogam   278
Sosu Sŏwŏn Tŭngnok   466
Source Materials on Korean Politics and Ideologies   314

South Korean Interim Government Activities. See: Republic of Korea Economic Summation
Stele Chinois du royaume du Ko Kou Rye 125
The Story of Korea 172
Studies in Korean Etymology 402
A Study of the Fu-yu 209
A Study on Lo-lang and Taifang 210
Sudo Kyŏngch'al Paltal-sa 324
Sugihara Chōtarō-shi Shūshū Kōkohin Zuroku 144
Summation of the United States Army Military Government Activities in Korea: See: Republic of Korea Economic Summation
Sŭngjŏng-wŏn Ilgi. See entry 265
Synchronismes Chinois 484
Taedong Kinyŏn 267
Taedong Unbu Kunok 99
Taedong Yasŭng 281
Taedong Yŏjido 113
Taehan Kang-yŏk-ko 111
Taehan Yŏngam 75
Taejŏn Hoet'ong. See: Chugyo Taejŏn Hoet'ong
Taiin-gun Den: fu Ōhi no Ishō 341
Tang Chang Sŏ Hwa Ch'ŏp 282
Tang-ŭi T'ongnyak 285
Tan-gun Sinhwa ŭi Sinyŏn-gu 218
Tokubetsu Kōgi 185:III
Tongguk Chŏllan-sa 176
Tongguk Munhŏn Pigo. See Chŭngbo Munhŏn Pigo
Tongguk T'onggam 244
Tongguk Yi Sangguk-chip 245
Tonggyŏng Chapki 115
Tongmun Hwigo 280
T'ongmun-gwanji 283
Tongmun-sŏn 431

Tongsa Kangmok 238
Tongsa Nyŏnp'yo 485
Tosho Sōmokuroku 31
Tōyō 63
Tōyō Bunko Chōsen-hon Bunrui Mokuroku, fu Annan-hon Mokuroku 21
Tōyō Gakuhō 64
Tōyō Ongaku-shi 398
Tōyō Rekishi Daijiten 88
The Tragedy of Korea 309
Traité des fonctionnaires et Traité d l'armée 469
Transactions of the Asiatic Society of Japan 45
Transactions of the Korean Branch of the Royal Asiatic Society 46
The True Function of Education in . . . Korea 464
Tsūkō 147
The Unabridged Korean-English Dictionary 66
Undiplomatic Memoirs: The Far East, 1896-1904 258
United Nations Documents Index 315
Urimal Sajŏn. See: Chosŏnŏ Sajŏn
Voice of Korea 47
Wŏnbon Ch'unhyang-jŏn 455
Yakubun Taiten Kaitsū 473a
Yangban-jŏn 456
Yangch'on-jip 271
The Yi Dynasty Annals of Korea 96
Yijo Sillok 289
Yŏ Ŭn-hyŏng Sonsaeng T'ujaeng-sa 325
Yŏksa Hakpo 52
Yŏksa Ilgam 98
Yŏllyŏsil Kisul 286
Yongjae Ch'onghwa 136
Yupul Yang-gyo Kyodae ŭi Kiyŏn e Taehan Ilyŏn-gu 373
Zakkō 65

Index of Authors

Note: Reference is to page number

Allen, Horace N. 172
An Chae-hong 77
An Chŏng-bok 85
An Hoe-nam 161
Aoyagi Nammei [pseud.]. See: Aoyagi Tsunatarō
Aoyagi Tsunatarō 68, 85, 103
Arimitsu Kyōichi 50
Asami Rintarō 2, 117
Aston, W. G. 92, 172
Baba Koreichirō 52
Bank of Chōsen 111
Boot, J. L. (Mrs.) 143
Carnegie Endowment for International Peace 90
Carter, Thomas Francis 42
Ch'en Ch'ing-ch'üan 70
Chi Hŏn-yŏng 158
Cho Yun-je 158, 159
Ch'oe Ho-jin 114
Ch'oe Hyŏn-bae 148
Ch'oe Ik-han 126
Ch'oe Nam-sŏn 17, 27, 61, 62
Ch'oe Sang-su 161
Chŏng Hyŏn-jin 20
Chŏng In-bo 81
Chŏng In-ji 86
Chŏng In-sŏp. See: Zong In-sob
Chŏng To-jŏn 93
Chŏng Yag-yong 33, 144
Chōsen Ginkō 117
Chōsen Gyōsei Henshū Sōkyoku 117
Chōsen Sōtokufu 118
Chōsen Sōtokufu Keimu-kyoku 118
Chosŏn Kwahakcha Tongmaeng 114

Chosŏn Ŏ Hakhoe 18, 148
Chu Si-gyŏng 149
Chung, Henry 90
Clark, Charles Allen 133
Clement, Ernest W. 172
Cordier, Henri 4
Courant, Maurice 4, 42, 79
Crémazy, Laurent 111
Dallet, Charles 138
Des Rotours, Robert 169
Du Pont, Maurice 42
Eckhardt, Andreas 42, 143
Fujita Ryōsaku 46, 49, 54, 174
Fujita Tōzō 127
Fujiwara Ichiki 137
Fukuda Yoshinosuke 82
Gale, James S. 16, 60, 147
Gardner, Charles S. 26
Gaspardone, Émile 172
Gerow, Bert A. 41
Gompertz, E. and G. 6
Grajdanzev, Andrew J. 111
Grey, Arthur L. 112
Griffis, William E. 60
Grigsby, Joan S. 158
Haenish, Wolf 5
Ham Hwa-jin 144, 159
Hamada Kōsaku 47, 49
Hamel, Hendrick 91
Han Ch'i-yun 86
Han Hŭng-su 43
Harada Yoshito 47
Harrington, Fred Harvey 92
Hatada Takashi 24, 68
Hayashi Taisuke 69, 70
Hewes, G. W. 41
Higasa Mamoru 70
Hirai Takashi 47

Hirose Bin 7
Hoang, P. 172
Honey, W. B. 43
Hong Hŭi 135
Hong I-sŏp 70
Hong Ki-mun 149
Hong Kyŏng-mo 33
Horne, E. C. 173
Hosoi Hajime 71, 119
Hu Huan-yung 37
Hŭlbŏp. See Hulbert, Homer
 B. 94
Hulbert, Homer B. 60, 61,
 91, 94, 166
Hwang Sin 94
Hyŏn Sang-yun 136
Ikeuchi Hiroshi 47, 49, 52,
 75, 77, 80, 88, 104
Il-yŏn 80
Im Kwang-ch'ŏl 71, 120
Imai Kichinosuke 174
Imamura Tomo 127, 128
Imanishi Ryū 70, 71, 77, 82,
 88, 171
Inaba Iwakichi 71, 72, 104
Inaba Kunzan [pseud.]. See:
 Inaba Iwakichi
Innami Takaichi 163
Inzenaşi 89
Kanazawa, S. 25
Kanda Sōzō 50
Kaneseki Takeo 47
Kang Hyo-sŏk 62
Karube Jion 47
Katō, Bunjiro 25
Katsuragi Sueji 48
Kayamoto Kamejirō 50, 53
Kerner, Robert 5
Kida Teikichi 121
Kikuchi Kenjō 121
Kim Chae-wŏn 39, 44, 77.
 See also: Kim Che-won
Kim Che-won 75. See also:
 Kim Chae-wŏn.
Kim Chong-bŏm 115
Kim Chŏng-ho 33
Kim Ch'ŏn-t'aek 159
Kim Han-ju 115
Kim, Helen K. 167

Kim Hyŏk-che 17
Kim Hyŏng-gyu 150
Kim Kyo-hwan 161
Kim No-gyu 34
Kim Pu-sik 80
Kim Pyŏng-je 149
Kim Sa-yŏp 156
Kim So-un [pseud.]. See: Kim
 Kyo-hwan
Kim Sŏk-tam 115
Kim Su-jang 159
Kim T'ae-jun 160
Kim Tu-hŏn 126
Kim Yŏng-gi 44
Kim Yun-gyŏng 149
Kitagawa Sajin 28
Kiyono Kenji 47
Ko Ch'ih-feng 124
Ko Chŏng-ok 160
Ko Yu-sŏp 44
Koizumi Akio 48, 49, 50
Korea (Republic). Bureau of
 Public Information 169
Kubo Tenzui 72
Kümmel, Otto 43
Kuno, Yoshi S. 61
Kuroi Jodō 171
Kurumada Atsushi 171
Kusuta Onosaburō 140
Kwŏn Kŭn 94
Kwŏn T'ae-sŏp 115
Landis, E. B. 26
Lautensach, Hermann 31, 32
Lee Hi-seung. See: Yi Hi-sung
Lew, Hyungki J. 17
Lim Hwa 160, 161
Longford, Joseph H. 61
McCune, Evelyn B. 75
McCune, George M. 19, 27,
 75, 91, 92, 112
McCune, Shannon 5, 31, 32
McKenzie, F. A. 112
Maema Kyōsaku 151
Mayers, William F. 27, 170
Meade, E. Grant 112
Min Chu-myŏn 34
Min Pyŏng-do 156
Mishina Akihide 72, 82
Miyazaki Isogi 72

Mori Junzaburō 173
Mun Il-p'yŏng 156
Mun Se-yŏng 18
Murayama Chijun 140, 141
Mutel, Gustave 139
Mutsu Munemitsu 103
Nachod, Oscar 5
Nakamura Eikō 24, 89
Nam Su-mun 87
Nelson, M. Frederick 113
No Sa-jin 35
Nomori Takeshi 50, 52
Nukariya Kaiten 134
Ŏ Ch'ŏng 28
Ŏ Yun-jŏk 18, 137, 173
Oba Tsuneyoshi 53
Oda Sensei Shōju Kinen-kai 73
Oda Shōgo 7, 73, 137
Ogawa Keikichi 52
Ogura Shimpei 18, 151, 152
Osgood, Cornelius 126
Ōta Akira 77
Paek Ch'ŏl 156, 157
Paek Nak-chun. See: Paik, L. George
Paek Nam-un 82
Paik, L. George 139
Pak Chi-wŏn 162
Pak No-sik 34
Pak Ŭn-sik 124
Pak Yun-ch'ŏl 160
Pang Chong-hyŏn 150, 160
Pang Ŭng-mo 160
Parker, E. H. 76
Praesent, Hans 5
Rackham, Bernard 43
Rahder, Johannes 147
Ramstedt, G. J. 147
Reischauer, E. O. 19
Roe, Chungil Y. 167
Rogers, Michael C. 148
Ross, John 61
Rossetti, Carlo 113
Royds, W. M. (Mrs.) 4
Saitō Tadashi 51, 53
Sakurai Yoshiyuki 8
Sambo Hombu 104
Sands, William F. 91
Satō Taneji 24

Sekino Tadashi 38, 51, 52, 53, 54
Seno Umakuma 101
Shibutani Reiji 122
Shidehara Taira 73
Shiikawa Kamegorō 83
Shiratori Kurakichi 76, 78, 171
Sin Ch'ae-ho 81
Sin Chŏng-ŏn 63
Sin Sŏk-ho 138
Sin Suk-ju 96, 97
Sŏ Kŏ-jŏng 87, 157
Sŏk Chu-myŏng 150
Son Chin-t'ae 140, 162
Song Hŭi-gyŏng 97
Sŏng Hyŏn 44
Sŏng Kyŏng-nin 144
Song Wŏn-muk 34
Sŏng-nŭng 35
Sŏul Taehak Kuksa Yŏn-gu Sil 62
Sŏul Taehak Kuksa Yŏn-gu-hoe 63
Starr, Frederick 133
Sū Ching 89
Suematsu Yasukazu 24, 26, 83, 101, 138
Sugihara Sadakichi 54
Sugiyama Shinzō 54
Suzuki Takeo 123
Szczesniak, Boleslaw 43
Tabohashi Kiyoshi 97, 123
Taka Kenzō 105
Takada Seiji 137
Takahashi Tōru 135, 137, 138
Tanabe Hisao 144
Tazawa Kingo 47
Tchang, Mathias 173
Tewksbury, Donald G. 113
Torii Ryūzō 51
Trollope, Mark N. 5, 133
Tsuda Sōkichi 36
Tsuneya Morifuku 73
Tung Yüeh 105
Umehara Sueji 47, 49, 52, 54
Underwood, Horace 6, 167
Uragawa Wasaburō 140
Wilkinson, William H. 170
Winkler, Robin L. 91

Yanagi Sōetsu   55
Yang Chu-dong   157, 161
Yang Sŏng-ji   35
Yano Jin'ichi   72
Yi Chŏnggu   23
Yi Hi-sŭng   150, 157
Yi Il   99
Yi In-yŏng   62, 63
Yi Ki-su   115
Yi Kŏn-ch'ang   99
Yi Kŭng-no   151
Yi Kwang-sa   99
Yi Kwang-su   155, 162
Yi Kyu-bo   79, 87
Yi Man-ch'ae   139
Yi Man-gyu   116, 167
Yi Nŭng-hwa   134, 136
Yi Nŭng-sik   139
Yi Pyŏng-do   63, 100
Yi Sang-baek   136
Yi Sang-ch'un   161

Yi Sŏn-gŭn   81
Yi Sung-nyŏng   150, 151
Yi Sun-sin   59, 100
Yi Ŭn-sang   155, 162, 163
Yi Yŏ-sŏng   126
Yi Yun-jae   18, 158
Yoshida Eizaburō   55
Yoshida Tōgo   83
Youn, L. Eul Son   135
Yu Chi-ok   23
Yu Hŭi-ch'un   102
Yu Hyŏng-gi. See: Lew, Hyung-ki J.
Yu Sŏng-nyong   93, 102, 103
Yun Chi-sŏn   139
Yun Hi-sun   45
Yun, S. S.   173
Yun Ŭl-su. See: Youn, L. Eul Son
Yun Yong-gyun   138
Zaichikov, V. T.   32
Zong In-sob   158

www.ingramcontent.com/pod-product-compliance
Lightning Source LLC
Chambersburg PA
CBHW021705230426
43668CB00008B/728